DEVELOPED AND PRODUCED BY MILES KELLY PUBLISHING LTD IN ASSOCIATION WITH RIPLEY PUBLISHING

Executive Vice President Norm Deska
Vice President, Archives and Exhibits Edward Meyer
Archives Executive Assistant Viviana Ray
Researcher Lucas Stram

Publishing Director Anne Marshall

Managing Editor Rebecca Miles
Picture Manager Gemma Simmons
Picture Researcher Charlotte Marshall
Researcher Rosie Alexander
Text Geoff Tibballs
Editors Judy Barratt, Sally McFall
Interviews Gemma Simmons, Jo Wiltshire
Indexer Hilary Bird

Art Director Sam South
Design Dynamo Design
Reprographics Stephan Davis

Sales and Marketing Morty Mint

ISBN: 978-1-893951-31-0

No part of this publication may be reproduced in whole or in part, or stored in a retrieval system, or transmitted in any form or by any means, electronic, mechanical, photocopying, recording, or otherwise, without written permission from the publisher.

For information regarding permission, write to VP Intellectual Property, Ripley Entertainment Inc., Suite 188, 7576 Kingspointe Parkway, Orlando, Florida 32819
email: publishing@ripleys.com

Library of Congress Cataloging-in-Publication Data

Ripley's believe it or not! : prepare to be shocked! / [text, Geoff Tibballs].
        p. cm.
    Includes index.
    ISBN 978-1-893951-31-0
    1. Curiosities and wonders--Juvenile literature.
I. Tibballs, Geoff.
    AG243.R458 2008
    031.02--dc22
                                    2008009722

PUBLISHER'S NOTE
While every effort has been made to verify the accuracy of the entries in this book, the Publishers cannot be held responsible for any errors contained in the work. They would be glad to receive any information from readers.

WARNING
Some of the stunts and activities in this book are undertaken by experts and should not be attempted by anyone without adequate training and supervision.

Printed in China

Ripley's Believe It or Not!®

Prepare to be Shocked!

RIPLEY
PUBLISHING

a Jim Pattison Company

Contents

49

AMAZING!

WOW!

8

62

Soft

63

118

242

CRAZY!

LOOK OUT FOR

....Golf ball swallowing **snake**

Glow-in-the-dark cats.........

.......**Buffalo** who was **best man**

Jet-powered outhouse.............

.....Indoor **tornado**

Violin-playing **robot**...

COOL!!
CARVED PUMPKINS
Amazing imaginary and well-known faces carved from huge pumpkins.

146

GROSS!!
FAMOUS DEAD BODY PARTS 206
Discover the fate of Galileo's finger, George Washington's dentures, Einstein's brain, and many more body parts of the famous deceased!

OUCH!!
LIGHT LUNCH 106
Meet a man who snacks regularly on glass—eating a particularly tasty electric lightbulb!

215

HUGE!!
BIGFOOT TRUCK
A giant truck weighing more than 28,000 lb with tires measuring a colossal 10 ft (3 m) tall!

STRANGE!!
MAN GROWS HORN
A crusty horn has been growing on this Chinese man's head since 2006.

71

WOW!!
FOODSCAPES 164
Check out mind-boggling landscapes created entirely from edible produce.

Robert Ripley

Robert Ripley, creator of the world famous daily cartoon strip "Ripley's Believe It or Not!" combed the globe in a relentless quest for odd people, places, and things. In December 1918, while working as a sports columnist for the *New York Globe*, Ripley created his first cartoon collection of odd facts and feats.

The cartoons, based on unusual athletic achievements, were submitted under the heading "Champs and Chumps," but Ripley's editor wanted a title that would better describe the incredible nature of the content. So, after much deliberation it was changed to "Believe It or Not!" The cartoon was an instant success and the phrase "believe it or not" soon entered everyday speech.

Ripley's passion was travel and by 1940 he had visited no fewer than 201 countries. Wherever he went, he searched out the bizarre for inclusion in his syndicated newspaper cartoons, which had blossomed to reach worldwide distribution, being translated into 17 different languages and boasting a readership of 80 million people. During one trip Ripley crossed two continents and covered more than 24,000 mi (39,000 km) from New York City to Cairo and back to satisfy his boundless appetite for the weird.

Although Robert Ripley died in 1949 (after collapsing on the set of his weekly television show), his "Believe It or Not!" cartoons are still produced on a daily basis—just as they have been every day since 1918— making it the longest running syndicated cartoon in the world.

Robert Ripley examines a carved coconut head in San Juan, Puerto Rico, in 1940.

Ripley with the "flour girls" of Siam while on a trip to Bangkok in 1932.

Intrepid researchers follow in his footsteps, continually scouring the world and enabling Ripley's to remain the undisputed king of the strange and unbelievable.

With a huge database of incredible facts, people, and events, a massive photographic archive, a TV show syndicated around the world, and a warehouse stuffed with unique and fascinating exhibits, Ripley's is able to present a glorious celebration of the amazing diversity of our world, without ever passing judgment.

From the outset, Robert Ripley encouraged his readers to submit unusual material and photographs—his weekly mailbag sometimes exceeded 170,000 letters! Ripley was once commemorated by a memorial in his hometown church of Santa Rosa, California. The entire church was made from a single giant redwood tree… Today, there is still a team of people waiting to hear from you, collecting new amazing facts.

Believe It or Not!
by Ripley

Charly ROMANO

MAN WITH RUBBER ARMS

NOW APPEARING IN THE ODDITORIUM

This souvenir postcard of contortionist Charly Romano was on sale in the New York City odditorium in 1940.

Romano was one of many performers who showcased their feats at Ripley odditoriums across the United States.

MUSEUMS

Ripley's remarkable collection is now showcased in no fewer than 29 museums across ten countries. Recent openings include London, England and Bangalore, India. Ripley called his museums "odditoriums," and built the first one in Chicago in 1933. Exhibits here ranged from genuine shrunken heads from the Upper Amazon to *The Last Supper* painted on a dime, and the effect the new museum had on the visiting public was startling. According to Ripley himself: "At Chicago one hundred people fainted every day and we had to have six beds." By the time the New York City Odditorium was opened in 1940, visitors were getting used to the wonderful world of Ripley's—there were only three beds available and "hardly anyone fainted."

LOOK OUT FOR THE CRYSTAL CAR!

Now featured in the Ripley's London odditorium

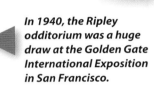

In 1940, the Ripley odditorium was a huge draw at the Golden Gate International Exposition in San Francisco.

This fully-functioning, sparkling Mini Cooper car has been decorated with a mural featuring American icons made from more than one million Swarovski lead crystals. It is currently on display in Ripley's new odditorium at Piccadilly Circus in the heart of London, England.

Ripley's opened a new odditorium in New York City's Times Square in 2007.

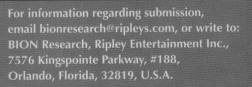

Anyone with a strange fact should contact...
www.ripleys.com

For information regarding submission, email bionresearch@ripleys.com, or write to: BION Research, Ripley Entertainment Inc., 7576 Kingspointe Parkway, #188, Orlando, Florida, 32819, U.S.A.

SHOCKING!

Zhang Deke can use his power as a human conductor of electricity to charge six 13-watt lightbulbs simply by placing them on his head and ears.

As the bulbs light up, he is even able to control their brightness. He has also cooked a fish, which he held in his hand as the current flowed through his body, in just two minutes!

Zhang, 71, a retired highway maintenance worker from Altay City, China, often exercises by hooking himself up to the electricity supply. With both hands holding live wires, he allows 220 volts of electricity to run through his body without any ill effects, even though it is the same charge that an electric eel delivers to kill a human.

He first discovered his extraordinary ability when he was 47. While changing a lightbulb, he accidentally touched a live wire, but instead of receiving a shock or being electrocuted, he felt almost nothing. He tentatively tried it again and eventually realized that his body could conduct electricity. In 1994, he was examined at the Chinese Academy of Sciences, where experts said he has an unspecified physical dysfunction.

Zhang administers his electrical therapy to help friends and relatives who are suffering from ailments such as rheumatism, arthritis, and lumbago. One friend had been bedridden for some time with lumbar hyperplasia, but nine months after receiving Zhang's shock treatment he was out riding a bicycle.

Zhang's incredible capacity to cook a fish with his body's electric current has amazed the world.

Zhang demonstrates his electrical abilities by lighting up a string of lightbulbs being worn by a friend.

Other shockers!

● Whenever Angélique Cottin, the "Electric Girl" of 19th-century France, went near an object, it moved away from her. Chairs twisted away from her when she tried to sit down, a heavy table rose into the air when she touched it, and if she tried to sleep in a bed, it rocked violently. People standing near her received electric shocks without her even touching them.

● Annie May Abbott, "The Little Georgia Magnet," toured the world demonstrating her ability to raise a chair with a heavy man seated on it, apparently just by touching it with her hand.

● Caroline Clare of Ontario, Canada, developed electrical powers soon after dramatically losing weight. Metal objects would jump into her hand and she gave an electric shock to anyone she touched. In one experiment, she passed a shock down a line of 20 people who were holding hands.

● When the fingertips of Louis Hamburger, a 16-year-old student from Maryland, were dry, he could pick up heavy objects simply by touching them. Pins dangled from his open hand as if they were hanging from a magnet.

● Brian Clements of the U.K., was so highly charged that he had to discharge his voltage into metal furniture before he touched anyone.

● Brenda Sheklian of Visalia, California, says that street lamps turn off when she passes under them and switch back on when she moves away. She also claims that her electrical powers can turn off the TV, blow lightbulbs, and freeze her computer.

Ripley's research ○○○○○○○○

How can some people possess special electric powers?

The human nervous system actually generates electricity. When we walk across a thick carpet, our body can build up around 10,000 volts, but because it can actually develop only a small electrical charge, the discharged current is equally insignificant. Yet so-called "electric people" are sometimes able to maximize their electrical potential.

Doctors believe that the ability to conduct electricity may be governed by a person's health and becomes more marked in the aftermath of a serious illness or disease. Other case studies suggest that the climate is responsible, with electrical activity at its liveliest during a heat wave. As yet, however, there are no definitive answers to a puzzle that has perplexed medical minds for more than 150 years.

The "Electric Man," Zhang Deke, all lit up.

9

DUCK OVERBOARD!

In January 1992, a stupendous storm washed three containers off a ship that was bound from Hong Kong to Tacoma, Washington. One container spilled its contents into the sea—no less than 29,000 bathtub toys!

Two-thirds of them bobbed off south through the tropics, landing months later on the shores of Indonesia, Australia, and South America. The remaining 10,000 plastic ducks, turtles, frogs, and beavers headed north and were soon off the coast of Alaska whereupon they turned back westward. Some of the ducks made their way south and were seen floating past Japan in 1995. Many, however, became trapped in the North Pacific Gyre. This giant clockwise spiral of water collects and gradually grinds the oceans' plastic debris. However, even this couldn't halt the plucky ducks, which eventually broke free and pressed on. They bravely steered a course for the Arctic where some became trapped in ice for several years.

They finally reached the North Atlantic in 2000 and, in the summer of 2007, more than 15 years and nearly 17,000 mi (27,500 km) after their journey's start, flotillas of ducks, bleached white by the sun and sea, hit the coasts of Great Britain and North America.

In 2007, retired teacher Penny Harris found the first plastic duck from the cargo to arrive in England when it washed up on a beach in Devon at the end of a 15-year round-the-world trip.

Global travels...

Between 1995 and 2000 ducks become trapped in slow-moving ice at the top of the world. **5**

Ship hit in storm in January 1992; container is washed overboard spilling 29,000 plastic bath toys. **2**

Ship leaves Hong Kong bound for U.S.A. **1**

Many of the toys are caught in the North Pacific Gyre and float in a 6,800-mi (11,000-km) loop from 1992 to 1995. **4**

In 2001 ducks are tracked in an area where the Titanic sank. **6**

19,000 toys bob along southward and wash up on the shores of Australia, Indonesia, and South America. **3**

After a 15-year journey, the ducks head south into the Atlantic and are caught in the Gulf Stream, which brings them bobbing toward the southwest coast of the U.K. in summer 2007. **7**

SAME DATE

Lila Debry-Martin of Kingston Peninsula, New Brunswick, Canada, gave birth to triplets on August 10, 2000—the same day that she had given birth to twins three years before.

BIRTHDAY BONANZA

Michele Rosciano, his son Giovanni, and his grandson Miguel were all born as the second child, on the same day, of the same month, in the same hour—just in different years.

HOCKEY RING

A Stanley Cup hockey championship ring that had been missing for more than 30 years has been found in the Gulf of Mexico. It belonged to former Toronto Maple Leafs' player Jim Pappin who later gave it to his father-in-law when he was traded to the Chicago Blackhawks. The ring was lost near Vero Beach, Florida, in the 1970s, but in 2007, a treasure hunter with an underwater metal detector found it with Pappin's name inscribed on the inside.

ANCIENT MUSHROOM

U.S. scientists say that a mushroom found embedded in a piece of amber in Myanmar is 100 million years old—an age that makes it 20 million years older than any other known mushroom fossils.

GOLFING DOUBLE

Two members of a foursome scored back-to-back holes-in-one at a New Jersey golf club in 2007—defying odds of more than 17 million to one! Immediately after nine-handicapper Thomas Brady landed an ace at the 179-yd (164-m) seventh hole at Forsgate Country Club in Monroe Township, Dennis Gerhart, a self-confessed "weekend hacker" who plays golf only 15 times a year, stepped up to the tee and emulated the feat.

CHIP AND PIN

In February 2007, grandmother Olga Mauriello of San Giorgio Cremano, Italy, found a live World-War-II-era grenade—without its safety pin—in a sack of potatoes.

WHALE FOSSIL

In early 2007, paleontologists discovered a near-complete five-million-year-old whale fossil beneath a vineyard in Tuscany, Italy.

CLOSE RELATIVES

Unbeknown to each other, Dorothy Caudle lived just 300 ft (100 m) from her sister Gladys Clark for an entire year. The sisters, who had not seen each other for 38 years, were living in the same senior care facility at Tempe, Arizona, but did not realize it until celebrations were held to mark Clark's 100th birthday in 2007.

SURPRISE LEGACY

Men carrying out plumbing work on Mike Sutton's new house in Bridport, Dorset, England, took up the cellar floor and found hundreds of artificial legs!

PETRIFIED FOREST

A forest of around 200 petrified trees has been discovered in Washington State, still standing on the spot where they were swamped by lava more than 15 million years ago. Clyde Friend used an excavator, a hammer, and a chisel to unearth the forest of preserved hickory, maple, elm, and sweetgum trees on his land near Yakima.

FRESH FRUIT

Archeologists in western Japan have unearthed a 2,100-year-old melon—with its flesh still on the rind. They believe it had been preserved for centuries because it had been in a vacuum-packed state in a wet layer below the ground, where it was immune to attack from microorganisms.

EGG RETURNED

A rare bird's egg was returned to a museum in the town of Salcombe in Devon, England, in 2006—43 years after it had been stolen. The bustard's egg arrived back in mint condition, accompanied by a letter signed only "John," apologizing for the theft in 1963.

JAILHOUSE ROCK

Hundreds of inmates at the Cebu Detention and Rehabilitation Center in the Philippines re-created the famous video dance routine to Michael Jackson's "Thriller." Their version proved so popular that by the end of 2007 it had been viewed more than 10 million times on YouTube—twice as many as had watched Jackson's original! The routine was an exercise program devised by security consultant Byron Garcia. Dancing is compulsory for all 1,600 inmates (except the elderly and the infirm) at Cebu and two former prisoners there have even gone on to become professional dancers.

HARRY'S HAT

Three-year-old Charlie Thomas from Cullompton, Devon, England, thought it would be a bright idea to put a traffic cone on his head so that he could look just like his hero, boy wizard Harry Potter... but when the cone stuck fast, he had to be cut free by six firefighters. After soap and tugging failed to remove the cone, the fire crews had to use cutting tools and pliers in a delicate half-hour operation.

HOTEL FALL

Joshua Hanson, of Wisconsin, plummeted 16 floors after falling through the window of a Minneapolis hotel in 2007, but survived because he landed on the roof overhang one floor up from the street.

UNUSUAL CASE

In 2007, a ten-year-old boy was hit by a car while walking to school in Lancaster, Pennsylvania, but escaped with only cuts and bruises because the violin case he was carrying took most of the impact.

BAD DAY

In 1945, Betty Lou Oliver of New York City survived a plane crash and a 1,000-ft (300-m) elevator fall on the same day.

DOUBLE STRIKE

Lightning can strike twice! On July 27, 2007, Don Frick of Hamlin, Pennsylvania, was at a festival when lightning struck the ground nearby, leaving a burned zipper and a hole in the back of his jeans—27 years to the day of his first strike. On July 27, 1980, he had been driving a tractor-trailer when the antenna was struck by lightning, injuring his left side.

BULL ATTACK

In 1912, 49-year-old "Granny" Anderson of Staples, Texas, had her intestines ripped out by a bull. A doctor washed the wound, replaced her innards, and sewed her up, and she went on to live to the age of 105.

UPSIDE DOWN

The pilot of a light airplane escaped injury in July 2007 when it landed on its roof at Darwin Airport, Australia. The plane was spun upside down by a fierce crosswind as it came in to land.

NAIL GUN

A three-month-old baby survived after being accidentally shot in the head by a nail gun. The boy was sitting on his mother's lap near a construction site in Delta, Colorado, when a nail fired from the gun ricocheted off boards and hit him in the head.

PLUGGED HOLE

Shot in the heart with a 3-in (7.6-cm) nail, 17-year-old Matt Robinson of Dexter, Missouri, survived the ordeal only because he didn't bleed. Miraculously, the nail plugged the hole it had made until a doctor could operate.

HANGING AROUND

An 85-year-old man fell from a fifth-floor window in Zhengzhou, China, in 2007—but was saved by a nail. The nail, located in the wall between the fourth and fifth floors, snagged Zhao Jinghzi's clothing and held his weight until help arrived.

GRASS DIET

Lost in the hot Canadian bush for nine days in July 2007, 78-year-old Norm Berg, of Alberta, survived by eating grass and leaves.

WHEELCHAIR RIDE

A wheelchair user was taken on a terrifying 50-mph (80-km/h) ride for 4 mi (6.4 km) along a U.S. highway in 2007 after his handlebars became wedged in the front grill of a truck.

Ben Carpenter, a 21-year-old muscular-dystrophy sufferer, was crossing the street in Paw Paw, Michigan, when the back of his motorized wheelchair was bumped by a truck leaving a gas station, the impact trapping the chair in the radiator grill. The truck driver then drove off down the highway, unaware that he had an involuntary passenger on the front of his vehicle.

Luckily, horrified passers-by saw Carpenter's predicament and alerted the police, who eventually managed to stop the truck. Carpenter was unhurt, having been held in place in his wheelchair by a seatbelt. Afterward he said: "It was quite a ride."

Incredibly, Ben Carpenter emerged unharmed from his high-speed ride... apart from losing his hat and spilling his soda.

The driver refused to believe there was a man stuck to the front of his truck... until he saw it for himself.

"It was pretty scary," said Ben Carpenter of his ordeal. "I tried to yell for help, but no one could hear me."

a Ben Carpenter crosses the road.

b A truck slowly pulls out of a gas station and hits Ben's wheelchair, which becomes attached to the front grill.

c Truck accelerates to 50 mph. Ben is carried along the highway.

d Passing vehicles call 911. Ben's chair is attached to the truck for 4 mi (6.4 km) before the police intervene.

BE OUR GUEST

When comedian and filmmaker Mark Malkoff's New York City apartment had to be fumigated in January 2008, he obtained permission to move into an IKEA store for a week.

Reasoning that hotels were too expensive, he lived, slept, and ate at the store in Paramus, New Jersey. Malkoff took full advantage of the free accommodation and fully furnished rooms at the IKEA store. He said the only problems were that the display sinks and toilets were not plumbed in (forcing him to shower in the staff locker room) and at night the lights in the store automatically came on at 2 a.m. Although his wife chose not to join him on his IKEA holiday, Malkoff had numerous visitors to his temporary in-store living quarters and even staged a housewarming party.

Mark sorts through his underwear drawer in one of the bedrooms.

Breakfast in Mark's IKEA pad was a relaxed affair.

Mark in his IKEA bedroom...

kitchen...

and bathroom.

BITE SIZE

Sid the grass snake looked to have bitten off more than he could chew when tackling a goldfish more than ten times the size of his head at a garden in Kent, England. However, by dislocating his jaw he was eventually able to devour the tasty meal and continue his campaign to snatch fish up to 8 in (20 cm) long from the pond.

ANCIENT TOOTH

Researchers in Spain have unearthed a human tooth that is more than one million years old. The fossil was discovered near Burgos and sets a new date for humankind's presence in western Europe—the previous oldest finds for the region being a mere 800,000 years old!

STONE RIDDLE

In September 2007, residents in northern England and in Scotland were puzzled to find strange stone heads left outside their homes in the dead of night. More than 50 gargoyle-like figures were deposited throughout a wide area, each bearing a carving that spelled out the word "paradox." A riddle was also attached. The culprit turned out to be eccentric artist Billy Johnson, who had hoped the recipients would use the cryptic clues to contact his website.

GIANT PENGUIN

Scientists have discovered fossilized remains of a sun-loving giant penguin that lived some 36 million years ago and, at 5 ft (1.5 m), was as tall as an adult human. The skeleton was discovered on the southern coast of Peru, indicating that it preferred the tropics to colder climes.

RING RETURNED

Clare Cavoli Lopez of South Euclid, Ohio, lost her class ring while scuba diving off the coast of South Africa more than 20 years ago. Her ring was found in 2007 by a professional diver in an underwater cave on Mauritius and returned to her.

MISTAKEN IDENTITY

Bones long thought to belong to Joan of Arc were recently discovered to be those of an ancient Egyptian mummy and its pet cat.

FISH CURE

British scientists believe that a tiny tropical fish could help find a cure for blindness in humans. The zebrafish has a unique ability to repair its own damaged and diseased eyes, and now researchers have identified that the special cells, which restore sight in zebrafish, can also be found in the human eye.

CHILI LOVERS

Across the Americas, people were eating chili peppers as long as 6,000 years ago. Recent discoveries from the Bahamas to Peru found starch microfossils of grains from chili peppers alongside remnants of corn, yucca, squash, beans, and palm fruit, suggesting that the ancients used recipes that aimed to make bland tastes more palatable.

DUNG DEAL

While examining two mountain plateaux in southern Suriname in 2005, mining company researchers discovered 24 new species of animals—half of which were dung beetles.

ALL THE EIGHTS

In 2007, a baby was born in Liverpool, England, at eight minutes past eight in the morning of the eighth day of the eighth month weighing eight pounds, and after her mother had been in labor for eight hours! The mother, Mel Byrne, was looked after by a midwife who delivered eight babies that day.

TRIPLE CELEBRATION

The golf-crazy Mackenzie family beat odds of 15 million-to-one to score three holes-in-one in the space of three days in 2007. Dad Ray, wife Gill, and their 14-year-old son Sam all landed aces at the Llanfairfechan Golf Club in North Wales.

AGED CLAM

A quahog clam estimated to be more than 400 years old was found in the waters off Iceland in 2006—which means that when it was young, William Shakespeare was writing his greatest plays!

FAT FEAST

Croatian conceptual artist Zoran Todorovic fed human fat and skin from liposuction clinics to visitors to his exhibition in Zagreb.

SICK REMEDY

In April 2004, a Chinese man was arrested on suspicion of stealing 30 corpses from graveyards, cooking soup from their flesh, and crushing the bones in an attempt to heal his sick wife.

PRESERVED FROG

A frog was found inside a chunk of amber in Chiapas, Mexico—where it has been preserved for as long as 25 million years.

SOMETHING FISHY

In January 2007, customs officials in Thailand found more than 1,400 turtles of various species and 33 arapaima fish being smuggled out of the country in a single suitcase.

BIRTHDAY TREAT

Each year on his birthday, Luang Phoo Budda Thawaro, dressed in a new orange robe, stands before worshipers at a monastery in Thailand—even though he has been dead since 1994.

In this annual Buddhist ceremony, the revered former abbot of Wat Krang Chu Si Charoensuk monastery, near Bangkok, is lifted from his glass coffin, cleansed, given a change of clothes and honored by the local community. His fellow monks are able to dress the corpse in a new robe and socks because his body has not decomposed. Instead it has mummified, supposedly because Luang Phoo dehydrated himself on his deathbed. Custom dictates that a monk who does not decompose after death should be preserved and worshiped.

Once Luang Phoo has been dressed, the congregation places tiny flakes of gold leaf on his face and families have their picture taken with him. When the ceremony is over, the monks carefully maneuver Luang's body back into his coffin, which is then returned to its place in the prayer hall. There he rests in peace until his next public appearance in 12 months' time.

Luang Phoo was a monk for more than 70 years. During his lifetime he survived wars, civil strife, dictatorships, and military coups. A hugely admired figure, his charisma drew worshipers to the temple from far and wide.

After prayers, the monks of Wat Krang Chu Si Charoensuk, each holding a fragile limb or shoulder, gently return Luang Phoo's body to his glass coffin.

Supported by his fellow monks, the newly clothed, mummified corpse of Luang Phoo Budda Thawaro is displayed before worshipers in Thailand.

MAN-MADE TORNADO

A museum in Stuttgart, Germany, has created its own 113-ft-high (34.4-m) tornado. In order to remove smoke from the building in the event of a fire, the Mercedes-Benz Museum has devised a system that uses 144 air jets to form a powerful tornado from 28 tons of air.

WATCH RETURNED

A World War I veteran's engraved watch was returned to the owner's family in 2007—nearly 90 years after William B. Gill lost it in France, where he served in the U.S. Army. It was later won in a poker game and then, with the help of a genealogist, returned to Gill's grandchildren in Sioux City, Iowa.

BLOOD BROTHERS

A bull that broke loose gored two American brothers—Lawrence and Michael Lenahan—simultaneously, catching one on each of its horns during the 2007 Running of the Bulls Festival at Pamplona, Spain.

BOWLING ALLEY

Italian archeologists working in Egypt have found an indoor bowling alley that is nearly 2,000 years old. A large room, with a shallow lane running into a pit and two heavy stone balls lying nearby, was found at an ancient site that lies 55 mi (88 km) south of the Egyptian capital, Cairo.

SEVENTH HEAVEN

Herbethe Elie of Birmingham, England, gave birth to her seventh baby in the seventh hour of the seventh day of the seventh month of 2007—in hospital delivery room number seven.

GREAT SURVIVOR

A 50-ton bowhead whale caught off the coast of Alaska in 2007 had a weapon fragment embedded in its neck that showed it had survived a previous attack over a century before. The 3.5-in (9-cm), arrow-shaped projectile, thought to date from around 1890, was found deep under the whale's blubber.

NEIGHBORLY ACT

After two days adrift in the Caribbean, John Fildes was rescued by a cruise ship, which, amazingly, was captained by a neighbor from his hometown—Warsash, England.

CAR KISSING

A Chinese woman won a car in 2007 by kissing it virtually nonstop for more than 24 hours. Zhang Cunying was one of 120 people taking part in the endurance contest at a Beijing shopping mall, where the competitors had to kiss Chevrolet cars through plastic nipples attached to the bodywork but without touching the car itself. The person lasting the longest was declared the winner. They were allowed a ten-minute break every seven hours and, in order to speed up elimination, were eventually made to stand on one foot with their hands behind their back. Zhang owed her success to her dance training, although she was so exhausted at the finish that she could not stand up unaided.

PARALLEL BIRTHS

Identical twins Nicole Cramer and Naomi Sale of Auburn, Indiana, both gave birth to a son at the same hospital on the same day—January 23, 2007.

LUCKY OMEN

After getting married on a Lake Michigan beach on August 18, 2007, Melody Kloska and Matt Behrs released a bottle containing their wedding vows. A few weeks later, it was picked up by Fred and Lynnette Dubendorf, of Mears, Michigan, who were also married on a beach—28 years to the day before Kloska and Behrs.

WAD A FIND!

In 2007, British archeology student Sarah Pickin discovered a 5,000-year-old piece of chewing gum at a dig site in western Finland.

CANNED FISH

A fish caught off the coast of Iceland in 2007 was wearing a tin can that had grown into its flesh. The fish must have looked into the can and become partly trapped. When fishermen first spotted the halibut, they thought it was wearing tribal jewelry.

SQUIRREL FIND

Squirrels in Placer County, California, dug up an ancient artifact in July 2007. The animals were rummaging around in soil at the Maidu Indian Interpretive Center—where it is illegal for human archeologists to dig—when they unearthed a 10,000-year-old carved tool.

JACKPOT JOY

After winning $10,000 on the Arizona Lottery in 2007, Barbara and Barry Salzman of Henderson, Nevada, immediately bought another ticket with their winnings and won the $15-million jackpot.

HIDDEN WINNINGS

In 2007, demolition workers at the Sands Casino in Atlantic City, New Jersey, discovered a staggering $17,193.34 in tokens, coins, and bills that had fallen underneath the slot machines.

HEADLESS CORPSES

Archeologists on the Pacific island of Vanuatu recently discovered a 3,000-year-old cemetery in which every single body they found had been decapitated.

IN A SPIN

Eight-year-old Patrick Grieves of Essex, England, accepted a dare from his sister to climb into the family's washing machine—and ended up having to be rescued by ten firefighters after becoming wedged fast in the drum.

VIKING SHIP

Professor Steven Harding of the University of Nottingham, England, found a 1,000-year-old Viking ship buried under the parking lot of a pub in Merseyside.

LONG GONE

In October 2006, authorities in Vienna, Austria, discovered the mummified body of Franz Riedl who had been lying dead in his bed for at least five years.

LOST ARMY

In March 2007, some 170 Swiss soldiers got lost and accidentally invaded Liechtenstein, a defenceless country of only 34,000 people.

FEUDING BROTHERS

Two brothers have divided the house that they share with barbed wire because they keep fighting. Taso Hadjiev and his brother Asen from Malka Arda, Bulgaria, have sued each other more than 200 times over the past 40 years but neither can afford to leave the family home—because all their money has been spent on lawyers' fees.

WRAPPED UP

A Kenyan air passenger flying home from China in 2007 was found to be wearing more than 100 items of men's and women's clothing! He told officials that he had been worried about being charged for carrying excess luggage.

SHELL SHOCK

An elderly lady in England used a live German World War I artillery shell, which could have exploded at any time, as a doorstop for 20 years. The 7-in-long (18-cm) device had been collected by Thelma Bonnett's grandfather in 1918 while he served with the Merchant Navy. Thelma had used it as an ornament for decades in her home in Paignton, Devon. However, a neighbor sounded the alarm in 2007, after which bomb-disposal experts were called in to the home to deal with the shell, which was packed with explosives and had its mechanism primed to fire.

GROUNDHOG DAY

A woman from Ohio has given birth to three children on the same date in different years—odds of more than 130,000 to one. Jenna Cotton of Marysville gave birth to sons Ayden and Logan in 2003 and 2006 respectively, followed by daughter Kayla in 2007—all on October 2.

SOLDIERS REBURIED

On November 25, 2007, historical re-enactors dressed up as Napoleonic soldiers and helped to rebury the bodies of 223 French servicemen of the Grande Armée who had died in 1812 near the town of Studenka, Belarus, during Napoleon's invasion.

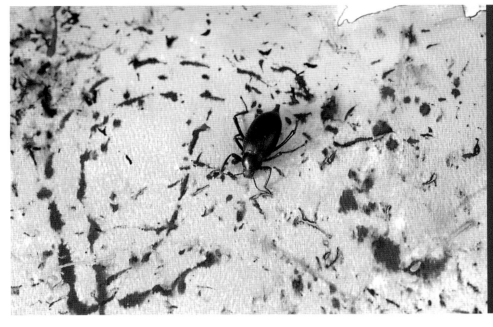

BUG ART

Los Angeles artist Steven Kutcher uses insects as living paintbrushes. He takes flies, cockroaches, and beetles in his hand and adds paint onto each leg, one leg at a time. He then releases them onto a prepared canvas, allowing them to create a trail of color. To ensure his insects come to no harm, he always uses water-based, nontoxic paints that wash off easily.

SKELETON IN LOFT

A man's skeleton was discovered in the loft of his family home in Bergholz-Rehbrücke, Germany, in 2007—22 years after his disappearance.

METAL ADDICT

The Swedish Employment Service granted disability payments to Roger Tullgren of Hassleholm, Sweden, because he is addicted to heavy-metal music. A heavy-metal fan since hearing Black Sabbath at the age of six, Tullgren attended 300 concerts in 2006, often skipping work to do so.

BODY FOUND

While researching a story in August 2007, Seattle-based author Peter Stekel discovered the frozen body of a World War II aviator on a Californian glacier.

CYANIDE TERROR

Nine villagers from Yangping, Henan, China, were killed in September 2007 when a floor collapsed and dumped them into an underground pool of cyanide that no one had known was there.

HARDENED CRIMINAL

Following an attempted carjack, police easily captured the fleeing suspect in Reno, Nevada, in November 2007, after he got stuck in wet concrete as he tried to make his escape through a construction site.

WALLET RECOVERED

A man who lost his wallet on a trip to the theater in 1964 got it back 43 years later. Construction workers renovating the Crest Theater at El Centro, California, discovered Epigmenio Sanchez's wallet jammed between the metal casings of a radiator.

DOUBLE BLOW

A man in Australia was attacked by a crocodile and then accidentally shot by his rescuer. Jason Grant had been collecting crocodile eggs at a reptile farm near Darwin when the saltwater croc seized him in his jaws. His colleague fired two shots at the crocodile and one struck Grant in the arm.

SNAKE'S TEE

When a python was taken to a wildlife sanctuary near Brisbane, Australia, with four bumps in its belly, veterinarians were amazed to see four golf balls show up on an X ray. The snake had swallowed the balls after apparently mistaking them for chicken eggs. Unable to pass the golf balls naturally, the snake underwent a successful operation to remove them and was later released back into the wild.

Birth of an Island

While sailing in the Vava'u group of islands Fredrik Fransson amazingly came across an island being formed right in front of his eyes!

Fredrik with the yacht Maiken anchored behind him.

FREDRIK FRANSSON ONBOARD
YACHT MAIKEN
BRISBANE, AUSTRALIA
AUGUST 11, 2006

We left Neiafu in the Vava'u group of islands in the northern part of Tonga on Friday, August 11, sailing toward Fiji. There was no wind, so we motored along toward an offshore island called Late Island.

Fairly soon we discovered brown grainy streaks in the water. It looked like heavy oil mixed with water. The surrounding water was strangely greenish, like a lagoon, not the deep bluish color that you normally see sailing offshore. As we got further southwest, the streaks turned into heavy bands of floating matter, until the whole horizon was a solid line that looked like a desert.

So far we didn't have a problem, as it was such a thin layer on the surface that it got pushed away by the bow wave, but when we entered the solid field it started to pile up and behaved like wet concrete. The sight was unbelievable; it looked like rolling sand dunes as far as the eye could see. Our speed went from 7 knots down to 1 knot as the pumice stones dragged along the waterline.

A field of pumice appears to rise out of the deep blue sea.

We turned around as quickly as we could and headed back the same way we came, toward clear water. As we hit clear water, we turned off the engine and figured out that it must have come from a volcanic eruption somewhere near. We were too far from land to contact anyone on the VHF radio, so our only options were either to sail south along the pumice rafts or to head back to the islands. I wanted to make sure that everything was OK with the boat before heading off for a longer passage, so we decided to head back toward land and anchor for the night.

The wake of the sailboat made a dramatic course through the volcanic pumice stones as Fransson steered through them.

curiosity overcame us and we headed toward the southern part of Home reef. The closer we came to the island, the clearer the smoke stood out from the surrounding clouds, and every so often a massive black pillar shot upward toward the sky. You could see particles raining down.

As the wind was pushing the volcanic smoke to the northwest, we decided to go in a bit closer. While the sun was going down, we motored up to within 1½ nautical miles of the island. Later, I put the coordinates to be 18°59.55 and 174°46.3W. The island was smoldering with steam, but it was possible to get a good picture of it.

You could clearly see the three mounds creating a crater with one side breaking off and opening up toward the sea. It looked like a big island made of black coal. We reached down and felt the water and it was warmer. Our concern at the time was to sail away from the island before it got too dark, as we didn't know if we would run into more pumice rafts.

AUGUST 12, 2006

We motored out early the next morning heading south-southwest until we encountered the pumice rafts and sailed along them until they were so broken up that we could safely steer through them. We collected a few stones, some as big as a soccer ball, but the bigger they were the more brittle they were, and with the motion of the sailboat they eventually broke into pieces.

Soon we could make out that one of the clouds on the horizon wasn't a cloud but actually a smoke stack from the active volcano. The two areas of volcanic activity in the area are Metis shoal and Home reef and the smoke came from the Home reef area. We were planning to sail south of both these areas, but

pumice raft —

new island —

The volcanic eruption sent pillars of smoke and particles into the air, but the new island was easily visible across the water.

When we were leaving Fiji in the middle of September, we heard on the radio an account of the pumice drifting up on beaches in Fiji. I have been told by another scientist at NASA that sometimes these islands do "disappear" with time as wind and wave action break them down. But the island that we found still shows up clearly on a satellite photo taken in the middle of October, so who knows.

This image from NASA taken in August shows the new island partially hidden by the plume of smoke erupting from the volcano. The pumice can clearly be seen.

MONSTER MUSHROOM

A monster white mushroom standing 27 in (70 cm) tall and weighing 41 lb (20 kg) was discovered growing near a coffee farm in Chiapas, southern Mexico, in 2007. The prize specimen of *Macrocybe titans* had grown to twice its normal size.

CORK SOURCE

Every nine years since 1820, the Whistler tree of Portugal has had its bark harvested for making corks—yielding enough to cork up to 100,000 wine bottles in a single harvest.

FIRST RAIN

After two years of abundant rain, grass began to grow for the first time ever on the desert-themed golf course at Cameron's Corner, Australia, in 2007. The unique course straddles three states—South Australia, Queensland, and New South Wales.

Ripley's research

The "hair" on the stone is thought to be the remains of a type of fungus that has been attached to its surface for hundreds of millions of years. Over that period, it has gradually extended upright and evolved into a hollow, pipe-shaped invertebrate fossil that resembles strands of white hair.

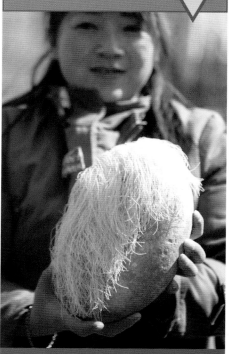

HAIRY STONE

A stone with thousands of 6-in-long (15-cm) strands of white hair growing on its surface went on display in Dalian, China, in 2005. The stone, which measured 8 in (20 cm) long and 6 in (15 cm) in diameter, was considered to be so rare that it was valued at $1,300,000.

LOTTERY TREE

People in Thailand flocked to visit a banana tree in Koh Sireh in 2007 in the belief that it could predict winning lottery numbers. Many claimed to have won prizes after rubbing a mixture of powder and water on the tree's trunk, then waiting to see what number the dried solution resembled.

IRON-EATING TREE

A sycamore tree in Scotland has literally "swallowed up" pieces of metal over the past 200 years. The Brig o'Turk iron-eating tree has engulfed all kinds of scrap left by the local blacksmith and has even enveloped a bicycle that a boy left against the tree when he failed to return from World War I.

SUDDEN DEATH

The rare *Puya raimondii* plant of Bolivia can take up to 150 years to bloom—and as soon as it does, it dies.

SPORE RELEASE

If a raindrop or a passing animal hits the giant puffball fungus, thousands of spores are puffed out of a hole in the top. In a single day, a giant puffball can release as many as seven billion spores.

STARTLING STONE

Visitors to a collectors' market in Haozhou, China, in April 2007, could hardly believe their eyes when they saw one of the exhibits—a strange marbled stone that looked like a huge slice of meat.

THUNDERSTRUCK

Approximately 1,800 thunderstorms take place across the Earth at any given moment, and the planet is struck by an average of more than 100 lightning bolts every second.

STORM POWER

A single lightning strike has enough energy to light 150 million lightbulbs. An average storm can discharge sufficient power to supply the entire U.S.A. with electricity for 20 minutes.

HUGE HARVEST

A tomato tree at Walt Disney World's Epcot Center in Orlando, Florida, boasts a one-year harvest of more than 32,000 tomatoes with a total weight of 1,152 lb (522 kg).

NOISY GROWTH

The Lady in the Veil mushroom from tropical Africa takes just 20 minutes to attain its full height of 8 in (20 cm). To achieve this, its cells expand at such a rate that they make an audible cracking sound.

RARE SNOWFALL

When snow fell in Buenos Aires in July 2007, it was the Argentine capital's first major snowfall since 1918. Thousands of people cheered and threw snowballs in the streets.

TRIFFID FIND

A dandelion discovered in Hampstead, New Hampshire, in 2007, stood a monstrous 49 in (1.2 m) tall—at least five times the height of the average dandelion plant.

ARABIAN CYCLONE

The first documented cyclone ever to hit the Arabian Sea landed in Oman on June 6, 2007, with maximum sustained winds of 92.5 mph (148 km/h) and affected more than 20,000 people.

EXPLODING FRUIT

When the fruit of the South American sandbox tree is ripe, it explodes with such force that the seeds can scatter nearly 200 ft (60 m) from the main trunk. The noise of the explosion fools some people into mistaking it for gunfire.

TAP TREE

In April 2006, a tree in San Antonio, Texas, began to spout a constant flow of clean, drinkable water. People visited the tree in the hope that it held miraculous healing powers and was spouting holy water, but it turned out that it had somehow tapped its roots into an underground water pipe.

TREE-MENDOUS SHOCK

When a 200-year-old chestnut tree was felled near the town of Bournemouth in Dorset, England, in 2007, villagers were amazed to find a perfect image of a tiny tree imprinted throughout the branch and trunk. Experts said the unusual phenomenon was caused by wood rot.

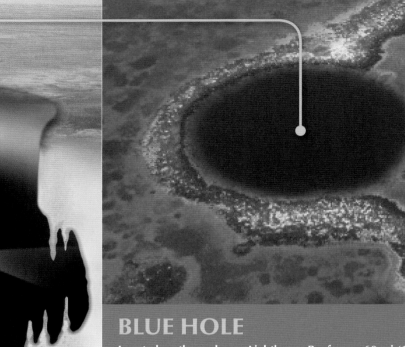

BLUE HOLE

Located on the undersea Lighthouse Reef some 60 mi (100 km) from Belize in Central America is a perfectly circular Blue Hole that measures 1,000 ft (305 m) across and 400 ft (123 m) deep. Filled with dark blue water, the hole was formed 15,000 years ago during the Ice Age when sea levels were lowered by more than 350 ft (107 m), exposing the limestone rock. As freshwater began flowing through the limestone deposits, huge underground caverns formed. Then, as the ocean began to rise again, the caverns flooded and the roof of one cavern collapsed to create this incredible sinkhole. With its breathtaking collection of stalactites, the Blue Hole is now a popular diving venue. At a depth of 130 ft (40 m) the temperature inside the hole is a constant 76°F (24°C).

FOG FOREST

A lush forest survives in Oman's Dhofar mountains with no rain! The cloud forest is surrounded by deserts and gets most of its water from seasonal fog.

WORM SHOWER

Clumps of live worms fell from the sky onto the streets of Jennings, Louisiana, in July 2007. They are thought to have been sucked up into the air by a waterspout seen 5 mi (8 km) away, and then dropped on the town.

TROPICAL ALASKA

It once topped 100°F in Alaska! On June 27, 1915, a temperature of 100°F (38°C) was recorded at Fort Yukon.

DRIFTING APART

North America and Europe are moving away from each other at about the same speed as a human fingernail grows—about 6 ft (1.8 m) every 75 years.

PURE GOLD

A lump of pure gold that is only as big as a matchbox can be flattened into a sheet the size of a tennis court. An ounce (28 g) of gold can be stretched into a wire 50 mi (80 km) long.

UNLUCKY STRIKE

A diver was killed in the ocean off Deerfield Beach, Florida, in 2007 after lightning struck his oxygen tank as he came to the surface.

UNDERWATER MOUNTAINS

The longest mountain range in the world is underwater. The Mid-Ocean Ridge extends about 40,000 mi (65,000 km) from the Arctic Ocean via the Atlantic to the Pacific off the west coast of North America.

SAFETY SALT

Ten per cent of all the salt mined in the world each year is used to de-ice freezing roads in North America.

ALASKAN TSUNAMI

In 1958, an earthquake followed by a rockslide in Lituya Bay, Alaska, triggered a huge tsunami more than 1,720 ft (525 m) high. As the area is relatively isolated and enclosed, the only casualties were two men in a fishing boat.

BOAT REVEALED

In April 2007, an earthquake near the Solomon Islands, measuring a powerful 8.1 on the Richter scale, pushed coral reefs around 10 ft (3 m) above sea level. It also tossed up a World War II torpedo boat that had previously sunk.

HOT BLAST

In July 1949, a sudden blast of hot air swept across an area of Portugal, causing temperatures to soar remarkably from 100 to 150°F (38 to 65°C) in just two minutes. The heat surge killed countless chickens on local farms.

CRYSTAL CAVE

Mexico's Cueva de los Cristales (Crystal Cave) is home to giant gypsum crystals that are more than 35 ft (11 m) long—over one third as long as the cave itself. By studying fluid samples embedded inside the crystals in the 970-ft-deep (290-m) cave, scientists believe the mammoth structures developed because the temperature there remained just below 136°F (58°C) for hundreds of thousands of years. Volcanic activity created the Naica Mountain some 26 million years ago and filled it with high-temperature anhydrite, which is gypsum without water. Above 136°F anhydrite is stable, but below that it turns to gypsum and, in this case, has formed majestic crystals.

SNOW DONUTS

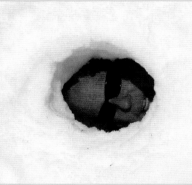

High in Washington Pass, Washington State, in March 2007, avalanche-control expert Mike Stanford found a series of perfectly shaped frozen snow donuts. They had rolled down the mountainside and frozen in place, the biggest being about 24 in (60 cm) high, large enough for Stanford to put his head through the hole in the middle.

Ripley's research

Snow donuts—or snow rollers—are rare phenomena that form at the base of steep slopes. When a clump of soft snow falls from a tree or off a rock face into hard-packed snow, and if conditions and temperature are just right, as gravity takes over, it pulls the snow down the slope and it rolls back on itself. Usually the center collapses and creates what is called a pinwheel, but if the hole stays open, it forms a snow donut.

RAINBOW ROCK

In a stunning natural spectacle, the earth at Chamarel, Mauritius, is divided into seven colors—red, brown, violet, yellow, deep purple, blue, and green. The phenomenon, which is at its most vivid at sunrise, is the result of mineral-rich volcanic rock cooling at uneven temperatures. Bizarrely, the different colors never merge even when it rains, and if mixed together artificially in a test tube, they separate into seven distinct colors again a few days later.

FOG PARTICLES

Particles of fog are so tiny that it would take seven billion of them to fill a teaspoon.

CHICKENS PLUCKED

A tornado in Britain traveled a distance of 100 mi (160 km) on May 21, 1950. The four-hour-long storm actually plucked some chickens completely bare.

ROOFS RIPPED

Lead nails ripped from roofs by a tornado were hammered by the wind into beams many yards away at Runanga, New Zealand, on April 20, 1956.

FOREST FLATTENED

A meteor exploded over Siberia's Tunguska River on June 30, 1908, unleashing the energy of 1,000 Hiroshima bombs and flattening 770 sq mi (2,000 sq km) of forest.

TOWN RESURFACES

Nearly 50 years after being submerged by the creation of an artificial lake, the underwater town of Adaminaby in Australia resurfaced following a prolonged drought in the area. The town was relocated in 1958 when Lake Eucumbene was created as part of the Snowy Mountains Hydro-Electric Scheme. Around 100 buildings were moved to the site of the new town on higher ground, some 300 mi (480 km) southwest of Sydney, but in February 2007 the lake's water level fell so much that the ruins of the old town became visible again.

WIDELY DISTRIBUTED

Gold has been located on 90 percent of the Earth's surface and is, with the exception of iron, the most broadly distributed metal on the planet. Gold is mined in such diverse settings as deserts, mountain ranges, the tropics, and the Arctic.

COLORED SNOW

Yellow snow and then red snow fell on areas of Russia within a few weeks of each other in 2006. The yellow blizzard was caused by airborne pollution from a gas and oil factory, and the red snow was the result of sandstorms in the neighboring country of Mongolia.

ICE BLOCK

In January 2007, a massive block of ice—thought to be a hailstone weighing more than 50 lb (22 kg)—fell from the sky and crushed a car belonging to Andre Javange in Tampa, Florida.

THICK ICE

Ninety percent of the world's total amount of ice is in Antarctica and at the South Pole where it is nearly 2 mi (3.2 km) thick.

OCEAN PRESSURE

The water pressure at the ocean floor, 2½ mi (4 km) deep, is equivalent to sitting under 14 fully loaded cement trucks.

COLORED POOLS

Scattered along the salt flats on the coast of Senegal are a series of small pools filled with different colored water, including red, orange, black, and white. They have been created by women workers digging for salt, which they collect by hand, load into sacks, and sell to neighboring countries. The variety of colors is a result of the high mineral concentration in the soil, the colors being intensified by the shallowness of the water in the pools.

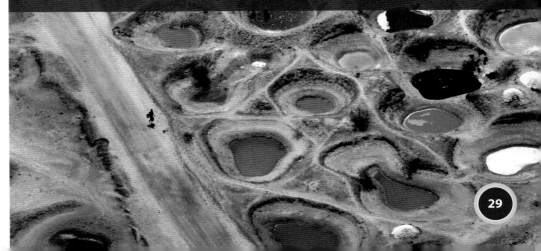

CROCODILE ATTACK

Veterinarian Chang Po-yu lost his arm to the jaws of a saltwater crocodile in Shaoshan Zoo in Kaohsiung, Taiwan, on April 11, 2007.

The vet's forearm was bitten clean through when he reached through iron railings to remove a tranquilizer dart from the 440-lb (200-kg) reptile. Two bullets were immediately shot into the neck of the crocodile, which then dropped the arm. But this story has a doubly remarkable ending. First, the crocodile was unharmed by the gunshots as the bullets didn't penetrate its hide, they merely shocked the croc into opening its mouth; and second, a team of surgeons operated for seven hours to reattach the arm—successfully!

What was it like, Mr. Chang?

Reptilian Tales

CROC PLUNGE
Believe it or not, a crocodile suffered nothing worse than a broken tooth after falling from the 12th floor of an apartment block in the Russian city of Nizhny-Novgorod. It was the third time that the pet croc, named Khenar, had tried to escape his captivity by climbing through a window.

GREAT ESCAPE
Australian rancher David George spent a week clinging desperately to the branches of a tree to avoid being eaten by crocodiles. Stranded in crocodile country after falling off his horse and hitting his head, George climbed a tree and stayed there for six days and nights, terrified by the red eyes of the hungry crocodiles that were circling expectantly below. Surviving on just a packet of cheese-and-ham sandwiches and a few sips of water, he was eventually spotted by rescuers and winched to safety.

DEADLY HEAD
A man in Prosser, Washington State, was hospitalized after being bitten by the decapitated head of a rattlesnake. Danny Anderson beheaded the 5-ft-long (1.5-m) rattler with a shovel, but when he reached down to pick up the severed head, it bit his finger, injecting venom. He took the head to a hospital, and by the time he arrived his tongue was swollen and the venom was spreading. He was released after two days' treatment. The bite was thought to be a reflex action from the snake, as, believe it or not, snake heads can still be dangerous up to an hour after being separated from the body.

HEARTY MEAL
U.S. scientists have discovered that some snakes can survive without food for up to two years by digesting their own hearts. Snake hearts then quickly rebuild themselves after a nutritious meal.

"I am a veterinarian and a director of the zoo. When I anesthetized and treated the crocodile, the animal took my left-hand away suddenly. It was a huge shock in my mind, my limb felt pretty numb.

My left-arm caused extreme pain, but I told myself that I must live, I want to take my arm back, and do my best to connect it again.

My associate helped me to stop bleeding by pressing on the top of the arm until the ambulance came. When I was on the way to the hospital, the police helped me to take my arm back from the crocodile's mouth.

Right now it's still hard for me to accept this serious damage. I have gone through six large operations and countless small operations. At present, my left arm has no sensation, and the injury is still in the process of recovery. I still need lots of recuperative treatment—for at least two years. Although I can't work right now, I still hope that I could continue to work in the administration or management of the zoo, the treatment of animals... and so on, in the future.

June 2007"

IN THE SURGEON'S OWN WORDS...

Dr Yin Chih Fu is an orthopedic surgeon at the Kaohsiung Medical University Hospital. He was one of the surgeons who worked on Chang Po-yu's arm. Ripley's tracked him down, and here is his account of what happened after the arm was severed.

"The zoo had done a great job to preserve the arm. It arrived at the E.R. in a clean plastic bag in iced water. This method of preservation is critical if reattachment is to be successful. Everyone had also acted fast. The arm was in surgery just 30 minutes after it had been retrieved from the crocodile and that greatly improved its chances.

First of all, I washed the arm with copious amounts of distilled water—about 350 fl oz (10,000 ml) of water in all—because an animal's mouth is so dirty and the risk of infection is high.

We reattached the bones first to make the arm stable. This had to be quick because we had to be able to repair the arteries as soon as possible to get oxygen to the tissue before it decayed. Even so, we had to take out some dead tissue. Then we reconnected the major veins, and afterward the nerves. The muscles were joined next, and, lastly, the skin.

Chang Po-yu had to be on high doses of antibiotics to stave off infection, but after just one month he could move his elbow and shoulder. He may need more surgery in the future, and must wait for his nerves to regenerate and muscles to heal, but eventually he should be able to grasp with his hand.

It's so important to never give up."

TASTY TOY

A pet bearded dragon, named Mushu, was treated by a veterinarian in Jacksonville, Florida, in 2007—after swallowing a 7-in (18-cm) rubber lizard.

RED SHEEP

To cheer up drivers sitting in highway traffic jams in 2007, a Scottish farmer dyed his flock of sheep red! Andrew Jack sprayed his 54-strong flock before releasing them on to the hills next to the busy M8 highway.

MATERNAL PRIDE

A lioness separately adopted three baby antelopes at Kenya's Samburu National Park over the course of a few months. Normally, a young antelope would make a delicious meal for a big cat, but this tenderhearted lioness was fiercely protective of the calves. One day, while the lioness slept, a male lion ate one of the calves. When she awoke from her slumber, the adoptive mother-of-three became grief-stricken and paced around the bush roaring in anger.

PAINTING PUPS

An art gallery in Salisbury, Maryland, staged an unusual exhibition in 2007—the artists of the exhibits were all dogs! Encouraged by dog-trainer Mary Stadelbacher, the canine Canalettos paint their masterpieces by chewing on a rubber bone with a hole drilled in the middle to hold a paintbrush. In this way they daub paint on the canvas. Each original work is signed with a black paw print in the corner and some of the doggy paintings have already sold for $350.

PIG-ASSOS

Pigs at a farm in Devon, England, paint works of art on large canvasses with their snouts and trotters. They got into art by accident, when they knocked over some tins of non-toxic paint after running amok at a craft fair.

UGLIEST DOG

After finishing second in 2006, Elwood, a Chinese Crested dog, from New Jersey, went one better in 2007 by being crowned the World's Ugliest Dog in the annual contest at Petaluma, California. With the award came a prize of $1,000, no wonder his owner Karen Quigley thinks he's cute.

SALES DOG

A dog in Pingdong City, Taiwan, is so clever that she serves customers in her owner's nut shop. The dog—named Hello—can open the refrigerator, pick up the nuts, put them on the counter, and collect money from customers. She also goes shopping by herself, waits patiently in line, and when it is her turn to be served, she puts her front paws on the counter, and gives a bag containing money and a shopping list to the waiting shopkeeper.

SNAKE SHOCK

While searching for snakes with his granddaughter in 2006, a man in Orion, Illinois, captured a two-headed bull snake.

BEST FRIENDS

In 2007, two rare Sumatran tiger cubs and two baby orangutans became inseparable friends in the nursery room of an Indonesian animal hospital. Whereas in the wild, a young orangutan would represent a tasty snack for a tiger, here the abandoned quartet regularly curled up together to sleep.

NEW TONGUE

The tongue louse, a parasite that lives on snapper fish, crawls into the mouth of a fish, eats its tongue, and then itself acts as the fish's tongue for the rest of the fish's life.

ONE OF A KIND

A calf was born in Litchfield, Nebraska, in 2007 with six legs and both male and female sex organs! The extra front and back leg extended from its pelvic area but did not reach the ground. The extra sex organs indicated that twin embryos may have fused during the animal's development.

LOBSTER LOVERS

In April 2007, a group of animal-lovers paid nearly $3,400 to buy 300 lobsters from a Maine fish market—then set them free, putting them back into the ocean.

WHALE SIZE

A blue whale's aorta—the main artery that supplies blood to the body—is so wide that a fully-grown human could swim through it.

BRAND NEW TAIL

Winter, a two-year-old bottlenose dolphin at the Clearwater Marine Aquarium in Florida, has been fitted with a prosthetic tail. The tail, which helps her to swim naturally, has a silicon sleeve that fits over her stump and a joint made of titanium. She lost her tail fin after becoming tangled in a crab trap at sea.

TWIN FREAKS

A tiger at Tianjin Zoo, China, gave birth to twin cubs in 2007—one orange, like a normal Bengal tiger, and one white. The mother is a mixed-blood tiger and it appears that, by a genetic freak, each of her cubs has inherited her different colors.

FRENCH-SPEAKING

To strike up a rapport with their new Siberian tiger, staff at the Valley Zoo, in Edmonton, Alberta, had to find a French-speaking keeper. The tiger, named Boris, was born at a zoo in Quebec and only answers commands that are spoken in French.

SWAN LAKE

A swan on a lake in Germany has fallen in love with a plastic pedal boat. Petra the black swan circles the swan-shaped boat and makes amorous noises at it. She is so in love that when the boat didn't fly south for the winter, neither did she.

LONG LUNCH

Few birds have an appetite to match that of baby robins—they eat 14 ft (4.3 m) of earthworms every day.

PARROT LOVE

A German ornithologist has set up a dating agency—for parrots. Rita Oenhauser runs a bird sanctuary outside Berlin and has brought romance to more than 2,000 pairs of parrots. Courtship between these colorful birds can take up to three months, but once together, loved-up parrots will stay faithful to each other for life.

CONFUSED COCKATOO

Pippa, a 17-year-old cockatoo from Nuneaton, England, spent two weeks trying to hatch a bowl of chocolate Easter eggs! Her owner, Geoff Grewcock, said she saw the delicious-looking eggs on a table and climbed straight on them, because she was going through a "maternal stage." Geoff decided to let her stay on the eggs until she got off them herself—two weeks later.

GARLIC DIET

Keepers at a zoo in Shanghai, China, have been feeding their penguins garlic to help fight breathing problems and other illnesses associated with the country's rainy season. The keepers hide the cloves of garlic in the penguins' usual meals of fish.

WATCH THE BIRDIE!

A pelican resident in St. James's Park, London, England, took a radical departure from its usual diet of fish when it decided to try pigeon instead. The pelican, one of five famous pelicans in this park that lies adjacent to Buckingham Palace, was performing its usual photocall for visiting tourists when it amazed them by scooping a nearby pigeon into its beak. The hapless bird struggled in the beak for a full 20 minutes before the pelican finally swallowed it.

FISH FOOD

A black swan at Shenzhen Zoo in southern China astounds visitors by regularly feeding his fishy friends. When zookeepers bring the swan his feed, the colorful carp rush over to the bank and open their mouths. The swan then takes a morsel of food and drops it into each hungry mouth.

Cool Cat

Odin, a six-year-old white Bengal tiger who lives at the Six Flags Discovery Zoo in Vallejo, California, has no qualms about diving into water after a piece of meat thrown in by his trainer. Most cats shy away from water, but Odin loves a cool dip, especially at dinner time. Some scientists believe that because tigers evolved in eastern Asia they dislike excessive heat and may use a refreshing swim as a way to keep cool.

PET RESCUE

When a man climbed a 60-ft (18-m) pine tree to retrieve his pet cockatoo, he himself had to be rescued by a coastguard helicopter. William Hart, from Montgomery County, Texas, had scaled the tree after the bird, Geronimo, escaped from its cage.

IN A FLAP

After shooting a duck for dinner, a hunter told his wife to put it in the refrigerator, which she did. But they didn't eat the duck that night, and when the wife opened the refrigerator door two days later, the duck was still very much alive! Initially, she was shocked at seeing it look up at her, but then she took the injured bird to an animal hospital in Tallahassee, Florida, where it was treated for wing and leg wounds.

MOP MOTHER

Guzzle the goose could be a little shortsighted, because he adopted a mop as his mother while being treated at an animal care clinic in Kent, England.

EXTRA FLIPPERS

A dolphin captured off the coast of Wakayama, Japan, in October 2006 had an extra set of flippers!

BATH RELIEF

After accidentally setting fire to her home in Northumberland, England, a Rottweiler puppy survived by jumping into the bath and gulping air through the plughole. Peggy had caused the fire by switching on the kitchen stove as she tried to reach her owner's chocolate birthday cake.

COW-NIVORE!

A cow in Chandpur, India, eats chickens! When 48 chickens went missing in a month, farmers suspected local dogs—until one night they saw their friendly cow, named Lal, creep in and devour several live chickens.

PURR-FECT PASSENGER

A cat in Wolverhampton, England, amazed passengers by traveling on a bus nearly every day for three months in 2007. The cat jumped on the number 331 bus, always sat at the front, and traveled for two stops before getting off near a fish-and-chip shop.

DONKEY DIAPERS

In Limuru, Kenya, the town council is trying to keep the streets clean by ordering local tradesmen to put diapers on their donkeys!

CROC COSTUME

U.S. zoologist Brady Barr studied a group of crocodiles in Tanzania up close while wearing a life-size croc costume to disguise the fact that he's a human!

CROSSBREED

A dog in a Chinese village appeared to give birth to a kitten in 2007. The first two puppies in the litter were normal but the third looked just like a cat. Vets in Jiangyan City said that it was really a puppy—it yapped like a puppy—but looked like a cat because of a gene mutation.

PRICKLY PROBLEM

It looks like mom, it feels like mom, it even smells like mom, but it's actually a brush! However, four tiny, orphaned hedgehogs at a wildlife park in Hampshire, England, knew no better and took a fancy to the center's cleaning brush, because its bristles reminded them of their absent mother.

WHAT A HOOT!

Four tawny owl chicks at a wildlife park in Hampshire, England, were given a stuffed toy owl as their surrogate mother. To keep warm, the orphaned chicks snuggled under the wings of the fluffy toy, which had to be washed regularly because it received so much love and affection.

TALKING CAT

A cat in China is able to say his own name! The two-year-old cat, from Beijing, says his name, Agui, repeatedly when he becomes nervous or frightened.

SINGING DOG

A dog has been adding his bark to the hymn-singing at a chapel near Llanelli, Wales. Teddy the Golden Retriever goes to the chapel every Sunday with his owner Nona Rees and joins in with the rousing hymns—although he sometimes falls asleep during the sermons.

MUSICAL DOG

A dog in Xi'an, China, sings along with the ringtone on his owner's cell phone. Dangdang yaps along to the rhythm of the music whenever Mrs. Zhang's phone rings.

RUBBER LEG

A tortoise at Longleat Safari Park in Wiltshire, England, was fitted with a rubber tire and wheel to replace a leg she lost in the wild.

PIGHEADED

A piglet in Queensland, Australia, is certain he will grow into a bull! Although he was a fraction of their size and weight, Charlie the feral piglet made himself at home with two big bulls, who even let him cuddle up to them for warmth.

PARROT JOKER

An African gray parrot belonging to a New York artist has a vocabulary of 950 words and can even crack jokes! When he saw another parrot hang upside down from its perch, N'kisi squawked: "You gotta put this bird on the camera!" He also uses words in their proper context, with past, present, and future tenses.

HORSEPLAY

A dangerous horse has finally calmed down—after learning how to play soccer. Sixteen-year-old Kariba regularly used to throw off riders until horse psychologist Emma Massingale, of Devon, England, soothed the stallion's temper by getting him to kick a ball around.

BLOOD PUMP

Because of its height, a giraffe's arteries feature special valves to help pump blood all the way up to its head. Without these valves, a giraffe's heart would need to be as big as its entire body.

PORKY PUPPY

After losing its own puppies, Hui Hu, a dog in China's Chongqing municipality, found an ideal replacement—a pig. The arrangement works both ways, as the devoted pig follows its foster mother everywhere.

BABY LOVE

A Chihuahua dog has been caring for a baby chick at a house in Guiyang City, China. Far from resenting the new pet, Huahua treated the chick as her baby and whenever it strayed too far, she would pick it up gently in her mouth and bring it back to her bed.

DOLPHIN AID

A Florida dog has been trained to sniff out dead or injured dolphins. Cloud, a female Black Labrador, works with her owner, marine biologist Chris Blankenship, who came up with the idea for a dolphin-sniffing dog after some 80 dolphins became stranded off Marathon Key in 2005. Around 30 of the animals died, mainly as a result of dehydration, but they could have been saved had they been located earlier.

WONDER WEB

A spider's web created in Texas in 2007 measured more than 200 yd (183 m) long! The web at the Lake Tawakoni State Park trapped millions of mosquitoes and was so vast that it totally engulfed seven large trees and dozens of bushes.

CHEWED CASH

A pooch named Pepper was in the doghouse in 2007 after eating $750 in cash. The dog was staying with owner Debbie Hulleman's mother in Oakdale, Minnesota, when it found a purse and chewed the contents. It spat out some money and when the family went to clean up the dog's mess outside the house, they noticed a $50 bill hanging out of one pile of poop. They gradually recovered $647 from both poop and vomit, and exchanged the cash for clean currency at a bank.

SQUIRREL ARSONISTS

Squirrels started two fires in eight days at the home of Alan Turcott, of Blue Island, Illinois—by knocking loose and chewing electrical cables.

ACTUAL 1:1 SIZE!

GIANT TOAD

A huge cane toad— believed to be the biggest ever found in Australia's Northern Territory—was captured near Darwin in March 2007. Its body was 8 in (20.5 cm) long and it weighed 30½ oz (861 g). Cane toads were introduced into Australia in 1935 to control scarab beetles, a sugar-cane pest. They have since become a pest themselves, as they have spread across the country, with their toxic skin poisoning millions of native animals along the way.

THREE EYES

In 2007, a piglet at a Chinese farm was born with two faces. The mutant had one extra-large head, two mouths, and three eyes!

BLESSING IN DISGUISE

Having a leg amputated after getting it caught on a fence would be a disaster for most ducks, but not for Stumpy—because, owing to a rare mutation, he was born with four legs! In fact Stumpy, from Hampshire, England, can actually waddle much faster in pursuit of his lady-friend now that he has only one extra leg to carry.

EXTRA NOSE

A calf in Merrill, Wisconsin, was born in 2007 with two noses. Lucy has a smaller nose on the top of the first, and both noses are functional. Owner Mark Krombholz noticed the extra nose only when he fed her a bottle of milk.

FOSTER PIG

When three tiger cubs at a zoo in Guangzhou City, China, were rejected by their mother, they found an unlikely surrogate mom—a pig. Not only did the cubs gently suckle the pig's milk, they even enjoyed playing with their piglet foster brothers and sisters.

MORE PORK

A piglet born in Croatia in 2007 had a little extra of just about everything. The piglet, nicknamed Octopig, had six legs, two penises, and two anuses. He was so unusual that farmer Ivica Seic decided to keep him as a pet.

NAIL HAT

Yang Decai of Hunan, China, has been attacked so often by an angry owl that he protects himself by wearing a special hat that is fitted with nails protruding from it.

SEVEN-LEGGED LAMB

A lamb born in Christchurch, New Zealand, in 2007 was not just one in a million—it was one in several million. The lamb was born with seven legs, making it an extremely rare polydactyl, meaning many-legged animal.

FREAK CALF

When Howard Gentry saw eight legs protruding from his pregnant cow, he thought she must be giving birth to two calves. Instead, the fully grown limbs—complete with hooves—all belonged to one eight-legged calf that was stillborn at Gentry's farm in Glasgow, Kentucky, in 2007.

MOOSE ASSAULT

In March 2007, a moose rammed and downed a low-flying helicopter near Gustavus, Alaska! The animal had been shot with a tranquilizer dart, but instead of slowing down it charged the hovering helicopter, damaging the tail rotor and forcing it to the ground.

RESCUE DOG

An Italian animal-lover has trained Newfoundland dogs to jump out of helicopters and rescue people who are drowning in the sea. Ferrucio Pilenga, from Bergamo, has a team of expert canine swimmers patrolling Italy's beaches, where they have already saved a number of lives.

DOGWATCH

A 196-lb (89-kg) Newfoundland dog is the latest recruit to the lifeguards in Cornwall, England. Bilbo's training paid off when he prevented a tourist from entering dangerous currents by swimming in front of her to stop her going out any further to sea. Bilbo has his own lifeguard vest with safety messages written across it.

CAUGHT ON CAMERA!

Wondering what his pet tomcat, Mr. Lee, got up to when he went through the cat flap, Jürgen Perthold decided to find out—by fitting a tiny camera to the animal's collar.

"He goes out the whole day," says Mr. Perthold. "Sometimes he returns hungry, sometimes not, sometimes with traces of fights, and sometimes he also stays out all night. It gave me the idea to equip the cat with a camera."

At first Mr. Lee was not keen on wearing the "CatCam" but he soon got used to it, and his adventures around his home in Anderson, South Carolina, have attracted worldwide attention.

The 2½-oz (70-g) camera, which takes one photo a minute for 48 hours, has shown Mr. Lee looking longingly at bird feeders, exploring garages, hiding under cars with other cats, and even encountering a snake. It has also revealed that the tabby has a girlfriend, although he faces stiff competition from a black tom.

Mr. Lee is not the only cat to be the star of his own feline soap opera. In Los Angeles, California, Julie Peasley has fitted a lightweight camera to the collar of her gray-and-white tuxedo cat, Squeaky. Within days, she had discovered that he likes to hide in the basement of the house next door.

With CatCam, no cat's secret will ever be safe again.

ELE-VISION

For a TV documentary *Elephants: Spy in the Herd*, a miniature, remote-controlled camera was mounted on a little mobile platform and covered with dry elephant dung. The camouflage was so effective that one elephant picked up the dung cam and walked around with it still filming.

PENGUINS UNCOVERED

In 2004, scientists obtained amazing images of penguins underwater by strapping miniature cameras to the birds' backs. They found that penguins swim together with at least one other bird on about a quarter of their dives for food.

ROBOT SHARK

A robot shark was built for the U.K.'s BBC series *Smart Sharks*, containing a hidden camera that filmed sharks live in their natural habitats.

PIGEON SPIES

During the 1970s, the CIA strapped cameras—weighing as little as only a few coins—to the chests of pigeons and released the birds over enemy targets. An earlier test, with a heavier camera in the skies over Washington, D.C., failed after two days when the overburdened pigeon was forced to abandon his flight and walk home!

FLYING HIGH

TV producers strapped a miniature camera weighing almost 1 oz (25 g) to a golden eagle and were rewarded with magnificent shots as the bird soared through the air.

Mr. Lee wears his owner-made CatCam.

A bird table, but no birds...

Snakes alive!

Squeaky wearing his camera.

A Squeaky-eye view of home.

Ripley's ask Julie Peasley:

"**Why did you first fit Squeaky with a camera?** Initially, I wanted to track Squeaky after he went missing for three days in 2005. Since he's an outdoor cat, I don't know where he gets off to all day. I thought that with a camera I could at least see what he is seeing and never lose track of him.

Did you make the camera yourself? No, Squeaky wears a spy cam available online for about $50.

Did he have any objections to wearing it? No, he hardly notices his new "jewelry" and, after many days wearing it, couldn't care less.

How often has Squeaky worn his camera? Five or six times. I like to put it on him first thing in the morning when he goes outside because that's when he makes his rounds of the grounds.

What is the strangest thing Squeaky has caught on camera? I found it interesting that he photographed the two-year-old child from next door looking into the apartment window.

Does Squeaky do anything sinister while out on his travels? Squeaky gets in a lot of territorial matches with other cats. If you consider squeezing through the open window of a neighbor's house sinister, he's guilty. Squeaky's brought home critters, too—a lizard, lizard tail, rat, bird, mouse, moth, grasshopper, and caterpillar.

What is your favorite picture taken by Squeaky? Hmm... it's really hard to pick a single favorite. My favorites are any that show his chin and whiskers—like a true cat-point-of-view genre of photography!

Where is Squeaky's favorite place to go? His favorite places include the upstairs balcony and any apartments that happen to have their doors open; the neighbor's yard; the neighbor's house; the neighbor's basement; under cars; in the hedge; behind the apartment building; and strolling around the carport. If his paw can open it, he goes in it."

It's a jungle out here!

Hmm... friend or foe?

I wonder what's in that hole.

KING HOG

A 1,050-lb (475-kg) monster hog, measuring 9 ft 4 in (2.85 m) long, was killed in Alabama in 2007—by an 11-year-old boy. Armed only with a pistol, Jamison Stone pursued the beast for three hours, shooting it eight times before finally firing the fatal bullet. The dead boar was converted into 2,800 sausages.

BUG SNIFFERS

Bill Whitstine of Safety Harbor, Florida, teaches dogs to sniff out bedbugs. One of his students, Abbey the Beagle, is such an expert that when she smells bedbugs, she sits down next to them and even points her paw at the affected area.

INFLATABLE COLLAR

Dogs in California who can't swim can wear a new inflatable dog collar. The collar—called the Float-a-Pet—fits over the dog's head and contains light-emitting diodes to help locate the animal when dusk falls.

TATTOOED FISH

Fish in Singapore are being tattooed. A tattoo laser is used to create patterns on the fish's body, including hearts, polka dots, and stripes. The tattooists maintain that the procedure does not harm the fish.

COLLIE WOBBLE

Kyle, a 14-year-old collie, who is partially blind and is also hard of hearing, survived a 50-ft (15-m) plunge at a Scottish waterfall—called Dog Falls. Despite being the place of Kyle's misfortune, the spot actually gets its name because the water falls in the shape of a dog's leg.

FISHING BATS

Whereas most bats prefer to eat insects, the bulldog bat from Central and South America is an accomplished fisherman. It trails its extra-long legs in the water and grabs fish with its huge hooked claws.

MONKEY BUSINESS

Monkeys are trained to assist in Thailand's coconut industry, because a single monkey can climb through the trees and easily pick hundreds of coconuts a day.

DISTINCTIVE BULL

The main attraction at a zoo in Guangzhou City, China, is a five-legged bull. The animal looks perfectly normal—apart from an extra leg growing on its back.

DINNER DATE

A wolf captured in Albania in 2007 became best friends with its dinner! A donkey was put in the wolf's cage as a prospective meal, but instead of hunting it down and eating it, the wolf made the donkey its friend.

TABLE MANNERS

Gorillas have table manners. A conservation group tracking western lowland gorillas in Africa has discovered that, after eating, they politely wipe their hands and faces with leaves—in exactly the same way that humans use table napkins.

HIGHWAY ROBBERY

In 2007, motorists in the Orissa state of India reported that a wild elephant refused to let their vehicles pass unless they gave him food. The elephant stood in the highway, forcing vehicles to stop, and moved aside only when fed with vegetables or bananas.

HEROIC CHIHUAHUA

A tiny Chihuahua saved the life of a one-year-old boy who was attacked by a rattlesnake. Booker West was playing in his grandparents' backyard in Masonville, Colorado, when the snake lunged, but Zoey the Chihuahua jumped in the way and took the bites. Happily, the brave dog survived.

BUSY BURROWS

In 1900, a single prairie-dog town in Texas covered 25,000 sq mi (64,750 sq km) and had a whopping estimated population of 400 million animals!

LION KISS

The owner of an animal refuge in Cali, Colombia, is on kissing terms with a fully grown lion! Ana Julia Torres rescued Jupiter the lion from a traveling circus seven years ago and now he repays her kindness by tenderly hugging her with his giant paws through the bars of his cage, and by planting a kiss on her mouth.

LONG EARS

Nipper's Geronimo, an English lop-eared rabbit owned by the Nipper family of Bakersfield, California, has ears that are more than 2½ ft (76 cm) long.

ZOO CLOWN

A German zoo has hired a clown to cheer up its gorillas, orangutans, and chimpanzees. Zoo chiefs hired local entertainer Christina Peter to keep the animals amused after research found that apes tended to become sick or aggressive when bored.

LANGUAGE BARRIERS

When Milo the Jack Russell terrier became trapped in a drain in England in 2007, its rescuers had to talk French to it because the dog used to belong to a family in France and it couldn't understand a word of English.

Ripley's research . . . .

Reports of winged cats have occurred sporadically over the years.

In 1966, a winged cat was said to be swooping down on farm animals at Alfred, Ontario, Canada. The animal was shot dead, and when exhumed, its "wings" were found to be nothing more than matted fur. It also had rabies, which accounted for its bizarre behavior.

The owner of the cat in China (right) is convinced that her pet sprouted wings after being harassed by female cats on heat. However, the cause is more likely to be either a genetic mutation or a rare hereditary skin condition called Feline Cutaneous Asthenia. This ailment results in the skin on the cat's shoulders, back, and haunches becoming abnormally elastic and forming pendulous, wing-like folds or flaps that sometimes contain muscle fibers.

Winged Cat

A cat in China has grown wings! Granny Feng of Xianyang City, was amazed to see what started out as two bumps on her cat's back grow into 4-in-long (10-cm) wing-like sprouts in less than a month in 2007. She said that the wings, which contain bones, make her pet look like a "cat angel."

PARROT LOOKOUTS

During World War I, parrots were kept on the Eiffel Tower in Paris, France, to warn of approaching German aircraft. Owing to their acute sense of hearing, the birds could detect enemy planes long before they came into the range of human lookouts.

SERIAL SWALLOWER

Taffy the Springer Spaniel needed an operation in 2007 after swallowing his 40th pair of underpants. The 18-month-old dog, which belongs to vet Eubie Saayman of Staffordshire, England, has also gulped down 300 socks, destroyed 15 pairs of shoes, and once ate the keys to the family's Mercedes car.

WEIGHTY WHIPPET

Wendy, a dog from Central Saanich, Canada, has a mutated set of muscular growth genes, making her "double-muscled" and twice the weight of an average Whippet.

NEW SPECIES

Scientists have discovered that hammerhead sharks can reproduce without having sex. The news was announced following studies of a female shark at Henry Doorly Zoo in Nebraska that gave birth to a pup in 2001 despite having had no contact with a male.

BEFORE

AFTER

BALL OF WOOL

Victa the sheep had a woolly coat that was five times his own body weight. Having not been sheared for up to three years at his backyard home in Melbourne, Australia, his wool had become so thick that he had problems bending down to eat. Luckily, Victa was rescued by animal protection officers and given a long-overdue shearing, after which he perked up considerably.

TWIN TURTLE

An aquarium in East Norriton, Pennsylvania, displayed a red-eared slider turtle that had two heads. The reptilian oddity had a pair of front feet on each side, but just one pair of back feet and only one tail.

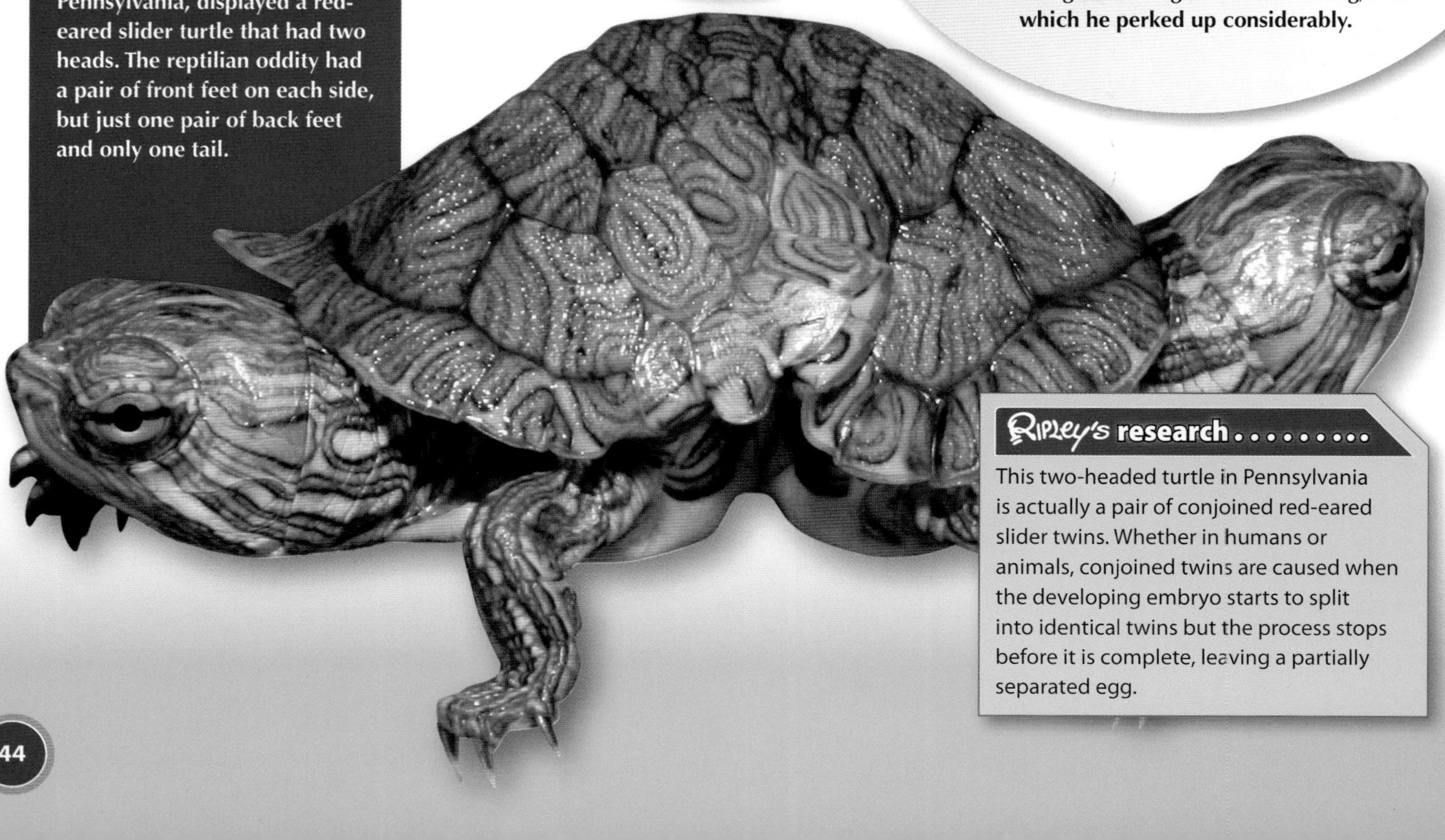

Ripley's research . . . .

This two-headed turtle in Pennsylvania is actually a pair of conjoined red-eared slider twins. Whether in humans or animals, conjoined twins are caused when the developing embryo starts to split into identical twins but the process stops before it is complete, leaving a partially separated egg.

Ripley's research....

With a zebra for a mother and a horse for a father, Eclyse is living proof that children inherit the genes of both parents. Most zebra-horse crossbreeds have stripes across their entire body but, by a freak of nature, Eclyse is only partially striped.

IT'S A ZORSE!

Visitors to a German safari park don't know quite what to make of Eclyse, its star attraction. Her head and rear are striped like a zebra, but the rest of her body and legs are snow white. The reason she looks so strange is that she's a "zorse," her father being a zebra and her mother a horse. While most zebra–horse crossbreeds sport stripes across their entire body, Eclyse has only two striped patches, giving her a truly unique appearance.

PAW AND ORDER

Alex, a 13-year-old Golden Retriever of Memphis, Tennessee, had an attorney appointed to represent his interests in a custody battle after his owner's death!

HAPPY HOMECOMING

Twenty months after disappearing from the Tighe family residence in Hallam, Nebraska, during a tornado, Harley the cat suddenly returned home in January 2006.

MUTANT MICE

Mutant mice created by scientists in Philadelphia, Pennsylvania, can grow back their toes and limbs and repair their severed spinal cords.

ELEPHANT'S BUZZWORD

Despite a huge difference in size and even though their skin is believed to be too thick for them to feel pain from a sting, African elephants are frightened by bees. Researchers have found that entire herds will steer clear of the sound of buzzing bees, and if bees get up elephants' trunks the animals go berserk.

LADYBUG'S BALL

A New York City apartment complex released 720,000 ladybugs onto its premises in October 2007 to help clear the grounds of parasitic insects.

MYNAH OFFENCE

A mynah bird was placed in solitary confinement at a zoo in Changsha, China, after being rude to visitors. After calling tourists stupid and ugly, eight-year-old Mimi had to stay in a darkened cage for 15 days and listen to recordings of polite conversation in an attempt to improve her behavior and language.

FOOD CYCLE

Leaf-cutting ants from South America actually grow their own food. They forage for plants and leaves, carry them home and then chew the pieces into a form of compost, which they proceed to spread on the floors of their underground chambers. Eventually, fungus grows on the compost and is eaten by the ants.

EXPERT MIMICS

Australia's lyrebirds mimic a huge range of natural and artificial sounds including other birds, dog barks, car alarms, musical instruments, and even revving chainsaws!

BACK TO LIFE

A hamster in Dagenham, England, was miraculously brought back to life after being accidentally cooked. Christmas the hamster was charred when the oven on which his cage was standing was turned on by mistake. When firefighters arrived, he was lying on his back with his legs in the air and his tongue hanging out, but after some oxygen, a rub of his tummy, and a few sips of juice, amazingly he was resuscitated.

PAMPERED PET

A wealthy New York hotel magnate left $12 million in her will to her dog. Leona Helmsley doted on her Maltese terrier, Trouble, and also stipulated that when the dog dies, it should be buried next to her.

HIDING PLACE

A New Jersey cat survived a house fire in 2007 by hiding in the furniture. The owners of the house in West Orange thought the cat must have perished, but were amazed to find their pet had wedged itself into the couch.

KISS-OF-LIFE

A man saved the life of his bulldog puppy by giving her the kiss-of-life after she had fallen into an icy lake while chasing ducks and geese. The puppy, named Lucy, had a blue face and paws by the time Randy Gurchin pulled her from the wintry water in Sarpy County, Nebraska, but he revived her by closing her mouth, placing his mouth over her nose, and then breathing into her lungs while pushing on her chest.

JUMBO JOB

City officials of Barisal, Bangladesh, hired circus elephants to help them to demolish illegal buildings in March 2007. With a lack of mechanical demolition tools at their disposal, officials called in the elephants, who demolished the buildings in minutes.

PATTERN CONTROL

Female North American side-blotched lizards control the patterns of their offspring's camouflage by releasing different amounts of hormones into their eggs.

Dances with Buffalo

Some families keep dogs, others keep cats, but the Bridges family of Quinlan, Texas, have a truly unusual pet—a 1300-lb (590-kg) buffalo named Wildthing.

Wildthing has his own room in the house, where he eats and sleeps, and is so tame that he follows his master, R.C. Bridges, everywhere and even used to dance with him. They are best friends and, when Wildthing turned two in 2007, the family staged a birthday party in his room,

draping it in ribbons and making a cake of feed and icing shaped like a buffalo patty, topped with a candle.

R.C., a cowboy since childhood, started raising the baby buffalo in 2005. Helped by his son Lloyd, he "halter broke" the young bull even though Wildthing could kick and push with the strength of a fully grown animal. Since then, R.C. has taught Wildthing to pull a plow, and also a chariot on which he takes the family for rides. Wildthing will happily pull R.C.'s daughter

Taylor along on a sleigh and another son Will has learned to ski behind him.

"Wildthing has so much energy and personality," says R.C.'s wife Sherron, who reveals that the buffalo likes to play with a basketball and to take baths. Unfortunately, Wildthing has become too big to dance with—and he still has another 700–800 lb (315–360 kg) to gain before he's fully grown.

R.C. Bridges began training Wildthing when the buffalo was two months old.

Wildthing tucks into a birthday meal in his own special living quarters.

When R.C. and Sherron renewed their wedding vows in 2006, they had their wedding photos retaken with Wildthing as best man.

Wildthing spends much of his day in the house, but he also has a pen in the yard.

Wildthing rarely leaves R.C.'s side. Even when R.C. sits down, Wildthing will lie down next to him.

In Sherron Bridges' own words...

"When we're away from the house for a couple of hours or more, Wildthing will call out to the truck as we pull into the driveway. You'll hear him grunting and he'll run and bounce with excitement because he sees R.C. is in the truck. Grunting is his call to R.C. to come out and feed or brush and scratch him. As long as Wildthing can see R.C., he is just fine.

Wildthing can get his feelings hurt by R.C. telling him he can't come in the house. Wildthing will then pout by walking away or even going to lie down. We won't let him in the house if he is all wound up, because he could hurt you just by slinging his head around, even if it's just to warn you to leave him alone. If R.C. has to tell him off for scratching on the side of the house or horning at the windows, he pouts.

Healthy buffalo usually live for about 40 years. We would be lost if anything happened to Wildthing, and Wildthing would be lost if anything happened to R.C."

The Bridges family with their big baby, Wildthing. He still has a lot more growing to do.

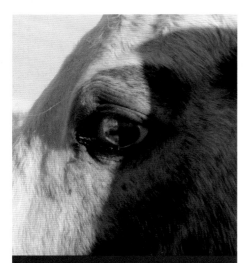

COLOR SPLIT

Peavey, a horse belonging to Ann Huth-Fretz of Tiffin, Ohio, has a two-tone eye, with the colors split straight down the middle!

SNAKE SLAIN

When a deadly viper slithered into the intensive care ward of a Croatian hospital, 80-year-old patient Miko Vukovic, who was recovering from heart surgery, jumped from his bed and beat the snake to death with his walking stick.

FIRE RESCUE

Jango, a Golden Retriever from Trail, British Columbia, Canada, saved his family from a fire by barking as the house filled with smoke. The dog then continued to bark to help the Unger family navigate their way to safety through the flames.

CARING CAT

A nine-year-old boy with Type 1 diabetes was saved from having a possible seizure by the attention of his cat. Mel-O climbed the ladder to Alex Rose's loft bed in his home in Morinville, Alberta, Canada, walked on his chest, swatted his face and purred in his ear until he got out of bed. When he went to his mother, his glucose levels were found to be dangerously low. Nobody knows how the cat managed to sense low blood sugar.

MILK BOOST

Romanian farmers have boosted milk production by playing music to their cows. Cowhands have set up CD players in the stables, and the music relaxes the animals so much that they even come in alone from the fields just to listen to more tunes.

CLIFF ORDEAL

A dog survived for two weeks on a ledge 100 ft (30 m) high in Devon, England, in 2007, by eating a dead bird and drinking from a waterfall. Bush the Staffordshire bull terrier had disappeared from his owner's sight when he ran over the edge of the cliff in pursuit of a deer.

JELLYFISH INVASION

In November 2007, billions of jellyfish washed into a salmon farm in Northern Ireland killing every one of the 100,000-plus fish.

HIDDEN PASSENGER

Arriving in her hotel room in Niagara, Ontario, Canada, after a two-hour flight from New Brunswick, Mary Martell opened her suitcase—and was amazed to find her cat Ginger inside. The cat had jumped into the case while Mrs. Martell was packing and had even escaped detection by airport security.

DOLPHIN RESCUE

Dolphins rescued surfer Todd Endris from a deadly shark attack off the coast of Monterey, California, by driving the shark away and surrounding the 24-year-old until help could arrive. Endris had been attacked by a 15-ft-long (4.5-m) great white shark, which had rammed him three times and was about to swallow his right leg when he managed to free himself. As the shark moved in for the kill, the bottlenose dolphins swam to his rescue and managed to keep the predator at bay. Talking to journalists, Endris described the rescue as "truly a miracle."

FISHING SETTER

A Croatian fisherman decided to sell his dog because it kept embarrassing him by catching more fish than he did. Whereas Slobodan Paparella reels in the occasional fish while out with his pals, his Irish setter Lipi would leap into the water and catch dozens.

TWO-FACED

A two-faced calf, named Star, was born recently at a dairy farm in Rural Retreat, Virginia. The curious creature had three sets of teeth, two lower jaws, and two tongues, but only one mouth. It also had two noses with separate airways, but only a single eye socket with two eyes in it!

ODD EYES

A two-year-old cat in Riyadh, Saudi Arabia, has different-colored eyes—one brown and one blue. Appropriately, the cat is a mix of Persian and Siamese.

DOGGY DUDE

The owner of a leather goods shop in Suzhou City, China, dresses her pet dog in T-shirt and jeans to welcome customers. The dog greets them with a friendly bark and bows courteously when they leave.

LION CHASE

Drivers in Wakefield, Ohio, are used to their cars being chased by dogs, but in November 2007 they were hotly pursued by a lion. Pike County sheriff's deputies responded to a 911 call of a lion "attacking" vehicles on U.S. 23 after the 550-lb (250-kg) beast, named Lambert, had escaped from its pen.

DOG SCENT

A firm in London, England, has launched a perfume for dogs. Petite Amande, which features blackcurrant, mimosa, vanilla, and almond, is designed to appeal to the canine nose and comes with a matching shampoo.

Troubled Triplets

Triplet puppies were born in Virginia in 2007, without any front legs—the first case of its kind in the world. Yet with the aid of daily physiotherapy at a New York animal shelter to strengthen their muscles, the brave little Chihuahuas were soon getting around by standing upright and hopping on their back legs.

JAR ORDEAL

A cat survived for 19 days with a peanut-butter jar stuck on her head. Thin and weak through lack of food, the feral cat was saved by the Cain family of Bartlett, Tennessee, who used oil to pry the jar off the animal's head and then nursed her back to health.

STRONG LEGS

Believe it or not, one leg of a mosquito can support 23 times the insect's weight—while standing on water.

PIE SNATCH

The 2007 World Pie Eating Championships were thrown into disarray after the organizer's dog woofed the pies. While Dave Williams, who won the title in 1995, was looking after the precious tournament pies at his home in Lancashire, England, his pet dog Charlie managed to sneak in and eat at least ten of them.

Ripley's research . . . .

TWO-FACED: Animals usually form two heads or faces because of a condition called axial bifurcation—an abnormality that occurs when an embryo is damaged in the womb. This can result in the formation of a lesion, causing some parts to develop in duplicate. Polycephalic (two-headed) animals rarely live very long.

TROUBLED TRIPLETS: The birth defects in the Chihuahuas below are thought to have been caused by excessive inbreeding—breeding between close relatives. Breeders of domestic animals use inbreeding to maintain desirable characteristics within the breed, but it can sometimes lead to genetic disorders and physical defects. While three of the puppies were born without front legs, the other two in the litter were normal.

COLOR SPLIT & ODD EYES: The condition to describe one eye that is a different color from the other is called heterochromia. It is caused by an excess or lack of pigment within the eye and can be inherited or acquired through mutation, disease, or injury. The rarer condition of sectoral heterochromia produces different colors within the same eye.

Hair-raising Yarn!

Victoria Pettigrew hated throwing away the hair from her pet Chow's brush after grooming. So one day she decided to spin it into yarn. Her idea has prompted pet lovers across the U.S.A. to wear their pets' hair with pride—in bed, to the shops, and even to the beach.

When Victoria's beloved 16-year-old Lhasa Apso dog, Karly, died in 2001, she spun her fur and knitted it into a small scarf. Now customers send hair from their dogs and cats to her company—VIP Fibers of Denton, Texas—and she spins it into yarn before sending it back to them as maybe a pair of mittens, a scarf, a blanket, a pillow, or, for the more daring, a fun-fur bikini. Such items are proving to be popular keepsakes with which owners can remember their adored pets.

Dog fur is up to 80 percent warmer than sheep's wool, but has to be thoroughly cleaned so that when the yarn gets wet, it does not smell like a wet dog. First the hair is washed in shampoo, then it is put through a process that removes the enzymes that cause odor, and finally it is soaked in softener and conditioner.

Victoria also spins yarn from alpacas, rabbits, horses, and even hamsters, although it may need several years' fur collection to create a hamster blanket!

From raw fibers through being spun into finished yarn, the pet hair undergoes a thorough cleaning process.

Victoria's friend Gary used her company to make his hat from his cat Teddie's hair.

Ripley's ask

How much yarn has VIP Fibers spun in its seven-year history? To date, we have spun 1,531,926 yards of pet yarn. We have created hundreds, if not thousands, of finished Fur-ever Keepsakes from a portion of this yarn.

Do you make every item personally? No, in the past the company has had up to four employees. Currently, we have one. In addition, my husband Stephen comes in to card fiber on a part-time basis—I perform all other tasks.

How much fur does it take to make a sweater? General rule of thumb is 2½ lb (1.1 kg) of raw fiber for a basic, large sweater. However, we do not recommend making an entire sweater from 100 percent "canine cashmere," as dog hair is up to 80 percent warmer than wool. A sweater constructed completely from dog hair would simply be too warm to wear.

Is there any specific type of animal fur you like to work with? My favorite fiber is any from a beloved and spoiled pet! They have the nicest fur!

What is the weirdest thing you have been asked to make? We were asked to make three dog-fur bikinis for a TV show last year.

What is the most peculiar animal fur you have worked with? Fur belonging to a Bengal tiger.

DOGGIE DUDES

Four-legged surfing dudes get the chance to shine at the annual Loews Coronado Bay Resort Surf Dog Competition in California. Forty-seven canines took part in 2007, the contest being divided into two sections—the first purely for dogs and the second for dogs and humans surfing together on the same board at the same time. Prizes included a gourmet doggie room service meal at the resort and a basket filled with dog treats.

TIGER ATTACK

A stray dog had a lucky escape in January 2008 when it wandered into the tiger pit at Memphis Zoo in Memphis, Tennessee. The 50-lb (23-kg) female retriever-mix jumped over a railing and a wall before swimming across a moat to the center of the enclosure, where it was attacked by a 225-lb (100-kg) Sumatran tiger. Seeing the incident, zoo workers used fireworks and air horns to distract the tiger and, despite being held in the tiger's grasp for several minutes, the dog escaped with nothing worse than puncture wounds to its neck and shoulders.

TOO HEAVY

Young gannets are fed so much fish that they are unable to fly. On leaving the nest, they have to fast for a couple of weeks until they are light enough to get airborne.

AUTO SHEEP

Too old to be able to walk alongside his animals, a resourceful Greek shepherd named George Zokos has trained his flock of sheep to follow his car instead.

FAKE BURIALS

Animal experts have discovered that gray squirrels fake food burials in order to confuse their rivals if they think they are being watched. To protect their winter food stocks from potential thieves, squirrels put on an elaborate show of burying non-existent nuts and seeds, even covering them over with soil to dupe any thieving onlookers.

ACTUAL 1:1 SIZE!

Burly Beetle

There is a beetle that is longer than an adult human hand! The titan beetle (or giant long-horned beetle) of the Amazon rainforest can grow up to 8 in (21 cm) in length, including its antennae. Its mandibles are so strong that they can snap pencils in half and cut into human flesh.

Enter the Vault

MAD MARKINGS

Pete the monocled dog was owned by Harry Lucenay in the 1930s. His startling natural markings helped launch his movie career—Pete was a star in the popular "Our Gang" short films of the 1930s.

CONJOINED CALVES

In March 1932, Dr. M.T. Cook of Cumberland, Kentucky, delivered these live conjoined calves that belonged to Gravil Cornett, of Dione, Kentucky.

◀ FASHIONABLE FELINE
Mickey was a Maltese cat who was given a whole new wardrobe every Easter by his owner, New Yorker Joseph Orlando. This outfit, from his 1950 collection, features puffed sleeves and a fetching hat.

DOG STAR
In 1950, the Horden twins of East Falls, Pennsylvania, were the proud owners of a black dog named Rip who had a perfect white-star marking on his chest.

SKILLFUL SHEEP

In the early 1930s, Clarence Bosworth of Cayton, California, was the proud owner of a sheep that could walk on its front legs.

HORNED ROOSTER

This rooster, owned by Jesse Parker of Dequeen, Arkansas, in the early 1930s had two horns sticking out of the top of its head.

FAT CAT

This 1935 photograph shows a cat of considerable proportions that was owned by A.M. Turner of Wimbledon, England. The fat feline weighed a whopping 35 lb (16 kg).

RAT TRAP

In the cold winter of 1934, C.H. Watson of Cuba, New York, found this rat that had frozen to death when it made the fatal mistake of licking an icy iron bar.

BEAKLESS BIRD

This chicken with no beak was owned by the Milbank Creamery in South Dakota in 1932.

TWO-NOSED DOG

This setter with two noses was owned by John Glenn of Benton, Arkansas, in the 1940s.

Ted, a four-year-old terrier owned by Bill Vandever from Tulsa, Oklahoma, is seen here climbing 10 ft (3 m) up a tree to retrieve his ball in 1944.

CANINE CLIMBERS

Elmer, a dog from Connecticut, used to report for duty at his job working for a construction firm. He would regularly climb the ladders onto the roofs of buildings in the mid-1950s.

TALENTED PARROT

Alex, an African gray parrot, could identify 50 different objects, seven colors, five shapes, and quantities up to six. His owner, Dr. Irene Pepperberg of Waltham, Massachusetts, said he was the intellectual equivalent of a five-year-old child. His last words to her before his death in 2007 were: "You be good. See you tomorrow. I love you."

GRASS ADDICT

A dog in Oxfordshire, England, needed life-saving surgery after vets discovered a pound of grass in its stomach. Pie, a Rottweiler–German Shepherd cross, had become so addicted to eating grass that he was unable to digest it and ballooned to three times his normal weight.

ANIMAL BRIDE

To atone for past acts of cruelty to dogs, a 33-year-old Indian farmer married a female dog in a traditional Hindu ceremony in the southern state of Tamil Nadu in 2007. The canine bride, who was bathed before the wedding, wore an orange sari and a traditional floral garland.

UNTIMELY DEATH

A kangaroo met an unusual death in Victoria, Australia, after it swam out to sea and was attacked by a marauding shark. Kangaroos usually venture out to sea only if they are ill or in danger.

WEIGHTY WORMS

If we weighed all the earthworms in the U.S.A., they would be about 55 times heavier than the combined weight of all the American people.

SOARING CINDY

Cindy, a five-year-old greyhound from Miami, Florida, can jump a bar that is 5 ft 8 in (173 cm) above the ground. Cindy took up high jumping after being rejected for greyhound racing.

CASH RETRIEVER

A British charity, Canine Partners, is training dogs to use cash machines on behalf of their disabled owners. The scheme was inspired by wheelchair-bound Gulf War veteran Allen Parton who was struggling to retrieve his cash from an ATM when his Labrador Endal jumped up to reach for the card, money, and receipt with his mouth.

WHALE EXPLOSION

A build-up of gases caused a dead sperm whale to explode onto the streets of Tainan, Taiwan, in January 2004 as it was being delivered to a research center.

SPOTTED HOUSE

Dog-lovers Goran and Karmen Tomasic of Pribislavec, Croatia, were so upset when their pet Dalmatian, Bingo, was run over by a car that they painted their house white with black spots in his memory.

CAT POST

A cat has been appointed a stationmaster in Japan. Dressed in a railwayman's cap, seven-year-old Tama and his two feline assistants welcome passengers at the unmanned Kishi station on the Wakayama Electric Railway.

SNAIL TRAIL

The sticky discharge produced by snails as they move along offers the snail such strong protection that they can slide along the edge of a razor blade without cutting themselves.

CHIMP CHAMP

A chimpanzee outscored college students in a series of short-term numerical memory tests in Japan. When the numbers were flashed on a computer screen, five-year-old Ayumu proved faster and more accurate than the humans in memorizing the numbers in the correct sequence.

IN THE DOGHOUSE

When animal control officers visited the home of a 70-year-old woman from Corpus Christi, Texas, in December 2007, they found that she was living with 237 dogs. It took six hours to round up all the animals.

CLEVER CARP

A pet carp in China can understand human speech and even responds to its own name. Owner Fang Peng from Pingsai, Guizhou Province, says the fish—called Submarine—has been trained for four hours a day over a period of six years.

VARIED DIET

The ruffed grouse of North America enjoys a varied diet, from salamanders and snakes to flies and watercress. It eats on average at least 518 different kinds of animals and insects and 414 different plants.

CONSTANT COMPANIONS

When Arthur the cat died, the Bell family's pet dog, Oscar, missed him so much that he dug up the cat's garden grave and dragged his body into the house. Owner Robert Bell of Wigan, England, found the dog curled up beside the dead cat in his basket. Oscar had even licked Arthur clean.

COOL CAT

It looks like a wild animal but behaves like a domestic cat. Created by crossing two exotic breeds—a Serval and a Leopard cat—with an ordinary cat, the Ashera is a new breed of domestic cat that resembles a mini-leopard but is playful and affectionate. It grows up to 30 lb (14 kg) in weight and costs a far-from-ordinary $22,000.

DOG MEAT

Oven-ready dogs hang at a street market in Lianzhou, China. Dog meat is a popular dish in this part of China, where consumers believe it keeps them warm in winter, but public opposition to the practice is growing.

TWICE LUCKY
In 2007, Aniki, a four-year-old male Rottweiler, survived for 29 days lost in the woods of Mount Seymour, North Vancouver, Canada, before being rescued by a passing hiker. It wasn't Aniki's first brush with death. In the past he had been hit by a car, resulting in a metal pin being inserted in his left hip.

FIRE RESCUE
Laney, a black Labrador, repeatedly bit the foot of 13-year-old Christopher Peebles to wake him up and save the boy and two of his friends from a house fire in Portage, Indiana, in January 2008.

EASY RIDER
A dog has become a celebrity in Guangzhou City, China, because he can balance on the back of a bicycle. Gougou balances on the bike as his owner Mr. Liu rides through the city. If he needs to pee, he taps Mr. Liu on the shoulder with one of his front paws.

SMART SEAGULL
A seagull turned into a persistent shoplifter by regularly wandering through an open door into a shop in Aberdeen, Scotland, and helping itself to a packet of potato snacks. The bird would wait until there were no customers around and the shopkeeper was standing behind the cash desk.

EAGLE-EYED
Bari Airport in Italy has paid $15,000 to hire Cheyenne, a six-month-old hand-reared golden eagle, to keep its runway free from wildlife. The airport had previously been forced to close the runway because of foxes hunting for mice and rabbits.

SHED ORDEAL
A cat locked in a garden shed survived for two months by licking condensation off the windows. Emmy, from Devon, England, was shut in when she followed her owner into the shed, which he then locked up for the winter.

CRANE IMPOSTER

Staff at a wild bird reserve in Gloucestershire, England, rear Eurasian Crane chicks using crane costumes and crane heads made out of litter-pickers so that the birds do not get too accustomed to humans.

NAIL SCULPTOR

These sculptures of a life-size moose and bison are made entirely from nails. They are the work of artist Bill Secunda from Butler, Pennsylvania, who specializes in creating metal creatures. The moose is made from 95,000 welded nails, weighs 1,800 lb (815 kg), stands 7½ ft (2.3 m) tall, 12 ft (3.6 m) long, and has antlers that are almost 9 ft (2.7 m) wide. The bison, made from 30,000 cut and framing nails, weighs 1,100 lb (500 kg) and is 6 ft (1.8 m) tall, 3 ft (90 cm) wide, and 8 ft (2.4 m) long.

HUNGRY WOLF

In December 2007, customers at a crowded bar in Villetta Barrea, Italy, were shocked when a wolf strolled in, ate a steak sandwich, and walked out again. The hungry beast, which came from the nearby Abruzzo National Park, had been driven to drastic measures by a spell of cold weather.

COURAGEOUS KITTENS

An elderly Chinese woman was saved in 2006 when eight family cats fought off a giant cobra that was trying to slither into her bed. As the deadly 6-ft (1.8-m) serpent made its way across the floor, the cats surrounded it, the mother cat stamping on the snake's head and the seven kittens biting its body and dragging it out of the house. As the cats pinned the snake to the ground, the old woman's son beat it to death.

HEAD STUCK

A cat in Cambridgeshire, England, got its head stuck after trying to pull a mouse out of a jelly jar. The cat was found wandering next to a road with the jar on its head and the mouse just in front of its nose. The cat eventually freed both itself and the mouse by smashing the jar.

RAPID GROWTH

In just two weeks, the monarch butterfly caterpillar grows to 2,700 times its birth weight. If a 7-lb (3.2-kg) human baby gained weight at the same rate, it would weigh more than nine tons.

NO SWEAT!

Camels can lose up to 30 percent of their body weight in perspiration and still survive. By contrast, a human would die of heat shock after sweating away just 12 percent of his or her body weight.

PIG COUNTRY

There are more wild pigs than people in Australia, which has a population of 21 million people and 23 million feral pigs.

GIANT RAT

In 2007, researchers in a remote jungle in Indonesia discovered a hitherto unknown species of giant rat that is about five times the size of a typical city rat and has no fear of humans. A 2006 expedition to the same stretch of jungle had uncovered dozens of new species of palms and butterflies.

PET FOX

Instead of behaving like a wild animal, Cropper the fox lives indoors with Mike Towler and his family, eats from a dog bowl, and curls up with the household cats. Towler from the town of Tunbridge Wells in Kent, England, tamed Cropper over a period of several months after the fox contracted a memory-damaging disease that left him unable to make a home or recognize prey.

BIG BONE

Walking along the beach in the village of Dunwich in Suffolk, England, in 2007, Daisy the miniature wire-haired Dachshund stumbled across a bone that was as big as herself. The bone—measuring 13 in (33 cm) long and weighing 8 lb (3.6 kg)—was a fossilized thigh section of a two-million-year-old mammoth.

TODDLER SAVED

When R.C., a German Shepherd–Husky cross, discovered two-year-old Vincent Rhodey outdoors in the freezing cold wearing only a T-shirt, he instinctively sat on the youngster and saved him from hypothermia. The boy had strayed from his home in Canonsburg, Pennsylvania, but R.C. curled up with him for nearly an hour to keep him warm until they were both found.

MONSTER PYTHON

Fluffy, a huge python bought in 2008 by Columbus Zoo, Ohio, has a body as long as a small truck and as thick as a telegraph pole. Fed 10 lb (4.5 kg) of rabbits a week, Fluffy is 22 ft (7 m) long and is thought to be one of the biggest snakes currently in captivity.

LIVING DEAD

When Gan Shugen of Chengdu, China, went to cook a chicken that he had kept in a freezer for two days, he was shocked to find it was still alive. The bird—a gift from a relative—was wrapped in a thick plastic bag with its legs tied, leading Gan to assume it was dead. Instead, despite 48 hours in sub-zero temperatures, it poked its head out of the bag and was soon able to stand.

DEEP BREATH

Armadillos can hold their breath for up to six minutes. That is how they are able to poke their noses deep into the ground in search of insects.

BLUE HAZE

The wings of the *Morpho sulkowskyi* butterfly have a self-cleaning texture that repels water and reflects light to give it a bright blue appearance.

LOUD HOWL

The scream of a howler monkey can be heard up to 5 mi (8 km) away. It is so noisy that the sound of a family of howlers traveling through the forest has been mistaken for a thunderstorm.

POOCH HOOCH

Pet-shop owner Gerrie Berendsen of Zelhem, the Netherlands, has devised a new beer— for dogs. The nonalcoholic brew is made from a mix of beef extract and malt.

BUSHY-TAILED BURGLAR

A squirrel with a sweet tooth raided a Finnish grocery store at least twice a day to steal chocolate candy eggs with a toy inside. The manager of the store in Jyvaskyla said the squirrel always carefully removed the foil wrapping, ate the chocolate, and left carrying the toy.

THE STING

Octopuses have been known to remove the stings from captured jellyfish and attach them to their own tentacles to use as an added weapon.

SKINNY PIG

The latest designer pet is the skinny pig, a hairless breed of guinea pig first created for laboratory testing 30 years ago. As they are naked, skinny pigs need to be kept warm on cold days, but will also burn if left in the sun for too long without protective suncream.

SWOLLEN TONGUE ～～～～

A dead humpback whale was found washed up on the coast of Alaska in 2007 with its tongue swollen to the size of a car. Scientists investigating the death of the whale think that a collision forced air into its tongue and caused it to swell.

ARTISTIC GORILLAS ～～～～

Gorillas at Franklin Park Zoo in Boston, Massachusetts, are keen finger-painters. Keepers at the zoo claim that the finger-painting helps to keep the apes intellectually stimulated; and it earns them money too—one of their artworks sold for a whopping $10,000!

KITTEN SAVIOR ～～～～

Zacheri Richardson-Leitman of Cairns, Queensland, Australia, had time to rescue his whole family from a blaze, despite being in bed asleep when his mattress caught fire. How did he do it? His ten-week-old kitten scratched at his face to wake him up and alert him to his burning bed.

RUNT OF THE LITTER

Part of a litter of 14 in Gansu, China, this piglet was born with one eye, four eyeballs, and a long nose that made it look like a baby elephant.

MYTHICAL BEAST?

When Phylis Canion found a strange animal dead outside her Cuero, Texas, ranch in August 2007, she thought it was a chupacabra, the mysterious beast blamed for killing 30 of her chickens. The state mammalogist suggested it was more likely to be a gray fox suffering from an extreme case of mange.

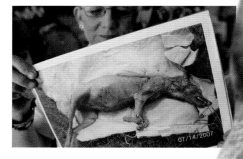

Ripley's research •

What is a chupacabra?

Nobody knows for sure whether the chupacabra is an undiscovered breed of animal or just a myth. The chupacabra gets its name, which is Spanish for "goat sucker", from its habit of attacking and drinking the blood of livestock. Dozens of sightings of the beast have been reported from Maine to Chile. Descriptions of it vary from a hairless doglike creature to a spiny reptile that hops like a kangaroo and has red glowing eyes. Some witnesses claim that it has wings. In 2006, a farmer from Coleman, Texas, killed a weird creature that mauled some of his chickens and turkeys. It was described as a cross between a dog, a rat, and a kangaroo, but was thrown out with the trash. Around the same time an evil-looking, rodent-like creature with fangs was found dead alongside a road near Turner, Maine, but the carcass was picked clean by vultures before anyone could examine it. In 2004, a rancher near San Antonio, Texas, killed a hairless doglike creature that was attacking his livestock. The Elmendorf Beast, as it became known, was in fact a coyote.

NEW SPECIES

Scientists in Indonesia identified 20 new species of sharks and rays during a five-year survey of catches at Indonesian fish markets.

HEROIC HOUND

A Golden Labrador saved a woman's life in 2007 by giving her the Heimlich maneuver. Debbie Parkhurst of Cecil County, Maryland, was eating an apple when a piece got stuck in her throat. Her choking alerted her two-year-old dog Toby, who stood on his hind feet, put his front paws on her shoulders, pushed her to the ground, and began jumping up and down on her chest, an action that dislodged the apple from her windpipe. As soon as Mrs. Parkhurst started breathing again, the dog stopped jumping and began licking its owner's face to stop her from passing out.

CAT COMFORT

A New York couple paid out more than $3,000 in taxi fares for the journey to their new home in Arizona—just so their two cats could travel in comfort. Pensioners Betty and Bob Matas were afraid that their pets would suffer in the cargo hold of a plane, so they opted to make the 2,500-mi (4,025-km) journey to the Southwest by cab, with the cats resting comfortably in carpet-lined cages in the back of the vehicle.

FELINE STOWAWAY

Taking delivery of a consignment of motorcycle helmets from China, the owner of a shop in North Carolina opened the box to find a cat inside. The animal had managed to chew its way into the cardboard box somewhere in Shanghai and had somehow survived the 35-day sea voyage despite being trapped in a cargo crate without food or water.

ODD COUPLE

When Mozambique was flooded in 2002, a dog from the village of Caia became firm friends with a wild monkey. The two played together and the dog even let the monkey ride on its back.

DUNG GIFT

The Valley Zoo, at Edmonton, Alberta, Canada, sells an unusual line in Mothers' Day presents—20-lb (9-kg) bags of composted animal dung. The zoo says the compost—made from the droppings of elephants, zebras, camels, and antelopes—is the ideal gift for keen gardeners.

NURSING HOME

Japan has opened a nursing home for dogs! Owners pay to keep their aging pets at the home in Tochigi, where the dogs have veterinary care as well as a team of puppies to play with in order to help them keep fit.

HEART SHAPE

A Chihuahua puppy was born in Japan in 2007 with a large heart-shaped pattern on his coat. Shop-owner Emiko Sakurada said the dog, named Heart-kun, was unique.

PIG WEDDING

Two pet pigs were married in Taiwan in 2007 with the blessing of a church priest. Farm owner Xu Wenchuan decided to reward his male pig, Xu Fuge, for all the hard work he does welcoming guests at the farm restaurant, and advertised for a suitable bride. Two parrots acted as bridesmaid and groomsman at the ceremony.

FOWL PLAY

Two chickens in China have become addicted to playing soccer! Owner Mrs. Zhang found an abandoned football and decided to give it to the competitive bantams for fun. Since then they play with the ball every day and can even perform sliding tackles.

ELEPHANTS' PICNIC

In 2007, two elephants escaped from a circus and went strolling around the town of Newmarket, Ontario, Canada, eating grass and trees in neighboring gardens during the early hours of the morning. A woman who saw them couldn't believe her eyes!

SWALLOWED TEETH

A Jack Russell terrier was rushed into surgery in 2007—after eating his owner's false teeth! The dog, who was named Desmond, swallowed Marjorie Johnson's dentures one morning while she was in the bathroom at her home near Newcastle, England. Veterinarians had to open up the dog's stomach to retrieve the teeth in an operation that lasted three hours.

STUCK DUCK

Eighteen firefighters, three fire trucks, a Land Rover four-wheel drive, and a rescue boat were used in a three-hour rescue to save a trapped duck near Birmingham, England. As crews raced to the scene from 35 mi (56 km) away, residents feared a child had drowned, but it turned out the casualty was Daffy, a white Aylesbury duck who was stranded in a drainage tunnel.

CAT-LOVING DOG

Ginny, a Schnauzer–Siberian husky cross, rescued more than 1,000 cats in her lifetime. She had the unique accolade, for a dog, of being named Cat of the Year at the 1998 Westchester Cat Show, in New York. When she died in 2005, at the ripe old age of 17, her memorial service was attended by 300 cats. Her owner, Philip Gonzalez from Long Beach, New York, never trained her—she just knew instinctively when a cat was in trouble. "Ginny loved cats," he said. "And cats loved Ginny."

MUMMIFIED DOG

In 1980, a mummified dog was found lodged 20 ft (6 m) above ground in a tree near the Georgia–Alabama state line. The hollow tree created perfect conditions for the animal to be preserved some 20 years after its death. The dog became so popular that it was later given its own name—Stuckie.

DARK DISCOVERY

Scientists at Rice University in Houston, Texas, and Rensselaer Polytechnic Institute in Troy, New York, have created a material so dark that it reflects only 0.045 percent of all light shined upon it, making it 100 times darker than the paint on a black car. The new material is made of sheets of carbon rolled into microscopic tubes just one atom thick.

Researchers have spent years trying to create the ideal black material, which absorbs all the colors of light and reflects none of them. An alloy of nickel and phosphorus developed in London, England, in 2003, reflected 0.16 percent of light, but that was bettered in 2008 by the American team led by Dr. Pulickel Ajayan and Professor Shawn Lin.

Choosing carbon—one of nature's darkest materials—as their base, they built a "forest" of vertically aligned carbon nanotubes, hollow cylinders made entirely of carbon atoms. Each nanotube measured about one-hundredth of an inch long—and that was 300,000 times greater than its width! After a year of experimentation, they found that the complex setup reflected only a tiny fraction of light.

It is hoped that by absorbing nearly all light, the new material could be used in the collection and storage of solar energy. As it reflects very little, it could also help to improve optical instruments such as telescopes.

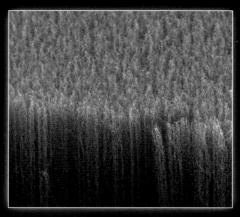

A slide shows the structure of the carbon-based creation to a magnification of 2,500.

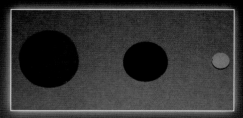

The new dark material (center) compared with a National Institute of Standards and Technology reflectance standard (left) and a piece of glassy carbon (right).

Ripley's research •••••••••••••••••••••••••••••

Astronomers believe that visible matter—such as stars, galaxies, gas, and dust—makes up only a small fraction of the mass of the universe and that the majority is made of stuff that we cannot see, or dark matter. Although it sounds mysterious, dark matter is simply the name given to anything that cannot be seen through an astronomer's telescope, because it does not emit or reflect enough light to be detectable. Instead, scientists can only estimate where it is by its effects on visible matter through gravity.

Dr. Pulickel Ajayan (left) and fellow researcher Lijie Ci exhibit a piece of the dark material. The carbon substance absorbs more than 99.9 percent of light shined upon it.

MULTI-PURPOSE

The Wenger company of Basel, Switzerland, has produced a Swiss Army Knife with no fewer than 85 different tools capable of performing more than 100 functions. The knife weighs 2 lb 11 oz (1.2 kg), is just under 9 in (23 cm) wide, and its features include seven blades and three types of pliers, plus screwdrivers, saws, wrenches, tweezers, a can opener, and a key ring.

TOP 10 UNIQUE FEATURES OF THE KNIFE ▼

1. Bicycle chain rivet setter
2. Cupped cigar cutter with double-honed edges
3. Fish scaler, hook disgorger, line guide
4. Laser pointer with 300-ft (90-m) range
5. Golf divot repair tool
6. Nail file, nail cleaner
7. Tire tread gauge
8. Toothpick
9. Golf club face cleaner
10. Watch caseback opening tool

SIBLING BIRTH

A Canadian girl could give birth to her own brother or sister. The girl's mother, Melanie Boivin of Montreal, Quebec, has frozen her eggs so that Flavie, who cannot have children naturally, can later conceive.

LIGHTNING HEAT

The spark from lightning can reach more than 5 mi (8 km) in length and raise the temperature of the air by 50,000°F (27,000°C).

SYNTHETIC TREES

A U.S. scientist has invented an artificial tree to clean up the atmosphere and combat global warming. Dr. Klaus Lackner of Columbia University says his trees would be a thousand times more effective than living trees at cleaning the air, and that just one could remove 40,000 tons of carbon dioxide in a year.

SPACE ODDITY

Hat-P-1, a planet that circles a star 450 light years away, is larger than Jupiter but less dense than cork. If it could be placed in water, the entire planet would float.

SLOW SEASONS

Because the planet Uranus is tilted to 98 degrees on its axis (meaning that it is practically lying on its side), it has the longest seasons in the solar system—winters and summers each last for the equivalent of 21 Earth years.

SUPER SLEUTH

In just 25 years of searching for supernovae, Robert Evans of Australia has found more with his backyard telescope than all the astronomers in the 400 years before him.

RESTRICTED VIEW

In the 1760s, French astronomer Guillaume Le Gentil prepared for eight years to record the transit of Venus across the face of the Sun —only to have clouds block his view on his last chance to see it for a century.

CLOUD SPRAYS

British professors John Latham and Stephen Salter have designed a fleet of yachts that would pump fine particles of seawater into clouds, thereby thickening them to reflect more of the sun's rays back into space and so reducing the impact of global warming.

MOON PULL

Even though the Moon is 239,000 mi (385,000 km) away, it has hundreds of times more gravitational pull than the action of a person hugging you.

DAZZLING SUN

In just one second, the Sun produces 35 million times the amount of electricity used annually by the whole of the U.S.A.

SPACE GROWTH

Astronauts grow taller by several inches while in space, but gravity shrinks them to their normal size when they return.

JUPITER YEAR

There are almost 10,400 Jupiter days in a Jupiter year. The planet spins through a day in 9 hours 50 minutes (Earth time), but takes almost 12 Earth years to complete its orbit around the Sun.

LONG DAYS

A Venusian day is longer than a Venusian year. This is because Venus takes longer (243 days) to spin on its axis than it does to orbit the Sun (224.7 days).

FLYING HOVERCRAFT

An inventor from New Zealand has devised a hovercraft with wings that flies 6 ft (1.8 m) above the water. Rudy Heeman has spent 11 years designing the Hoverwing, a two-passenger vehicle with an ability to lift off that leaves other water-based craft in its wake. It sets off like an ordinary hovercraft but on reaching its top speed of 60 mph (97 km/h), its wings can be extended, enabling it to take to the air.

SPEED SURFER

A Swedish pensioner is able to surf the Internet many thousand times faster than anybody else in the world, thanks to a connection installed by her son. Seventy-five-year-old Sigbritt Lothberg of Karlstad has a 40-gigabits-per-second connection, so she can download a full-length movie in less than two seconds.

SOCK RIDDLE

The Bureau of Missing Socks is the first website devoted exclusively to solving the riddle of what happens to single missing socks— with explanations from the occult to aliens.

IMAGINARY FRIEND

A man from Newport, Wales, who tried to sell his imaginary friend on eBay in 2007 attracted bids of more than $3,000. The seller, calling himself "thewildandcrazyoli," decided to sell his pretend friend, Jon Malipieman, because at 27, he had grown out of him.

PEANUT GEMS

Scientists at the University of Edinburgh, Scotland, say they can turn peanut butter into diamonds. They claim that the carbon in peanut butter can be transformed into precious gems by subjecting it to pressures of five million atmospheres—that's higher than the pressure found at the center of the Earth.

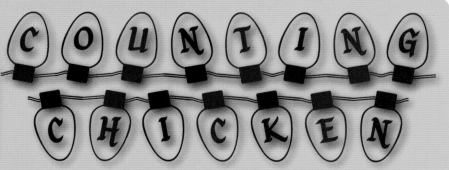

COUNTING CHICKEN

A hen in Shenyang, China, can apparently do simple arithmetic. The bird's owner says the chicken can peck the answer to simple calculations when he points to numbers on a board and asks her questions. She also knows and can point to the 26 letters of the alphabet when asked to do so.

SEARCH DEVICE

Police in Strathclyde, Scotland, have introduced an Unmanned Airborne Vehicle (UAV) to help search for missing people. The lightweight portable device is able to carry out searches using photography and video, its advantage being that it can be safely flown in weather conditions that prevent traditional aircraft from leaving the ground.

GIANT COIN

A 220-lb (100-kg) gold coin the size of a pizza was produced by the Royal Canadian Mint in 2007. Worth $2 million, the coin featured maple leaves on one side and Queen Elizabeth II on the other.

ELECTRIC CHARGE

Human sweat is able to create an electrical charge in coins that have two different alloys—like the Canadian Toonie or the 1 and 2 euro coins.

CONVERTED CART

Bill Lauver of Middleburg, Pennsylvania, converted an electric golf cart into a remote-controlled snowplow so that he could clear his driveway of snow from the comfort of his living room.

TRUTH GLASSES

A New York company has brought out a pair of sunglasses that can tell whether people are speaking the truth. The lie detector eyeglasses can monitor conversations in real-time and provide an LED display of the truthfulness of people around the wearer with 95 percent accuracy.

MULTI-TASK TOILET

The prize in a 2007 contest held by a U.S. plumbing company was an HDTV, DVD player, game system, laptop computer, digital music player, exercise machine, cooling fan, and refrigerator—all connected to a toilet.

PHONE CHANTS

To raise funds, Brazil's Xavante tribe records traditional chants for cell-phone ringtones.

DISCARDED GEAR

A North American website shows pictures of clothing that have been discarded on sidewalks across the world. These include T-shirts, sneakers, baseball caps, and even a prosthetic leg in Singapore.

BEER LAUNCH

A student from North Carolina has invented a refrigerator that throws cold cans of beer to drinkers. John Cornwell spent $3,000 devising the Beer Launching Fridge, which, when activated by remote control, rotates an arm to line itself up with its target and then catapults the can up to 10 ft (3 m) away.

SOLAR HEATING

A Chinese farmer obtains hot water from a device made of beer bottles connected by lengths of hosepipe. Ma Yanjun from Shaanxi Province, has attached 66 beer bottles to a board on the roof of his house. Sunlight heats the water as it passes slowly through the bottles and it eventually flows into his bathroom as hot water.

CANNED BURGER

A Swiss firm has invented a cheeseburger in a can. The burger is meant for trekkers, who have to heat the can in a water container over a fire for two minutes, and then eat.

ROBOT WAITER

Japanese engineers have invented a robot 3 ft 8 in (1.2 m) tall that can serve breakfast. Called Twendy-One, the robot has long arms and 241 pressure sensors in each hand, enabling it to perform such chores as picking up a loaf of bread without crushing it, putting toast on a plate, and fetching ketchup from a refrigerator.

QUICK CHANGE

A new invention means that women can now switch from flats to stilettos without having to change shoes. The shoes have a retractable high heel that disappears when driving, but then extends again at the push of a button.

SLEEP EASY

Designers in the U.K. have developed a pair of pajamas that regulate body temperature to help the wearer enjoy a good night's sleep. Made from a special material, the invention follows research showing that a person's body temperature changes constantly throughout the night, affecting his or her sleep pattern.

PERFECT EGG

Scientists in Britain have developed an egg that times itself so it is always boiled to perfection. Choosing from cartons labeled "soft," "medium," or "hard," shoppers buy eggs that are marked with lion logos in heat-sensitive invisible ink. The ink turns black as soon as the egg is ready—this takes from three minutes for soft-boiled to seven minutes for hard-boiled.

VACUUM SHOES

A new pair of shoes has been invented that vacuums as you walk. The "Shoover" has a tiny rechargeable vacuum cleaner inside the base that collects dust while the wearer walks around the house.

THIN SET

The Japanese company Sony unveiled a new flat-screen television set in 2007 that is about the same width as a coin.

LIGHT MOVERS

All electrons and protons moving through the wires, cables, and transistors of the Internet have a combined weight of less than 2 oz (57 g).

THINK SMALL

Korean nanotechnology researchers used lasers and microscopic materials to create a copy of Rodin's sculpture *The Thinker* that is only twice the size of a red blood cell.

BELT CONVENTION

The Niagara Aerospace Museum in Niagara Falls, New York, holds an annual convention dedicated to rocket belts—jet packs that can propel a person into the air.

ROBOT FLY

Scientists at Harvard University have created a life-size robotic fly. Weighing only 0.002 oz (60 milligrams) with a wingspan of $1^{3}/_{16}$ in (3 cm), the minute robot's movements are modeled on those of a real fly. It is hoped that the mechanical insects might one day be used as spies or for detecting dangerous chemicals.

INVINCIBLE OPPONENT

Computer scientists at the University of Alberta, Canada, have created a program for playing checkers that cannot be beaten. The program's name is Chinook.

ROBOTIC VIOLINIST

A Japanese company has built a robot that can actually play the violin. Created by the Toyota Motor Corporation, the 5-ft-tall (1.5-m) robot has 17 joints in its hands and arms to give it human-like dexterity. At the product launch, it used its mechanical fingers to push the strings correctly while bowing with its other arm to give a near-perfect rendition of Edward Elgar's "Pomp and Circumstance."

DOUBLE VISION

Zou Renti introduces his robot twin at a conference on intelligent robots and systems in Beijing, China. To make it appear more human, the robot has a lifelike skin made of silica gel. In case you're still not sure, the robot is the one on the right.

BIONIC HAND

Born without the lower part of her left arm, Lindsay Block of Oklahoma City, Oklahoma, demonstrates her new i-LIMB bionic hand—a prosthetic device that looks and works like a human hand. It has individually powered fingers that can grip objects and works via small electrodes taped to the skin of the wearer's forearm, which transmit signals to tiny electric motors that power the false hand's movements.

SWELL IDEA

Scientists in Naples, Italy, have invented a new weight-loss pill that swells up to the size of a tennis ball in the stomach. The pill, which is made out of diaper material, makes people feel full for about two hours.

EYE TEST

English scientist Sir Isaac Newton (1643–1727) once slid a needle into his eye socket to create spots in his vision so he could study the results for an optics experiment.

SLOW START

Invented by King Camp Gillette, the safety razor first went on sale in the U.S.A. in 1903, but only 51 were sold in the first 12 months. In 1904, Gillette sold 90,000!

ROBOT RESCUE

The U.S. Army is developing a robot that can carry a wounded soldier from a battlefield. BEAR (Battlefield Extraction-Assist Robot) can lift more than 300 lb (135 kg) and is able to climb stairs holding a human-sized dummy.

TALKING PLANTS

New York University students have invented a device whereby plants that need watering telephone their owners for help. Activated by moisture sensors placed in the soil, the plant sends a signal of "I'm thirsty" over a wireless communication network. When the owner answers the call, the plant's "voice" (an audio file) relays the problem. The plant also calls back after being watered to say "Thank you." Each type of plant is given a different recorded voice to match its biological traits.

MOUSE IN A MOUSE

Americans Christy Canida and Noah Weinsrein created a computer mouse housed inside a real mouse! They used the skin of a dead rodent bought from a pet shop.

CAFFEINE RUSH

U.S. firm Think Geek has manufactured a soap that releases caffeine into the user's system, providing the same energizing effect as two cups of coffee. Shower Shock is designed for people who do not have time for both a shower and a cup of coffee in their morning routine.

ARCTIC STUDY

Kristin Laidre, a researcher at the University of Washington, studies the depths of inaccessible parts of the Arctic Ocean by strapping scientific instruments to narwhals.

TRAINED BEES

Honeybees are being used to help find unexploded landmines in Croatia. Scientists at Zagreb University have been training the bees to locate explosive chemicals using the bees' keen sense of smell. The bees are trained to associate the smell of explosives with food so they settle on ground where mines are buried.

SPECIAL GOATS

A U.S. biotech company breeds goats that produce a nerve gas antidote in their milk.

LIGHT-BOILED EGG

English inventor Simon Rhymes from Chippenham, Wiltshire, has devised a machine that boils the perfect egg, using lightbulbs instead of water. The eggs are lowered into the machine and heated by four halogen bulbs. After cooking the egg, the gadget even slices off the top so that bread can be dipped into the yolk.

COOL FOR CATS

Nohl Rosen of Scottsdale, Arizona, runs a web radio station for cats that features interviews with veterinarians and pet owners, plus music approved by cats. The station manager of Cat Galaxy is Rosen's own cat Isis (she loves funk and Ozzy Osbourne). Her assistant and the station's program director are also cats.

INSPIRED BY NATURE

Scientists from Northwestern University, Evanston, Illinois, have created a new super-sticky material based on the natural adhesive powers of geckos and mussels. The material, called "geckel," is effective because it is made from coating fibrous silicone—a substance similar in structure to a gecko's foot—with a polymer that replicates the powerful "glue" used by mussels.

PIGEON CONTROL

Scientists in Shandong, China, have learned to control the flight of pigeons by implanting electrodes in the birds' brains. The researchers have designed a computer system that allows them to instruct the pigeons to fly left, right, up, or down.

Here, the cat on the right has the "fluorescent" gene and will glow under ultraviolet light, whereas the cat on the left does not.

The altered skin color of the "glow-in-the-dark" cat is clearly seen here—on the ears and nose, compared with the unaltered cat on the left.

Scientists in South Korea have created cats that glow red. Researchers at Gyeongsang National University manipulated a gene in two cloned white Turkish Angora cats to change the cats' skin color so that they would have a fluorescent glow under ultraviolet light.

GLOWING CATS

ALBINO BIRTH

At Jamestown, North Dakota, in 2007, White Cloud, North America's only female albino bison, gave birth to an albino calf, named Dakota Miracle. The chances of this happening naturally in the wild would be one in ten million!

ANT INTELLIGENCE

Scientists from the University of Bristol, England, have observed that army ants form living bridges to help get jobs done. When ants are foraging on rough ground, some of them use their own bodies to plug tiny holes and allow their fellow ants to walk over them. It was even discovered that individual ants choose which of them is the best size to lie across a particular hole.

HOMEMADE REACTOR

Thiago Olson, a 17-year-old high school student from Oakland Township, Michigan, built a functioning fusion reactor in his garage. It took him two years and more than 1,000 hours of research.

THE BEST MEDICINE

Scientists from Vanderbilt University in Nashville, Tennessee, believe that laughing for 15 minutes a day can help people lose weight. They say daily laughter can burn off up to 5 lb (2.3 kg) of fat a year.

ZOMBIE DOGS

In trials to develop suspended animation for humans, scientists in the U.S.A. have managed to bring dead dogs back to life. The Safar Center for Resuscitation Research in Pittsburgh, Pennsylvania, rendered the dogs clinically dead by draining their veins of blood and replacing it with an ice-cold salt solution. The animals stopped breathing, but three hours later they were revived with no ill effects after their blood was put back.

RAMPANT RAT

A prehistoric skull found in a museum in Montevideo, Uruguay, has led scientists to conclude that a rodent the size of a cow roamed the forests of South America four million years ago. The monster rat stood 5 ft (1.5 m) tall, was 10 ft (3 m) long and weighed almost a ton, making it 14 times bigger than any rodent alive today.

BARK ANALYSIS

Hungarian scientists have developed computer software that will enable humans to understand dog barks. Following the analysis of 6,000 barks, the amazing software can differentiate between a dog's various barks to be able to tell when it has seen a ball, when it meets a stranger, or when it wants to be taken for a walk.

FEARLESS MICE

Scientists at Japan's Tokyo University have created a mouse that is not scared of cats. The researchers succeeded in turning off the receptors in a mouse's brain that react to the scent of its chief predator. The result has been the creation of genetically modified mice who show no fear when coming face-to-face with cats.

SEE-THROUGH FROG!

Scientists in Japan have bred transparent frogs whose organs, blood vessels, and eggs can be seen clearly through their skins. Experts say the frogs will be invaluable for research into diseases such as cancer, because scientists can study organ growth and development without having to dissect the frog... which is good news for the frog, too.

THE HUMAN CANVAS

STOP! LOOK VERY CLOSELY AND SEE IF YOU CAN MAKE OUT THE BODY PARTS USED AS A CANVAS FOR THESE AMAZING PAINTINGS!

Chadwick Gray has to remain motionless for up to 15 hours at a time so that artist Laura Spector can paint him. Yet this is no ordinary still life, for the canvas is not a sheet of paper but Chadwick's body.

It is all part of the New York City collaborative team's Museum Anatomy project, which began in 1996 and sees them re-create old paintings onto a human canvas.

Chadwick admits he suffers for his art and enters almost a meditative trance in order to stay completely still for so long. Sometimes his feats of meditative endurance are made publicly. In 2001, for example, Laura painted a 19th-century portrait of a bride onto his body in the front windows of the Henri Bendel department store in New York.

Chadwick and Laura scour the storerooms of museums across the world for likely subjects, frequently looking for paintings that have been stored and hidden away from public view because of their controversial nature. Chadwick says: "We often had to convince conservative curators, and once, in Prague, even a panel of nuns, to allow us to reproduce rare paintings of the female form onto the often naked male body."

Once the body art is completed, Laura photographs Chadwick and the prints are developed to the same size as the original painting. The resulting photographs reveal a new work of art in which the painting acquires curves and sometimes leaves the canvas unrecognizable as Chadwick's human form.

"Chadwick had to shave his eyebrows for this painting, so the painted lady wouldn't have a mustache. Eyebrows take about three weeks to grow back."

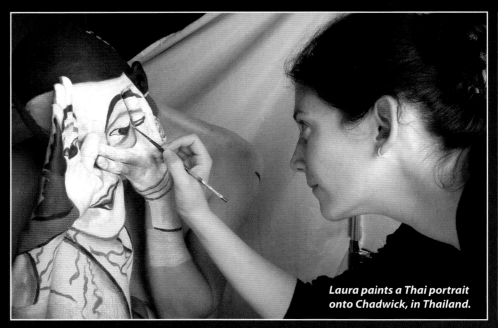

Laura paints a Thai portrait onto Chadwick, in Thailand.

The completed portrait of "Lanna Woman."

"The original painting from which this was created exists in catacombs underneath a convent in Prague, in the Czech Republic."

"It's rare to find 19th-century portraits in Thailand, so this piece was re-created from the wall of a temple in northern Thailand. The woman represented is the Thai version of Mother Nature—she can water the rice fields with her hair."

"This was our first painting on the body, created in San Francisco, where the painted eye matches up with Chadwick's real eye."

"This painting's original was lost during World War II, so we had to re-create it from a black-and-white photograph."

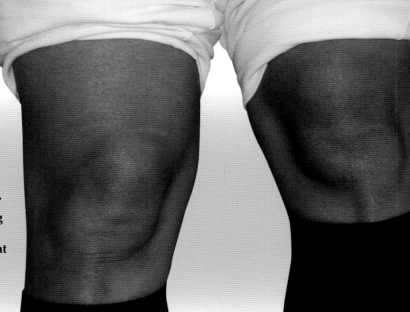

KNEE IMAGES

In December 2006, Amia Fore of Detroit, Michigan, was amazed when she looked in the mirror and saw what appeared to be a face on her right kneecap. A month later another "face" appeared—this time on her left kneecap, the features becoming more pronounced as the weeks passed. A spiritual advisor said the initial image was of Amia's first (unborn) grandchild and that the features would disappear once the baby was born.

HUMAN MAGNET

Romanian Aurel Raileanu often finds himself literally glued to the television. The Bucharest hospital worker has become known as the Human Magnet because spoons, books, lighters, and even a 50-lb (23-kg) TV set, all stick to him.

SWOLLEN FINGERS

Liu Hua from Jiangsu Province, China, had fingers that were thicker than his arms. His left thumb, index finger, and middle finger were deformed at birth and grew to a huge size before surgeons removed 11 lb (5 kg) of bone and tissue from them in 2007.

PENGUIN GIRL

As she had no forearms, only three toes on each foot, and a distinctive walk, diminutive Nany Mae Hill of Keyes, California, was billed in circus shows as the "Penguin Girl". After marrying 6-ft-tall (2.2-m) farmer Benjamin Hill in the 1940s, she wore her wedding ring on the middle toe of her left foot.

LEGLESS ACROBAT

Born in Ohio in 1844, Eli Bowen had no legs—just two small feet of different sizes growing from his hips. As a toddler, he used his arms for walking and would hold wooden blocks in his hands, enabling him to swing his hips between his arms. The strength he developed from walking in this manner helped him become a top-class acrobat.

SEAL AND CHIMP

Stanislaus Berent of Pittsburgh, Pennsylvania, had hands growing from his shoulders, but no arms—a condition known as phocomelia. Billed in shows as "Sealo the Seal Boy," his act featured a chimpanzee to which he fed cookies.

ROLE MODEL

Firefighter John Joseph Conway from Chicago, Illinois, underwent plastic surgery in India to make himself look like Hollywood star Bruce Willis. He spent $1,600 on the operation because he thought Willis' strong jaw was the ideal look for a firefighter.

LOBSTER BOY

Born in 1937, Grady Stiles Jr. from Pittsburgh, Pennsylvania, suffered from ectrodactyly, where the fingers are fused together in groups to form claw-like extremities. Consequently, he was billed in shows as "Lobster Boy."

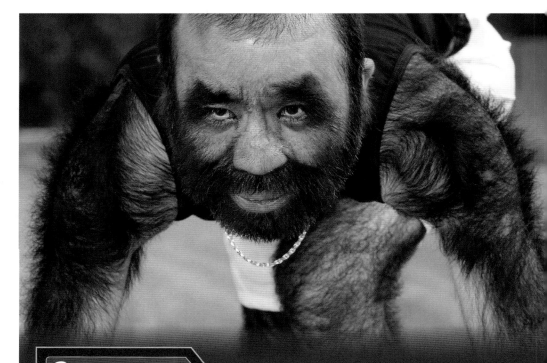

Ripley's research

Yu Zhenhuan suffers from hypertrichosis—or werewolf syndrome—a condition that produces excessive body hair. He has 256 hairs growing on almost every square inch of his skin. The condition is usually genetic and occurs in around one out of every ten billion people.

BODY HAIR

Yu Zhenhuan has thick hair covering 96 percent of his entire body—every inch except for the palms of his hands and the soles of his feet. His eyelashes are so long that they hide his eyes. Also known in his native China as rock singer King Kong, Yu has undergone five operations to remove hair from his nose and recently had another to remove a clump of hair from his ear because it was impairing his hearing.

HORNED MAN

An 88-year-old man from a village near Zhengzhou, China, has a horn growing from his head. It started in 2006 when he picked at a little bump on his head and it went on to grow steadily over the next few months. Doctors believe it is a form of hyperplasia, an excess of normal body tissue.

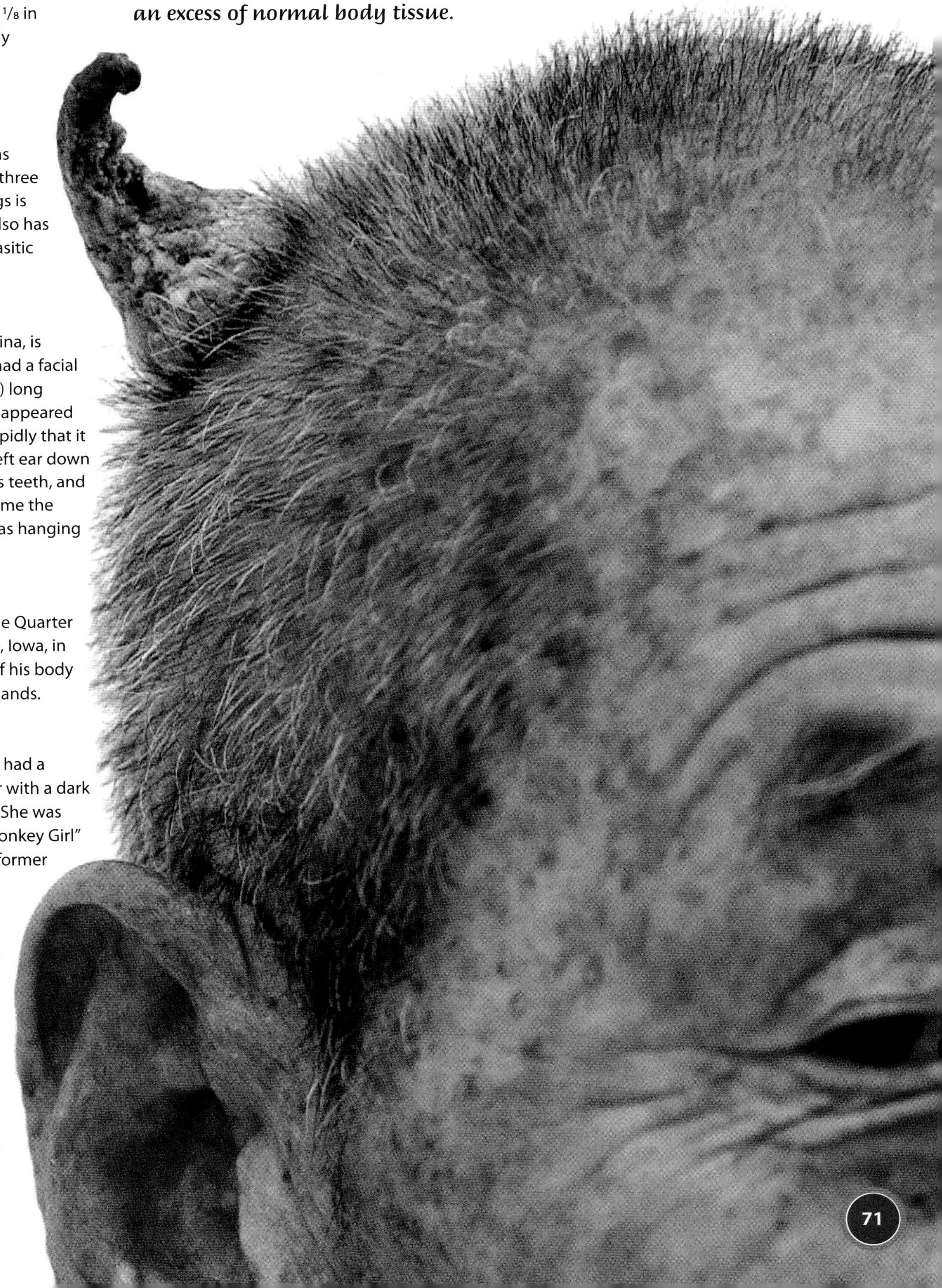

HAIR MOP

Thousands of prisoners donated their hair to help soak up spilled fuel following the crash of an oil tanker off the coast of the Philippines in August 2006.

BLADDER STONE

Doctors in Israel removed a bladder stone from Moneera Khalil that was the size of a grapefruit! The stone measured 5 1/8 in (13 cm) across and weighed nearly 2 lb 4 oz (1 kg).

EXTRA LIMBS

Rudy Santos of Bacolod City, the Philippines, has been promoted as "Octoman" on account of having three legs and four arms. One of the legs is missing below the knee and he also has the small head and ear of his parasitic twin attached to his stomach.

MASSIVE TUMOR

Huang Chuncai, 31, of Hunan, China, is only 4 ft 6 in (1.37 m) tall but he had a facial tumor that was nearly 2 ft (60 cm) long and weighed 33 lb (15 kg). It first appeared when he was four and grew so rapidly that it blocked his left eye, pushed his left ear down to shoulder level, knocked out his teeth, and deformed his backbone. By the time the tumor was removed in 2007, it was hanging down from his face.

QUARTER BOY

Johnny Gilmore—alias "Zandu the Quarter Boy"—was born in Marshalltown, Iowa, in 1913 with the entire lower part of his body missing. He used to walk on his hands.

STRANGE COUPLE

Percilla Lauther from Puerto Rico had a hormonal imbalance that left her with a dark beard and hair all over her body. She was billed in shows as "Priscilla the Monkey Girl" and in 1938 she eloped with performer Emmitt Bejano, "The Alligator-Skinned Boy," who suffered from ichthyosis, giving him scaly skin. Together they were promoted as "The World's Strangest Married Couple."

BABY TEETH

A baby in England was born in 2007 with teeth. Megan Andrews from Worthing, Sussex, stunned family by arriving in the world with seven teeth.

Tattoo Master

At InkLine Studio in New York City, Anil Gupta can reproduce a famous artwork as a tattoo without losing any of the intricate detail from the original painting. He has created postage-stamp-size tattoos of works by Michelangelo, Van Gogh, and Leonardo da Vinci, including a tiny copy of the *Mona Lisa* and this shoulder-width version of *The Last Supper*.

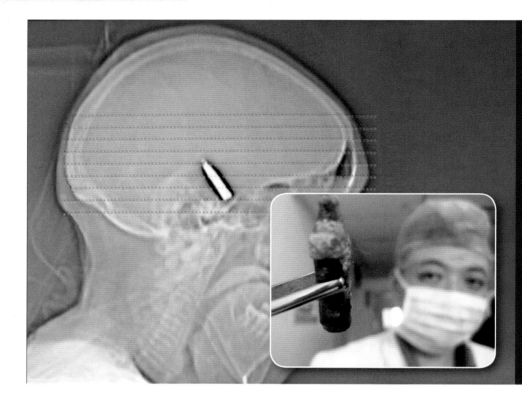

LONG SHOT

In 2007, a Chinese grandmother finally discovered the cause of the recurrent headaches she had been suffering for 64 years—a bullet had been lodged in her skull since 1943.

Jin Guangying was just 13 when she was shot in the head by the Japanese army while delivering lunch to her father, a soldier stationed in Jiangsu Province. Although she recovered from her ordeal, she went on to experience repeated headaches, during which she would babble incoherently, pound her head with her fist, and foam at the mouth. As her condition deteriorated, her family borrowed money to send her to hospital, where surgeons removed the rusty 1⅛-in (3-cm) bullet in a four-hour operation. One surgeon said that it was a miracle that she was able to survive for such a long time with a bullet in her head.

EAR NEST

A pair of spiders made their home in the ear of a nine-year-old boy. When Jesse Courtney of Albany, Oregon, felt a faint popping in his left ear, followed by an ache, doctors flushed out two spiders—one dead, the other alive. Jesse was given the spiders as a souvenir and took them to school to show his friends.

SWALLOWED HEAD

A man whose head was swallowed by a great white shark managed to break free from the 10-ft (3-m) monster by lunging at its face with a metal chisel. Eric Nerhus, 41, was diving for sea mollusks off the coast of New South Wales, Australia, in January 2007, when the shark grabbed him head-first. It snatched his head, shoulders, and chest into its mouth, but let go after being struck repeatedly with the chisel. Although the surrounding water was red with his blood, Nerhus escaped with a broken nose and deep bite-marks to his chest.

WEDGED TOOTH

An Australian rugby player carried on playing for more than three months... unaware that he had an opponent's tooth embedded in his forehead. It was only when Ben Czislowski complained of shooting pains that a doctor found the tooth of opposing forward Matt Austin, with whom Czislowski had clashed heads during a match in April 2007.

QUEASY RIDER

A Japanese motorcyclist carried on riding his bike for more than a mile before realizing that he had lost his leg. The 54-year-old office worker hit a safety barrier but it was only when he stopped a couple of minutes later that he noticed his leg had been severed below the knee.

PENCIL REMOVAL

A woman in Germany has had part of a pencil removed from her head—after living with it for 55 years. Margaret Wegner was four when she fell over while carrying her pencil. It punctured her cheek and part of it went into her brain, just above her right eye. She has endured nosebleeds and headaches most of her life, but now surgeons in Berlin have managed to remove most of the pencil, although a 1/12-in (2-mm) section was too deeply embedded for them to get out.

SPOON SUPPER

A woman accidentally swallowed a spoon 6 in (15 cm) in length while having a laughing fit as she ate a plate of spaghetti in a Sydney, Australia, restaurant in 2007.

DENTURE DRAMA

A 38-year-old Romanian woman swallowed her lover's false teeth during a passionate kiss. She was rushed to hospital with pains and X rays showed the teeth in her stomach.

Alien

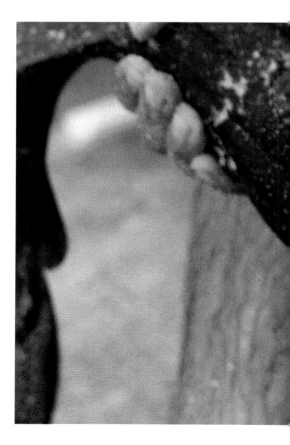

FACE BUGS

Doctors thought the painful bumps on Aaron Dallas's head might have been gnat bites or shingles... until the bumps started to move. That was when they discovered five botfly larvae living in an ⅛-in-wide (3-mm) pit near the top of his skull. The tiny parasites were probably placed there by a mosquito. "I could feel and hear them," said Dallas of Carbondale, Colorado. "I actually thought I was going crazy."

Intruders

Ripley's research . . .

The botfly is a hairy fly, the larvae of which live as parasites within the bodies of mammals, especially horses. There are about 150 species worldwide, but only one—*Dermatobia hominis*—attacks humans. The female botfly often uses a mosquito to carry her eggs to the host body and when the mosquito bites, the eggs fall off. The heat of the host body induces the larvae to hatch and they then start burrowing into and eating off the flesh for up to eight weeks, before leaving to pupate into an adult fly. They will thrive in any warm part of the body—even in the throat and nose. Since the maggot has strong, hooked spines, it cannot be removed just by squeezing. The best method is either to use a venom extractor syringe or to cover the wound with Vaseline, forcing the maggot up in search of air, and then to pull it out with tweezers.

SHARK ATTACK

Attacked by a 2-ft (60-cm) shark while he was snorkeling off the coast of New South Wales, Australia, Luke Tresoglavic had to swim 300 yd (275 m) to shore, walk to his car, and drive to a surf club... all with the shark still hanging on to his leg. The Wobbegong shark, which can grow up to 10 ft (3 m) in length, sank its razor-sharp teeth into Tresoglavic's flesh and refused to let go even though lifeguards flushed its gills with fresh water in a bid to loosen its grip. Tresoglavic was treated for puncture wounds to his leg but, sadly, the shark died as a result of the ordeal and was buried in the Tresoglavic family garden.

MEDICAL MISHAP

In 2007, a Brazilian woman discovered that the cause of her persistent stomach ache was a 2-in (5-cm) scalpel that had been left in her body when she gave birth by Cesarean section 23 years earlier.

HIDDEN TOWEL

When the body of Bonnie Valle from Canton, Ohio, was donated to science after her death in 2002, a green surgical cloth the size of a large hand towel was found behind her left lung. The rolled-up towel had apparently been left there seven years earlier during a surgical procedure on her lungs. Her family said that she had often complained of a funny feeling in her chest.

A BIG Difference

One of the tallest men in the world at 7 ft 9 in (2.36 m), Bao Xishun shakes hands with fellow Mongolian He Pingping who, at only 2 ft 5 in (73 cm), is less than one-third Bao's height.

Herdsman Bao was of normal size until the age of 16, when he experienced a sudden, unexplained growth spurt, as a result of which he reached his present height just seven years later. In July 2007, after searching the world for a suitable bride, 56-year-old Bao married 5-ft-5-in (1.68-m) Xia Shujuan, a woman from his hometown. She is nearly half his age and more than 2 ft (60 cm) shorter. For the wedding *(see right)*, it took 30 tailors three days to create Bao's outfit.

He Pingping was the size of an adult's palm at birth. Although his two sisters developed normally, he has grown very slowly because of a bone deformity.

Bao Xishun and Xia Shujuan married in 2007 in traditional Mongolian costume.

SHORT & TALL TALES! ▽

1 ft 8 in (51 cm)	Lucia Zarate, Mexico (1864–90). She weighed just 8 oz (227 g) at birth—about the weight of a lemon—and at the age of 12 her waist measured only 14 in (35 cm) in circumference. After finding fame as The Mexican Lilliputian with P.T. Barnum's circus, earning $20 an hour, she died of cold when the train she was on became stuck in a blizzard for a week in the Rocky Mountains.
3 ft 0 in (91 cm)	Michel Petrucciani, France (1962–99). Despite his lack of height, Michel became a brilliant jazz pianist, even though he was so fragile when he was a teenager that he had to be carried to and from the piano. His father made a special extension so that Petrucciani's feet could reach the pedals.
3 ft 4 in (102 cm)	Charles Stratton, Bridgeport, Connecticut, U.S.A. (1838–83). Better known as General Tom Thumb, a performer with P.T. Barnum's circus, Stratton married the equally small Lavinia Warren in 1863 and the happy couple stood on top of a grand piano in New York's Metropolitan Hotel to greet 2,000 guests.
8 ft 11 in (2.72 m)	Robert Wadlow, Alton, Illinois, U.S.A. (1918–40). Wadlow was 6 ft 2 in (1.88 m) by the age of eight and eventually grew so tall that he had to walk in leg braces. He was buried in a half-ton coffin that had to be carried by 12 pallbearers.
8 ft 9 in (2.67 m)	Eddie Carmel, Bronx, New York City, U.S.A. (1936–72). By the time of his death his standing-up height had dropped to 7 ft (2.13 m) owing to the crippling disorder kyphoscoliosis, or curvature of the spine.
8 ft 8 in (2.64 m)	Grady Patterson, DeKalb, Illinois, U.S.A. (1943–68). Patterson grew 12 in (30cm) in just one year, aged 13.

TALL STORY

At 8 ft 5 in (2.57 m) tall, Leonid Stadnyk, a former veterinarian from the Ukraine, has to sleep on two beds joined together lengthwise. He used to work on a cattle farm but had to quit after suffering frostbite—his feet measure 17 in (43 cm) in length and he could not afford to buy a pair of shoes to fit them. Yet before his growth spurt at age 14, following a brain operation, he was so small that at school he was nicknamed "Titch."

GERMAN GIANT ～～～∞

Known as "Le Géant Constantin," Julius Koch (1872–1902) of Reutlingen, Germany, had hands that measured 15 in (38 cm) long—more than twice the size of an average adult hand. He was believed to be more than 8 ft (2.4 m) tall, but his height had to be estimated because his legs were amputated after developing gangrene.

UNEQUAL TWINS ～～～∞

Born in Denton, Montana, Donald Koehler (1925–81) experienced an abnormal growth spurt at age ten and stood 8 ft 2 in (2.48 m) tall at his peak. Yet his twin sister was only 5 ft 9 in (1.75 m) tall—a height difference of 29 in (74 cm).

MIGHTY MING ～～～∞

U.S.-based Chinese basketball player Sun Ming Ming stands 7 ft 9 in (2.36 m) tall and wears size 19 shoes. He did not start playing his sport until he was 15, by which time he was already 6 ft 7 in (2 m) tall.

TINY TOT ～～～∞

When Edith Barlow of Yorkshire, England, was born in 1925, she weighed just over 1 lb (450 g) and was so tiny that for the first six months of her life she was literally wrapped in cotton wool that had been soaked in olive oil. By the time of her death, at age 25, she had grown to a height of only 1 ft 10 in (55 cm).

ADMIRAL DOT ～～～∞

Born in San Francisco in 1858, little Leopold Kahn was discovered by showman P.T. Barnum at age four and dubbed "The Eldorado Elf," later renamed as "Admiral Dot." At 16, Kahn was 2 ft 1 in (63 cm) tall, but he eventually reached 4 ft (1.2 m) and became a deputy sheriff and volunteer firefighter in White Plains, New York, making him the smallest man in the U.S.A. to hold either post.

HALF SIZE ～～～∞

When Frenchman Fabien Pretou married Natalie Lucius at Seysinnet-Pariset, France, in 1990, he towered over her in the wedding photos. For he was 6 ft 2 in (1.85 m) tall and she was half his height at 3 ft 1 in (94 cm).

LONG NOSE ～～～∞

Thomas Wedders, who lived in the U.K. during the 18th century, had a nose that measured 7½ in (19 cm) long. He put his pronounced proboscis to good use by joining a traveling freak show.

Tongue in cheek

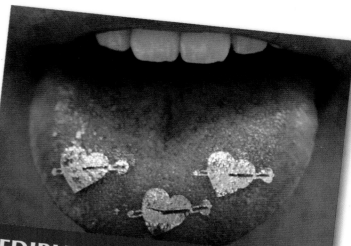

EDIBLE GOLD

A company in Japan has created edible gold shapes that can float in your coffee or decorate your tongue. As well as offering the height of luxury, the gold is said to help refresh the human body.

BEE BEARD

Steve Bryans of Alvinston, Ontario, Canada, had his face crawling with 7,700 bees at an annual bee beard contest at Aylmer, Ontario. The bees, which had been smoked into good behavior, were brushed onto competitors' faces and shaped with feathers into beards. They remained in place because they were attracted by their queens, who were caged and tied around the contestants' necks.

LONG WASH

Dae Yu Quin, a 41-year-old woman from Shanghai, China, has hair that is 14 ft 9 in (4.5 m) long. She has not cut it since she was forced to shave her head as a teenager following a scalp disease. It takes her half a day to wash and dry it!

EYE-POPPING

Claudio Paulo Pinto of Brazil, can pop his eyeballs out of their sockets a distance of at least 0.3 in (7 mm). He once had a job scaring visitors at a haunted house tourist attraction in Belo Horizonte.

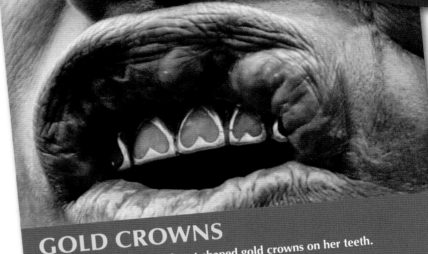

GOLD CROWNS

This Bolivian woman has heart-shaped gold crowns on her teeth.

TONGUE TWISTER...

TOUGH TEETH

Cai Dongsheng of Chongqing City, China, can break nails with his teeth. Protecting his teeth with gauze, he has so far snapped more than 22 lb (10 kg) of nails.

HICCUP ATTACK

Jennifer Mee of St. Petersburg, Florida, started hiccupping on January 23, 2007, and continued for 38 days straight.

ALBINO FAMILY

All four children of Canada's Mario and Angie Gaulin were born with albinism, giving them pinkish eyes and white hair.

TOTAL TATTOO

Lucky Diamond Rich, an Australian performer, has tattoos over every inch of his body—even inside his mouth and ears. Some areas have multiple layers of ink. He has been tattooed by 136 artists in more than 250 studios, in 45 cities and 17 different countries, involving a total tattoo time of 1,150 hours—that's nearly seven weeks.

LONG NAILS

Li Jianping of Shishi City, China, has let the fingernails on his left hand grow for 15 years—and now they are over 3 ft 3 in (1 m) long. He avoids crowded places and always sleeps with his left wrist under his head to stop that hand from moving.

MULTIPLE DIGITS

Jeshuah Fuller of New York City was born in August 2007 with six fingers on each hand and six toes on each foot.

BIG TONGUE

Stephen Taylor of the U.K. has a tongue that is 3.74 in (9.5 cm) long, enabling him to insert it into his nostrils!

MERMAID EFFECT

A woman from New Zealand with no legs is being fitted with a mermaid's tail so she can pursue her love of swimming. Nadya Vessey had both legs amputated by the age of 16, but has asked the company responsible for the special effects in the *Lord of the Rings* and *King Kong* movies to make her a prosthetic tail molded on to a pair of wetsuit shorts.

FINGER GROWTH

Lee Spievack of Cincinnati, Ohio, lost the tip of a finger in August 2005, but the finger grew back to its original length—and the fingernail on that finger now grows twice as fast as the rest.

SWOLLEN FINGERS

Liu Hua from Jiangsu Province, China, had fingers that were thicker than his arms. His left thumb, index finger, and middle finger were deformed at birth but grew to an amazing size before surgeons removed 11 lb (5 kg) of bone and tissue in 2007.

HUMAN BILLBOARD

Edson Alves from Tanabi, Brazil, makes a living by having advertisements tattooed on his body. He walks around with his shirt off, displaying more than 20 tattoos promoting local shops, restaurants, and businesses.

TONGUE SPLITTING

James Keen from Scottsville, Kentucky, shows off his split tongue. He had it split by a piercer using a scalpel heated by a blowtorch and no anesthetic. Although it is said to enhance the pleasure of kissing, the practice is now illegal in some U.S. states, where it is considered tantamount to mutilation.

Mohammed Rafi of Kerala, India, can twist his tongue at a 180-degree angle and roll it inside out by flipping his entire tongue backward. He can touch the tip of his nose with his tongue and can also roll it into all sorts of shapes—a flower, a shell, and even a boat.

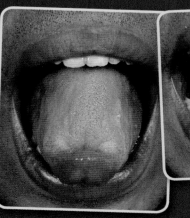
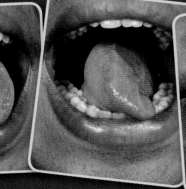
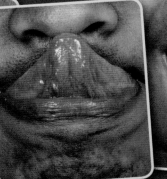
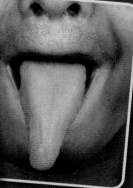

Enter the Vault

LITTLE AND LARGE

Extremes of tall and short people from West (left) and East (right) seen in the 1930s and 1880s respectively.

BITE ME!

This oyster shell grew up around an old set of missing false teeth!

CRANIAL HOPPER

In 1931, Alexandre Patty's party trick was to ascend staircases "walking" on his head! He called the technique "cranial hopping."

SAY WHAT?

Max Calvin, from Brooklyn, New York, never needed to fish for change. He could hold an astonishing 25 quarters in his ear!

CONJOINED TWINS

This photograph of conjoined twins, Mary and Arrita, was taken in 1924. The girls, from Mexico City, Mexico, were joined at the ribcage.

ON THE CHIN

Robert Dotzauer of Davenport, Iowa, was able to balance two heavy iron lawn mowers on his chin.

SUPERSIZE ME!

At one point, both Sam Harris of Farmersville, Texas, and Alice Dunbar of Dallas, Texas, were the heaviest man and woman alive, weighing 691 lb (313 kg) and 685 lb (311 kg) respectively.

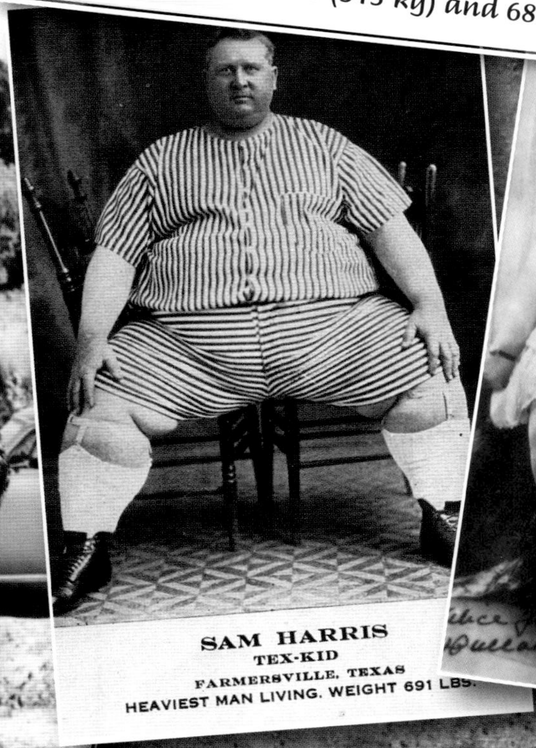

SAM HARRIS
TEX-KID
FARMERSVILLE, TEXAS
HEAVIEST MAN LIVING. WEIGHT 691 LBS.

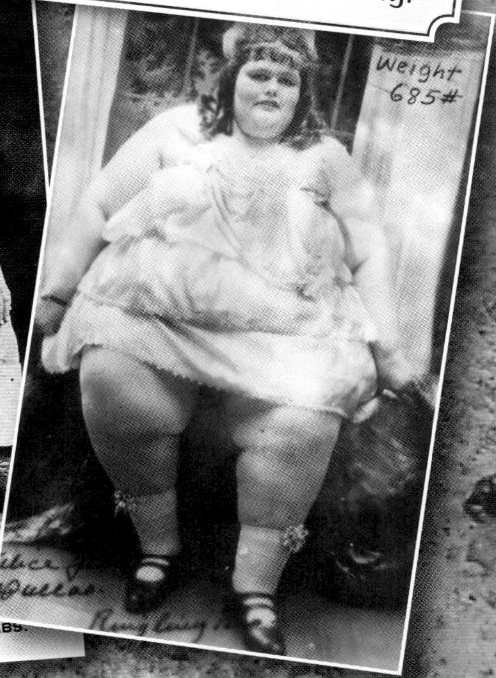

Weight 685#

HORIZONTAL STRENGTH ▼

Laurence J. Frankel was able to hold himself horizontally on stall bars with a 110-lb (50-kg) weight attached to his back.

◀ A REAL MOUTHFUL

Despite standing a mere 5 ft (1.52 m) in height, Jackie del Rio of Chicago, Illinois, managed to lift two tables and six chairs—with his teeth!

HUMAN FLAG ▲

Perry L. Biddle of DeFuniack Springs, Florida, is seen here performing his human flag impersonation on his 90th birthday in 1936.

PIERCING RECORD

Brent Moffatt from Winnipeg, Canada, pierced himself with 900 surgical needles in 2003 in an effort to break his previous body-piercing record of 702.

CURVED HORN

A Chinese grandmother has a 5-in (13-cm) horn growing out of her forehead. Ninety-five-year-old Granny Zhao of Zhanjiang City, says the horn, which curves downward and looks like the stalk of a pumpkin, grew from a mole three years ago. It causes her no pain but interferes slightly with her vision.

GREEN BLOOD

Surgeons operating on a 42-year-old man in Vancouver, British Columbia, Canada, were alarmed to discover that he had green blood! Tests revealed that he had taken too many doses of a headache pill, which had caused his blood to change color.

LOUD SNAP

Robert Hatch of Pasadena, California, snaps his fingers at a sound level of 108 decibels— almost as loud as a rock concert.

NECK TUMOR

Seventeen years after first discovering a strange growth on the back of his neck, 58-year-old Huang Liqian of Chongqing, China, finally had it removed in 2007. In that time it had grown into a huge neck tumor weighing an incredible 33 lb (15 kg).

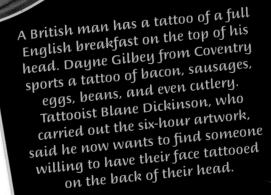

Egg on Face!

A British man has a tattoo of a full English breakfast on the top of his head. Dayne Gilbey from Coventry sports a tattoo of bacon, sausages, eggs, beans, and even cutlery. Tattooist Blane Dickinson, who carried out the six-hour artwork, said he now wants to find someone willing to have their face tattooed on the back of their head.

MAGIC TRICK

Actor Daniel Radcliffe, best known for his role as Harry Potter in the movies of the same name, can hold his hand on a flat surface and rotate it 360 degrees.

ABDOMINAL GROWTH

Chen Huanxiang of Wuhan, China, was admitted to a hospital in April 2007 for the removal of a whopping 110-lb (50-kg) abdominal tumor.

PIZZA HEAD

To mark the opening of his takeout pizza shop, Colin Helsby of Penmaenmawr, Wales, had a slice of ham-and-pineapple pizza tattooed on the back of his head. The tattooist took three hours to complete the artwork, which features three types of ham, chunks of pineapple, and strands of cheese dripping down Helsby's neck.

RARE CASE

Lydia Fairchild of Washington State, is one of only 50 people in the world known to be born with two different sets of DNA, a condition known as "chimerism." Doctors made the discovery in 2002 when she had to prove that she was her chidren's mother.

SHOCK DISCOVERY

Chinese surgeons operating on a 10-month-old baby girl from Zhoukou found grass growing on her right lung. The 1³/₁₆-in (3-cm) piece of grass was the same type as in the yard at home where she often plays. Doctors say it is possible that grass seed was blown into the baby's nose and through her respiratory system to the lung, where it found suitable growing conditions.

REPLACEMENT HORN

A man in the Yemen has grown two horns. Saleh, aged 102, had often dreamed he was growing a horn on his head and one finally sprouted on the left side 25 years ago. It grew to 1 ft 8 in (50 cm) before falling off but a second one has now grown in its place.

PARASITIC DRESS

Born in Albany, Georgia, in 1932, performer Betty Lou Williams had a parasitic twin protruding from the front of her torso. The twin consisted of two legs, one arm with three fingers, and a second arm that was little more than a single finger. Sometimes she dressed the twin in tiny clothes and off-stage she kept it hidden under a maternity dress.

LONG FINGER

Before surgery, Liu Hua of Jiangsu, China, had an index finger on his left hand that was 12 in (30 cm) long.

LEG BATTLE

Two men were feuding in 2007 over who had the rightful ownership of a severed leg. John Wood of Greenville, South Carolina, had the leg amputated after a plane crash, but kept it in a barbecue smoker so that he could be buried "whole" when he died. However, the smoker containing the leg was among items that Shannon Whisnant of Maiden, North Carolina, bought at an auction—and he wanted to keep it.

SUPERSIZE CYST

When Taquela Hilton of Kellyville, Oklahoma, ballooned to more than 560 lb (254 kg) with a 71-in (180-cm) waist, doctors thought that she was eating too much. Instead, the cause of her weight-gain was a 93-lb (42-kg) ovarian cyst, containing 12 gal (45 l) of fluid. After removing the cyst, one surgeon said: "This was like having a C-section to deliver a 12-year-old. It was a small adult that she was carrying around in her."

MAGNIFICENT MUMMIES

More than 2,000 human mummies line the walls of an underground crypt in Palermo, Sicily —all wearing their finest clothes. To make the spectacle even spookier, their jaws are loosely wired in place so that their mouths appear to be gaping wide at visitors.

Some are stretched out in niches carved into the limestone of the Capuchin Catacombs, but, owing to lack of space, others simply hang from hooks on the walls. The mummies are grouped according to age, sex, and social status, ranging from tiny babies in cribs and rocking chairs to adult lawyers in their best suits and soldiers in uniform. There are also hundreds of coffins, the sides of which have been cut open to reveal the deceased.

The monks of Palermo began mummifying their dead as a status symbol more than 400 years ago. The first Palermo mummification happened by chance. A monk, Brother Silvestro, died suddenly in 1599 and some months later it was found that the limestone and the lack of air in the crypt had combined to mummify his body. Thereafter, his fellow monks decided that they, too, wished to be mummified after death and soon the wealthier local townspeople began to express similar desires.

The practice was finally discontinued in the 1920s. One of the last people to be mummified was two-year-old Rosalia Lombardo, also known as the "Sleeping Beauty." Her family frequently visited her open coffin.

Although the dry air in the crypt has preserved many of the remains, body parts such as ears and hands have fallen off over the years, and other mummies are now little more than dressed skeletons.

Hundreds of dressed corpses line the walls of the crypt, having been embalmed by the Capuchin monks of the city. Surprisingly, there is no smell.

Ripley's research .....

The most common form of mummification in Palermo was for the bodies to be dehydrated in special cells for eight months after death, then taken out and washed in vinegar. However, during times of epidemic, the bodies were often dipped in arsenic or lime. Dr. Salofia, the Palermo medic who tended to young Rosalia Lombardo, injected chemicals to mummify her but took the details with him to his grave.

Many local people wrote wills naming the clothes in which they wanted to be buried, or stipulated that their clothes should be changed over a period of time. The Palermo mummies are all dressed as they had been in life. Consequently, some of the mummified monks have ropes dangling from their necks, because when they were alive they had worn the ropes as a penance.

MUMMY MEDICINE
In the 16th century, mummies were thought to possess medicinal properties that could prevent wounds from bleeding. Coated in honey, they were sold in powdered form as pharmaceuticals to be taken orally.

CORPSE EXPORT
During the American Civil War, mummies were imported to the U.S. so that the extensive linen in which they were wrapped could be manufactured into paper.

WELL PRESERVED
The mummy of a small girl born in the 2nd century AD was so well preserved when found near Rome, Italy, some 1,800 years later, that her fingerprints could be taken.

THICK WRAPPING
An ancient Egyptian mummy had more than 9,000 sq ft (835 sq m) of wrappings.

Although the clothes of the Palermo mummies have survived the centuries, many of the bodies themselves have been reduced to skeletons.

On the better-preserved bodies in Palermo, the flesh, the hair, and even the eyes have been mummified.

The mummified body of a child in the Capuchin Catacombs at Palermo. Whereas many of the adults were simply hung in rows, some of the children were arranged to adopt specific poses.

WEIRD ENTERTAINMENT

Aristocrats in 19th-century Europe used to buy a mummy, unwrap it, and invite friends over to view the curiosity. The regular exposure to air eventually caused the mummies to disintegrate.

BURIAL JARS

A tribe from Borneo keep their dead in huge earthenware jars. As the corpse rots, the bodily fluid is drained away and the dried remains are put in another container. The original jars are then re-used for cooking.

INUIT FAMILY

Eight well-preserved, 500-year-old mummies were discovered at an Inuit settlement in Greenland in 1972—a baby, a young boy, and six women. The bodies had been mummified naturally by the sub-zero temperatures and the dry winds in the cave in which they were found.

Mummies of Capuchin monks were dressed in priestly vestments so that their colleagues could pray to them after death.

MARRIED HIMSELF
A narcissistic Chinese man married himself before 100 guests in Zhuhai City, China, in 2007. Liu Ye married a life-sized foam cut-out of himself wearing a woman's bridal dress.

SAME DRESS
In 2007, Charlotte Middleton of Norfolk, England, became the sixth bride in her family to wear the same wedding dress. The chiffon and satin gown was first worn by her great grandmother in 1910.

THE CORPSE GROOM
Tulsi Devipujak of Anand, Gujarat, India, married her fiancé, Sanjay Dantania, in March 2007 even though he died in an accident before the ceremony. The bride's family dressed the corpse like a groom and conducted the marriage rituals on a decorated stage.

SHE'S MINE!
A couple in Merioneth, Wales, proved just how deep their love was—by getting married 500 ft (152 m) below ground in an abandoned slate mine. Kerry Bevan and Wayne Davies and their 15 guests wore traditional wedding attire with the addition of helmets and gum boots.

BAD LUCK
Seventy-five-year-old Phulram Chaudhary of Nepal married a dog in a local custom to ensure good luck. The charm didn't work, as he died three days later!

LONG DRESS
A Chinese man had a 656-ft-long (200-m) wedding dress made for his fiancée. Ken, the groom from Guangzhou, originally intended to make the dress 2,008 m (1¼ mi) long in tribute to the 2008 Beijing Olympics, but decided to reduce it to 200.8 m (658 ft). It took nearly three months to make and weighed almost 220 lb (100 kg).

LOVE IS IN THE AIR
Two high-rise window cleaners were married hanging in the air on their work platforms while guests cheered some 50 ft (15 m) below. Jiang Dezhang and Tie Guangju tied the knot in Yunnan Province, China, in August 2007 while sitting on wooden boards supported by ropes and pulleys. The best man and bridesmaid were suspended alongside.

HEN-PECKED HUSBAND

At the wedding of Terry Morris and Renee Biwer near Bismarck, North Dakota, in August 2006, the bridesmaid was a chicken! Henrietta the hen has been a pet of the groom's for 12 years and even stays in hotel rooms with the couple. The ceremony had a distinct barnyard feel to it, with the bride and groom riding in on horseback and saying their vows from the saddle.

ARBOREAL BLISS

Believing the ritual would ward off evil spirits, hundreds of people gathered in English Bazaar, India, in December 2006, to witness a marriage ceremony between two trees.

DIVORCE GIFT

In October 2006, a man in Vienna, Austria, spitefully cut off his ring finger and presented it—complete with wedding band—to his ex-wife after their divorce became final.

DONUT NUPTIALS

In addition to creating pastries, the employees of the Voodoo Doughnut Shop of Portland, Oregon, perform weddings in the bakery's chapel.

LUCKY OMEN

Sitting for a 2007 exam to become a firefighter, Alina Modoran, from Romania, wore her wedding dress. She had come straight from the church and had decided not to change out of her dress because she thought it would bring bad luck.

FUNERAL WEDDING

P. Sanjeevi Rajan of Port Klang, Malaysia, married his fiancée at his mother's funeral in 2007 to fulfil her dream of seeing him married.

DOG SUBSTITUTE

Dumped by her boyfriend two weeks before her wedding day, Emma Knight of Dorset, England, went ahead with the reception by wearing her $3,000 gown and dressing up her dog as the bridegroom.

NEVER A CROSS WORD!

When Aric Egmont of Cambridge, Massachusetts, wanted to propose to Jennie Bass, he decided to do so via a crossword puzzle. At his request, *The Boston Globe* Sunday magazine created a special puzzle where the crossword clues spelled out his proposal.

SERIAL HUSBAND

Sixty-eight-year-old Shehu Malami of Sokoto, Nigeria, has four wives and has been married a total of 201 times.

DUMMY RUN

When ventriloquists Eyvonne Carter and Valentine Vox married in Las Vegas, Nevada, their dummies—a baby doll and dog respectively—were present, too. The best man, maid of honor, bridesmaids, and ushers were all ventriloquists, accompanied by their dummies, and the ceremony was conducted by pastor Sheila Loosley—with her dummy, called Digger.

BALLOON WEDDING

Laura Dakin walked down the aisle at her wedding to Don Caldwell in 2006 wearing a dress made entirely out of twisted balloons. To add to the surreal nature of the Blue Hawaii-themed ceremony at the Viva Las Vegas Wedding Chapel in Las Vegas, Nevada, "Elvis" was on hand and the groom wore Hawaiian shorts. The couple met at a balloon-twisting convention and Caldwell (aka Buster Balloon) popped the question after stepping from a giant 6-ft (1.8-m) pink balloon.

At a wedding between two professional balloon twisters, it was only natural that even the bouquets were made of balloons.

It took the groom around eight hours to make the wedding dress from more than 200 white balloons. "I have worked on all sorts of projects before," said Don Caldwell, "but this was my first time making a life-sized, wearable dress."

87

FESTIVAL OF FIRE

To celebrate the feast of Saint Anthony (the patron saint of animals), horses and riders jump through burning pyres each January in the Spanish village of San Bartolomé de Pinares as part of the Las Luminarias de San Anton Festival. Cheered on by enthusiastic crowds, more than 100 horses and riders, some carrying small children, brave the flames from 30 bonfires laid out over the 0.6-mi (1-km) course. The controversial ceremony, which dates back hundreds of years, stems from the belief that running through fire will cleanse the village of disease.

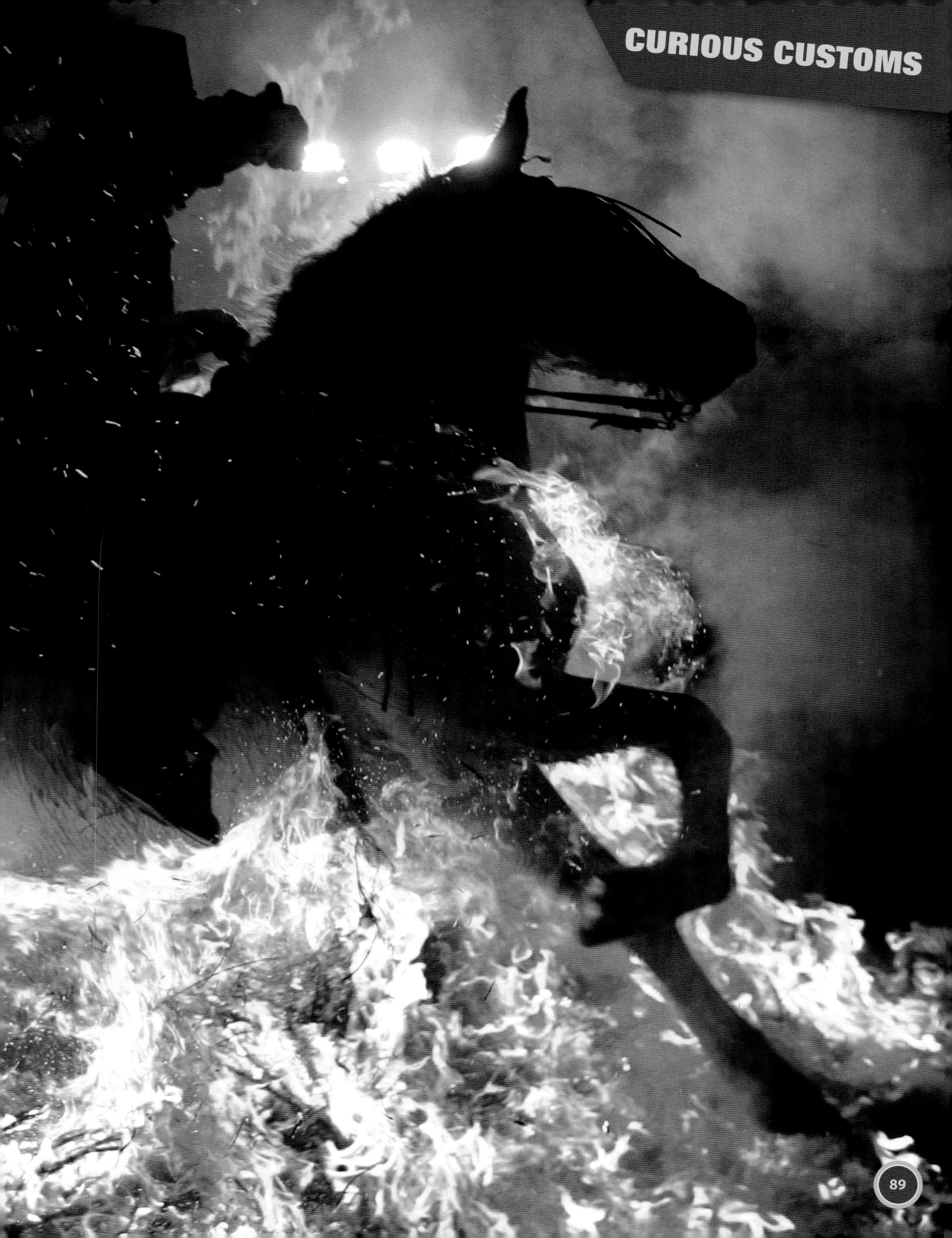

SAUNA BIRTH

Until the 1920s, babies in Finland were often delivered in saunas, because the heat was thought to be beneficial in warding off infection for the newborn and the mother.

BANNED NAMES

Malaysian parents are issued a list of names that they are not permitted to give their children—including Hitler, smelly dog, hunchback, and 007.

SLEEPYHEAD DAY

July 27 is Sleepyhead Day in Finland, where the last person in the house to wake up is dragged out of bed and thrown into a lake or the sea.

SACRED METEORITE

Members of Oregon's Clackamas Indian tribe annually make a cross-country pilgrimage to visit the 15.5-ton Willamette Meteorite, which they consider sacred, at the American Museum of Natural History in New York City.

FROG RITUAL

In Rangpur Province, Bangladesh, villagers perform mock weddings with frogs in the belief that the ritual will bring rain.

CLEAN SWEEP

Italians moving into a new home use a broom to sweep away evil spirits and sprinkle salt in the corners of the house to purify it.

PATRIOTIC DINER

Customers at a West Virginia diner join waitress Judy Hawkins in singing the American national anthem every day at noon. Hawkins works at the Liberty Street Diner in Charles Town and encourages customers to stop eating and sing along to "The Star-Spangled Banner."

SPINSTER SEAT

Icelandic superstition says that an unmarried woman who sits at the corner of a table will not marry for at least another seven years.

COMB CAUTION

The Japanese believe it is bad luck to pick up a comb with its teeth facing your body.

Crying Sumo!

In a popular Japanese contest, two sumo wrestlers hold two toddlers facing each other and coax them to cry. The first child to burst into tears is declared the winner. Most of the children who participate are under one year old. Crying Sumo, as it is known, is designed to promote the child's health as, according to Japanese belief, crying is supposed to be good for babies.

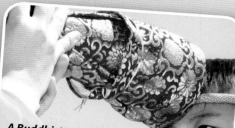

A Buddhist monk pushes a stamp on a child's forehead before the start of a Crying Sumo contest at a Japanese temple in 2004.

BALANCING ACT

Modern-day versions of traditional Japanese raftsmen, known as *kawanami*, ride on floating square logs during a festival in Tokyo. The custom dates back to the 17th century when agile Japanese lumberjacks were able to build rafts while standing on floating logs.

JUMPING DEVILS

At the El Colacho festival in Castrillo de Murcia, near Burgos, Spain, parents who want to protect their newborn babies from evil spirits lay them on the ground and allow grown men dressed as devils to jump over them.

SPITTING CONTEST ～～～

In a Sudanese marriage ritual, newlyweds have a milk spitting competition to decide who will become head of the household.

CAT CURSE ～～～

In some regions of France they believe that if a bachelor steps on a cat's tail, he will not find a wife for at least a year.

SWAN FOREBODING ～～～

To people in Scotland the sight of three swans flying together indicates that a national disaster is imminent.

TUSK CURRENCY ～～～

The 14 branches of the Tari Bunia Bank on Vanuatu's Pentecost Island have standard accounts, interest rates, and check books, and an unusual currency—pig's tusks. The tusks are paid into a customer's account, and the more they weigh, the greater their worth.

COUCH BALLOON

Kent Couch flew nearly 200 mi (322 km) over Oregon in nine hours in July 2007—in a contraption that consisted of nothing more than a lawn chair and 105 brightly colored, helium-filled balloons.

Inspired by Larry "Lawn Chair" Walters, who floated over Los Angeles, California, using weather balloons in 1982, the 47-year-old attached the bundle of 4-ft-round (1.2-m) balloons to his chair and took off from his gas station in Bend, Oregon. He carried a global-positioning device, a two-way radio, a digital camcorder, a cell phone, and a pair of sunglasses.

He also had instruments to measure his altitude and speed, plus four plastic bags, each holding 5 gal (19 l) of water, to act as ballast. To increase altitude, he simply released some of the water.

He traveled as high as 14,000 ft (4,267 m) as he floated eastward and said he could hear cattle and children as he drifted among the clouds. On the ground below, friends and family followed his progress in a convoy of vehicles.

His intended destination was Idaho, but with his water supply running low and mountains approaching, he decided to touch down in a field near Union, Oregon. He completed the descent by popping the balloons.

Afterward, Couch said he would love to do it again. "When you're laying in the grass on a summer day, and you see the clouds, you wish you could jump on them. This is as close as you can come to jumping on them. It was just like being on ice, nice and smooth."

HOW HIGH?

Jet airplanes	35,000 ft
Mt. Everest	29,000 ft
Mt. McKinley	20,000 ft
Kent Couch	14,000 ft
Bald eagles	10,000 ft

Ripley's ask

"

Where did your childhood dream of flying by balloon cluster come from? I believe my childhood dream came from a time when I was a kid at a birthday party and was asked to hold a cluster of helium-filled birthday balloons. I could feel the tug on my arm as they wanted to ascend to sky. I remember thinking if I only had a few more I could fly!

What did you fill the balloons up with in your 2007 ride? I used helium.

How long were you flying for? I flew for eight hours and 45 minutes.

Did you have any wobbly moments? Yes I did have two wobbly moments, one when I crossed a mountain range which had some wind vortices that were colliding with each other, making the balloons and chair kinda dance. The other time was when I was reaching out to retrieve a few balloons and my chair wanted to tip to the side I was leaning towards.

What is your most memorable moment of the flight? I think probably the most memorable moment in my flight was at about 14,000 ft looking down at the blue mountain range. For a moment, I felt so separated from the earth. It was just something about no noise, no people, relaxed in a lawn chair looking down at God's handiwork. Words have a hard time describing my feelings.

Was the balloon couch uncomfortable? The chair was pretty comfortable; however, I don't think I ever sat in one spot for that long. I wiggled around as much as possible.

How did you come back down to earth? I came back to earth by popping balloons one by one until I was satisfied with my descent rate.

Would you do it again? I would definitely do it again if the opportunity arises.

"

Ripley's research . . . . . .

The snake handler can perform this remarkable stunt by making use of his nasal cavity—the large air-filled space above and behind the nose. He puts the snake into his mouth, closes his throat, and, with nowhere else to go, the snake is forced upward into the nasal cavity, from where it slides down his nostril and out of his body.

SWIMWEAR SHOOT

In September 2007, 1,010 bikini-clad women assembled at Australia's Bondi Beach for a huge magazine photoshoot.

UNDERSEA FLAG

On August 2, 2007, Russian divers planted the country's flag 14,000 ft (4,267 m) below the North Pole, on the bed of the Arctic Ocean.

UPSIDE DOWN

It's not enough for 17-year-old circus performer Erik Kloeker of Cincinnati, Ohio, to juggle sharp objects, eat fire, lie on a bed of nails, and swallow swords—he can even juggle upside down! In September 2007, wearing special gravity boots and hanging from scaffolding on top of the USS *Nightmare* at Newport, Ohio, he managed to juggle three balls upside down for over four minutes—a tremendous feat of abdominal strength, co-ordination, and concentration.

FLYING FEATHERS

A mass pillow fight lasting 30 minutes was staged outside the City Hall in Toronto, Ontario, Canada, in May 2007. The air was filled with feathers as about 200 people hit total strangers with down-filled pillows. Many participants dressed up for the event, wearing bandannas, ski goggles, and capes.

SHARP PRACTICE

At a May 2007 exposition in Moscow, a member of Russia's special police lay on a bed of broken glass and nails as knives were dropped point-first onto his chest!

MASS KISS

In August 2007, Budapest, Hungary, was the place to be for 7,451 happy couples who kissed simultaneously during a week-long music festival.

HEAD OVER HEELS

Don Claps of Brighton, Colorado, was head over heels with joy in 2007. For on the TV show *Live with Regis and Kelly*, he performed an incredible 1,293 cartwheels in just one hour.

SNAKES ALIVE!

A folk artist in Nanjing, China, can push a snake into his mouth and then pull it out through one of his nostrils!

SMASHING TIME

Yang Yuyin from China's Jiangsu Province can split bricks with one hand. His goal is to split 10,000 bricks in seven hours.

DR. SIZE

In 2006, Isaac Nesser lay down and lifted the front of a van off the ground! He had no idea how much it weighed, but says that the average car weighs 2,000 lb (900 kg). Nesser, of Scottdale, Pennyslvania, has been lifting weights since he was nine, and his muscular physique—weight 362 lb (164 kg), chest 74½ in (189 cm), neck 23½ in (60 cm), biceps 29 in (74 cm), and forearms 22 in (56 cm)— have earned him the nickname Dr. Size.

GALLAGHER GLUT

A total of 1,488 people with the surname Gallagher turned up at Letterkenny, County Donegal, Ireland, in September 2007 for the Global Clan Gathering. The Gallaghers had traveled from Ireland and Britain, and also from New Zealand and the U.S.A.

PULLING PASTOR

The power of prayer helped Reverend Kevin Fast of Cobourg, Ontario, Canada, to pull two firetrucks, weighing a total of 69 tons, more than 98 ft (30 m). He achieved this in 1 minute 15 seconds, but needed two attempts, his first having been halted by a pothole near the finish line.

WRAPPED UP

New Zealander Alastair Galpin believes in keeping out the cold. In Auckland in 2006, he wore no fewer than 74 socks on one foot. On previous occasions he has worn seven gloves on one hand and 120 T-shirts!

DOLLAR CHAIN

On September 24, 2006, residents of St. Michael, Barbados, created a line of dollar coins that measured 1 mi 380 ft (1.73 km) long—adding up to more than $67,000!

BIG FOOT

In November 2007, the Sony Centre for the Performing Arts, in Toronto, Ontario, Canada, unveiled a stocking that measured 90 ft 1 in (27.5 m) long and 37 ft 1 in (11.3 m) wide from heel to toe.

APPLE PICKER

Fifty-year-old Claude Breton picked 30,240 apples, a total weight of 805 lb (365 kg), in eight hours in September 2007 at the orchard in Dunham, Quebec, Canada, where he works. Apple picking has been his passion for more than 30 years, and even when he works in a different job, he still spends his vacation picking apples.

SNAKE CHARMER

Snake man Jackie Bibby spent 45 minutes in a dry, see-through tub with 87 venomous rattlesnakes at Dublin, Texas, in 2007. Although the reptiles slithered all over him, none bit him. Bibby said afterward: "The key to them not biting is for me to stay still."

STRONG EYELIDS

Everyone else needs both hands to pick up two pails of water—but Li Chuanyong of Guangxi, China, can lift them with just his eyelids! He previously used his mighty eyelids to pull a car 16½ ft (5 m) along a road.

Enter the Vault

LONG BEARD ▶

Edwin Smith, a miner in the California gold rush of the mid-1800s, liked his beard so much that he let it grow for 16 years. It reached a length of 8 ft (2.4 m) and was so long that Smith had to hire a servant just to wash and comb it.

▲ TREE HOUSE

This tree dwelling in Horatio, Arkansas, belonged to Fred Brown, who was known as the Human Owl. Nobody knew who he was nor where he came from, but he lived in the tree for more than ten years.

▶ HIGH-RISE FRED

In 1940, Chicagoan Fred Steinlauf, 18, could be seen riding through the streets of his hometown blindfolded on a 10-ft (3-m) unicycle.

DOGGONE CLEVER

Peppy, a Dalmatian owned by Bill Fontana of Fort Frances, Oregon, rolled a log lumberjack-style for a full mile in one hour in 1954.

▲ TREE MAN

For a period during the 1930s, "The Monkey Man" of Portsmouth, Rhode Island, spent all day every Sunday standing in a tree watching the cars go by.

PIANO MAN

Arthur Schultz of Hamtramck, Michigan, gave piano recitals in the 1930s, playing the instrument with the backs of his fingers.

THE REGURGITATOR

In 1939, Dagmar Rothman performed at Ripley's New York City Odditorium astounding crowds by swallowing and regurgitating a live mouse. He smoked a cigarette before and during putting the mouse in his mouth, claiming that the smoke stunned the creature into lying still. Rothman could also place a whole lemon in his mouth.

△ CUT THE DECK

In 1931, New Yorker W.M. Wright could perform the astonishing feat of tearing a regular deck of playing cards into eighths with his bare hands. The resulting pieces of card were no bigger than his thumbnails.

DARING STUNT

U.S. daredevil performer Brad Byers from Moscow, Idaho, can place a deadly tarantula or scorpion in his mouth and blow soap bubbles at the same time.

METAL MAN

Believing that the metal would cure his abdominal pains and create pressure to induce bowel movements, 30-year-old Pradeep Hode from Diva, India, swallowed 117 coins over the course of a few months in 2007. Sadly, Hode's plan didn't work and he had to have surgery to remove the coins.

BULB SWALLOWER

Harry Rifas, a former paratrooper from Bronx, New York City, could swallow seven flashlight bulbs and then bring them up again.

GLASS-EATER

An Indian fisherman eats crushed glass as part of his regular diet. Dashrath, known to residents of Kanpur as the "Glass Man," enjoys glass bulbs and bottles with his dinner and also eats lead bullets. He says that he's never had any health trouble and doesn't believe that the glass or bullets are causing him any ill effects.

IRON JAWS

Cai Dongsheng of Chongqing City, China, can snap nails with his jaws. He demonstrated his strength in 2007 by clamping four nails in a vice, wrapping them with gauze to protect his mouth, and then gripping the nails fiercely between his teeth. In just two minutes he had broken the nails.

MULTI-TASKER

Ray Steele of Alva, Oklahoma, could whistle with his tongue sticking out—and chew gum at the same time!

Turning Tomato

Nicholas Huenefeld calls himself "The Human Ketchup Drinking Machine"—and with good cause. His personal bests are quaffing 13 fl oz (384 ml) of ketchup in just 33 seconds—or 46 fl oz (1.36 l) of the red stuff in six minutes!

In Huenefeld's own words…

" I started drinking ketchup after a $5 bet at a local restaurant. I drank the whole bottle at the table and found it to be no problem. Drinking ketchup doesn't really affect me, unless I drink massive amounts. The only time I was affected was after drinking 46 fl oz (1 l). It took me a weekend to recover and not feel bloated anymore. I am currently training to increase my metabolism, which will help me breathe quicker and drink more quickly and intensely. One of my goals is to simply hold every ketchup record there is and be known as the world's greatest ketchup drinker. "

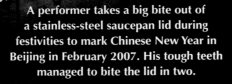

STEELY BITE

A performer takes a big bite out of a stainless-steel saucepan lid during festivities to mark Chinese New Year in Beijing in February 2007. His tough teeth managed to bite the lid in two.

HOT STUFF

Manuel Quiroz, a 54-year-old taxi driver from Mexico City, Mexico, can eat dozens of spicy chili peppers, as well as rub them on his skin, and even squeeze their juice into his eyes—without feeling any discomfort at all. Quiroz first discovered his awesome talent when he was just seven years old. "Chilies don't sting me," he says. "They have no effect. It's just like eating fruit."

BALL JUGGLER

Francisco Tebar Honrubia, alias Paco, a Spanish entertainer who has performed with New York's Big Apple Circus, can juggle five ping-pong balls—using only his mouth and sending them up to 50 ft (15 m) in the air. He says the secret of his art is not to let his mouth get too dry.

TRICK SHOT

While blindfolded, Larry Grindinger of Duluth, Georgia, spat a cue ball out of his mouth onto a 9-ft (2.7-m) pool table so that the ball bounced over five rows of balls and sank four balls in two pockets.

MUSICAL TONGUE

Adrian Wigley from the West Midlands, England, played an organ nonstop for two hours— but he didn't use his fingers. Instead, he used only his tongue to hit the keys.

MOUTH PORTRAIT

In Chennai, India, in 2006, S. Rajendran painted a portrait of the then Indian President A.P.J. Abdul Kalam using only his mouth—it took him 151 hours. He produced this amazing piece of art by holding the brush with his tongue.

FOUR BALLS

Sam Simpson of Avalon, California, could hold either a baseball or three billiard balls in his mouth all at the same time—a feat he demonstrated at the 1933 World's Fair in Chicago, Illinois.

GIANT CROSSWORD

A self-confessed crossword fanatic from the Yemen has created a giant crossword puzzle that is 178 times bigger than any other. Abdul-Karim Qasem spent seven years devising a crossword with 320,500 squares and 800,720 words in its accompanying clue book. He spent hours on end surfing the Internet to find information for his clues and answers, taking great care not to repeat any information in the puzzle.

HARD TO SWALLOW

A huge tank filled with more than 80 sharks and stingrays was the watery setting for for a startling performance by world-renowned sword-swallower Dan Meyer, aka "Captain Cutless." Meyer, from Nashville, Tennessee, made history by becoming the first person in North America to swallow a sword while submerged 15 ft (4.5 m) underwater at Ripley's Aquarium in Myrtle Beach, South Carolina. He successfully swallowed a 24-in (61-cm) solid steel sword in a feat made many times more dangerous by being underwater and surrounded by large fish.

CHINESE ACROBATS

Su Chuandong, a 63-year-old folk artist, from Wuhan, China, is able to float in a river while spitting fire. A former acrobat and lifeguard, he can also smoke, read a newspaper, and play the bugle while floating on the water.

SIMULTANEOUS SKIPPING

More than 3,000 people, ranging in age from ten to 68, assembled in the center of Changsha, China, in July 2007 to take part in three minutes of simultaneous skipping.

TOUR DE FAT

More than 3,600 cyclists, some riding homemade contraptions, took to the streets of Fort Collins, Colorado, in September 2007 for the Tour de Fat—an initiative aimed at promoting cycling as an alternative to driving. Many donned fancy-dress costumes, ranging from Miss Piggy to Fred Flintstone.

TRAM PULLER

In May 2007, Hungarian strong man Arpad Nick dragged a 70-ton tram more than 160 ft (49 m) through the streets of Budapest.

KING TOOTH

A Malaysian strong man nicknamed King Tooth pulled a seven-coach train using a steel rope clenched in his teeth. Rathakrishnan Velu hauled the 325-ton train 9 ft (2.8 m) along the track at Kuala Lumpur railway station in August 2007.

UNDERWATER HOOPER

Ashrita Furman of Jamaica, New York, hula hooped underwater for 2 minutes 20 seconds at a dolphin center in Key Largo, Florida, in 2007. While Furman was executing the stunt with a specially made metal hoop and breathing air from a portable scuba tank, the resident dolphins watched intently. "I think the dolphins thought I was totally crazy," said Furman afterward. "Who knows, maybe they'll try it themselves!"

PLANE DRAG

Using only his ears, Manjit Singh, 57, from Leicester, England, pulled a 16,315-lb (7,400-kg) passenger jet aircraft 12 ft (3.6 m) along the runway of East Midlands Airport in 2007. Prior to this event, his feats of strength included pulling a double-decker bus using only his hair and lifting 187 lb (85 kg) with only his ears.

STRONG EARS

Wang Lianhai from Qiqihaer, China, pulled a car for more than 650 ft (200 m) with his ears—but he was also riding a motorbike at the time! With his ears attached to metal clamps, which in turn were connected to steel wires, he pulled the 1¼-ton car, complete with its driver, along a street in Beijing in January 2007.

FREE THROWS

In August 2007, basketball-crazy Mike Campbell of Denver, Colorado, made 1,338 free throws in an hour—that's faster than one throw every three seconds. Throughout the 60 minutes he maintained a success rate of more than 90 per cent.

GO SLOW

Greg Billingham from Cheshire, England, deliberately ran the 2007 London Marathon in slow motion! Running one step every five or six seconds, he finished seven days after the rest of the runners.

NASAL POWER

A Chinese man pulled a 1²/₃-ton van and its driver more than 40 ft (12 m) with his nose. Fu Yingjie sucked one end of a thin rope through his right nostril and into his stomach, where he used his abdominal muscles to grip the rope and drag the van.

LOUD CLAP

A man in China can clap his hands almost as loud as the sound of whirring helicopter blades. Seventy-year-old Zhang Quan, of Chongqing City, has had his claps measured at 107 decibels—just three decibels lower than the sound made by a helicopter. Zhang does not clap very often, however, because the noise is so great that it hurts his ears.

HUG-A-THON

Utah college student Jordan Pearce hugged 765 people in just 30 minutes in 2007. However, the challenge was not all tender-hearted cuddles for the 18-year-old—a boy kicked and screamed to avoid being hugged by her, a man spilled his drink on her, and one girl refused to let go of her.

HAIR-RAISING

To celebrate India's 60th Independence Day in 2007, Siba Prasad Mallick of Balasore, pulled two motorcycles for a distance of 1¼ mi (2 km)—with his mustache. He began growing his 2-ft-long (60-cm) mustache seven years ago and keeps it strong by moisturizing it with mustard oil.

TREE-PLANTING

Farmers, students, and forestry officials in Uttar Pradesh, India, planted more than 10 million trees in one day on June 31, 2007!

FITNESS FANATIC!

No wonder the people of Xi'an, China, flock to see this man showing off his flexible body during morning exercise—he's 75 years old!

ONE-HAND WONDERS ▼

328 coins	Dean Gould, Felixstowe, England, 1993
205 beakers on 41 trays	Abul Hashani, London, England, 1986
25 tennis balls	Julius B. Shuster, Jeannette, Pennsylvania, 1931
23 clothes pegs	Alastair Galpin, Auckland, New Zealand, 2006
23 cups	Blanche Lowe, Tyler, Texas, 1940
20 baseballs	Julius B. Shuster, Jeannette, Pennsylvania, 1931
7 full milk bottles	Joe E. Wiedenmayer, Bloomfield, New Jersey, 1932

EGG-STRAORDINARY!

Guo Huochun from Zhejiang, China, can pick up and hold 12 eggs simultaneously in one hand—without any of them cracking.

EYE OF THE TIGER

Instead of being on the outside of a cage looking in at lions and tigers, Arnd Drossel put himself inside a cage and allowed the big cats to get a close-up. The daring stunt was all part of his 220-mi (355-km) roll through the German state of North-Rhine Westphalia in a ball of steel wire.

The 38-year-old performance artist made his unusual journey to raise money for, and awareness of, mental illness. In fact, psychiatric patients from clinics in the region helped him create the rolling globe, which measured just over 6 ft (1.8 m) in diameter, weighed around 265 lb (120 kg), and was constructed out of 250 bent stainless steel rods. When finished, it resembled a massive ball of steel wool.

Drossel set off in April 2007 from his birthplace of Dorsten and finished his roll-athon in his home town of Warburg. He covered around 13 mi (21 km) a day, propelling the ball by simply shifting his weight in a walking motion. As well as "walking," he ate and slept in the ball. Drossel passed through a number of towns on his journey, but, predictably, his most hair-raising moments occurred in the Stukenbrock Safari Park where he came face to face with the eyes of several tigers, not to mention the lions.

That was when—for the first time in his life—he was happy to be inside a strong, protective cage.

Arnd speeding past the famous Brandenburg Gate in Berlin.

Even a makeshift bed was relaxing for Arnd Drossel after a hard day's walking in his steel globe.

Arnd emerging after a night in his ball.

The journey took him across all kinds of terrain.

The tigers at Germany's Stukenbrock Safari Park are curious about the stranger who has rolled into their paddock.

JUNIOR COWBOY

Max Mobley of Kennett, Missouri, is one of the country's leading practitioners of Wild West arts—and he's only eight years old! Yet Max is no newcomer to his unusual hobby—he has been cracking and spinning ropes since he could walk.

MIGHTY ATOM

He stood only 54 in (137 cm) tall, but David Moyer of Reading, Pennsylvania, won 23 national titles in weight lifting, held national and world records, and could bench press more than twice his own weight.

SIMON SAYS

A total of 1,100 freshmen from the University of Miami gathered at the city's Bank United Center in August 2007 and simultaneously played the mimicking game "Simon Says."

KEEN TYPIST

Les Stewart of Mudjimba, Australia, spent 15 years typing out all the numbers from one to one million in letters, simply because he "wanted something to do." Between 1983 and 1998 he typed for 20 minutes every waking hour—on the hour—eventually filling 19,890 pages. Once he had finished, he threw all the pages out, except for the first and the last sheets. Stewart is no stranger to odd feats—he once put 3,400 stamps on a single envelope.

WIDE AWAKE

Tony Wright from Penzance, Cornwall, England, stayed awake for an incredible 11 days and nights in May 2007—a total of 266 hours. He prepared for the challenge by eating a diet of raw vegetables, fruit, nuts, and seeds, which, he says, helped his brain to stay awake and remain functional for long periods of time. He also fought off waves of tiredness by drinking tea, playing pool, and keeping a diary.

TEEN TEXTER

A 13-year-old girl who sends an average of 8,000 texts a month was crowned U.S. texting champion in 2007. Morgan Pozgar of Claysburg, Pennsylvania, beat off competition from 300 rivals to land the title in New York. She was not short of practice—she sends about 260 texts a day (roughly one every five minutes) to her friends.

CAR PUSH

In September 2006, Rob Kmet and Teri Starr of Winnipeg, Manitoba, Canada, pushed a Dodge Neon more than 50 mi (80 km) around a racetrack over a period of 21 hours. They trained for the event by lifting weights and jogging in the shallow water of a lake.

WEIGHT LOSS

In just one year, 42-year-old Manuel Uribe of Monterrey, Mexico, shed 440 lb (200 kg)! In early 2006 he weighed a colossal 1,235 lb (560 kg)—over half a ton—but within 12 months his low-carb diet had taken him almost halfway to achieving his ultimate goal of losing 1,000 lb (454 kg).

LONG LINE DANCE

In August 2007, more than 17,000 dancers formed an enormous line dance at the Ebony Black Family Reunion Tour in Atlanta, Georgia.

PRETTY PRANK

Walt, a prank-loving employee at a company in Washington, D.C., returned to the parking garage one day to find his beloved Jaguar car covered in 14,000 multi-colored sticky notes! Every inch of the car—including the tires—was covered except for the hood ornament and license plate. It had taken co-worker Scott Ableman and a dozen colleagues less than two hours to pull off the elaborate joke. Luckily, Walt saw the funny side and, once he'd cleaned off the windshield, drove the car home to show his family.

RUN OVER

Patrick Chege of Kenya, allows heavy trucks to run over his chest and gets up afterward without injury!

ON-AIR MILES

U.S. TV host Jimmy Kimmel commuted 22,406 mi (36,060 km) during one week in October 2007. He filled in every day for Regis Philbin on *Live with Regis & Kelly* in New York City and then jumped on a plane to host his late-night talk show in Los Angeles.

WOBBLE BOARDS

A total of 487 students, teachers, and adults at Eisenhower Junior High School in Taylorsville, Utah, gathered in November 2007 to form a huge wobble board ensemble. Popularized by the Australian entertainer Rolf Harris, wobble boards are musical instruments made of hardboards measuring 2 x 3 ft (60 x 90 cm). They are played by propping them between the palms of the hands and bouncing them back and forth.

BEER CARRYING

In 2007, Reinhard Wurz of Australia, carried 20 one-liter (32-fl oz) glasses full of beer for a distance of 130 ft (40 m).

SMASH HIT

Dan Wilson from Lodi, California, smashed 64 dinner plates on his forehead in 41 seconds in 2007. The 47-year-old father-of-eight, who also breaks bottles, bricks, and boards on his head, said of his achievement: "I wanted to do something famous before I die and as I don't have the brains, I thought I'd better use my body." He added that he spends about two hours psyching himself up before each challenge, concentrating all his energy on one quarter-sized spot at the top of his forehead.

DOMINO TOPPLING

A TV commercial filmed in Salta, Argentina, in 2007 featured 6,000 dominoes toppling in just 14 seconds. The domino trail took two days to construct and also involved 10,000 books, 400 tires, 45 dressers, and six cars.

CHECKMATE K.O.

In November 2007, German policeman Frank Stoldt was crowned world champion of the hybrid sport of chessboxing. Bouts are composed of up to 11 alternating rounds of chess and boxing, representing the ultimate test of brains and brawn. After fending off his American opponent's punches, Stoldt managed to clinch the title with a checkmate in the chess game of the seventh round.

MASS DRIBBLE

Led by the Indiana Pacers basketball team, around 4,600 people dribbled basketballs through Indianapolis in October 2007.

WORM DANCE

James Rubec performed a "Worm" break dance move along the turf of the Rogers Centre stadium in Toronto, Ontario, Canada, for more than 98 ft (30 m) in 2007.

BLINDFOLDED TEXT

New Zealand teenager Elliot Nicholls sent a 160-character text message in just 45 seconds... while blindfolded. The 17-year-old sends around 50 text messages a day and has worn out the keypads on four cell phones already.

GORILLA SUIT

Ferrari Formula One driver Kimi Raikkonen entered a powerboat race in the Finnish city of Hanko in July 2007 wearing a gorilla suit to disguise his identity.

ALL SCORED

Every soccer player in a 12-man squad scored when Bridlington Rangers Blues Under-13s beat Hutton Cranswick United 23–0 in a match in Yorkshire, England, in 2007. As the boys switched positions, even the goalkeeper scored three times.

TWISTER GAME

More than 1,400 people played a mass game of Twister at the Rogers Centre Stadium in Toronto, Ontario, Canada, in 2007.

Light Lunch

Wang Gongfu, of Lianyungang, China, eats glass twice a week. He ate his first glass cup when he was 20 and in the intervening 22 years he has eaten more than 440 lb (200 kg) of glass. His favorite is teacup glass, but he is also quite partial to electric lightbulbs.

Ripley's research

The risks associated with eating and swallowing glass depend on its size, shape, and sharpness, jagged pieces being far more dangerous than smooth. The human digestive tract can cope with many things—including bones in meat or fish—so small pieces of glass can travel right through the bowel and be passed out normally.

Sword swallowers must first eliminate the gag reflex, which they do by putting their fingers, then spoons, knitting needles, and eventually wire coat hangers down their throat. They must also relax their pharynx, esophagus, and the muscles of their neck, and make sure that the sword is lined up perfectly. Another trick of the trade is to lubricate the sword beforehand with either saliva or butter.

BALLOON JOURNEY

Five-year-old Kelvin Bielunski released a helium balloon from his school in Woodston, England—and three weeks later it was found by a soldier in Iraq, 2,500 mi (4,000 km) away!

WET CEREMONY

Taiwan's College of Marine Sciences staged its 2007 degree ceremony underwater! At the ceremony, which was held in the aquarium of the National Museum of Marine Biology, the university president wore a diving suit and handed out waterproof certificates to students whose graduation clothes were accessorized with flippers and oxygen masks.

HORSE SHOW

As a special attraction at the 2006 Stockholm International Horse Show in Sweden, Oliver Garcia of France rode his horse inside a massive plastic ball.

4,000 TRACTORS

In Cooley, County Louth, Ireland, in 2007, a total of 4,572 vintage tractors plowed a field simultaneously. All of the tractors involved were built before 1977, the oldest dating back 100 years. Farmers traveled from as far away as South Africa, Australia, the U.S.A., and Canada to take part.

IT'S THE PITS!

Breathing air provided by algae watered with urine, an Australian marine biologist lived for 13 days in an underwater steel capsule 10 ft (3 m) long submerged in a flooded gravel pit. Lloyd Godson's survival at a depth of 15 ft (4.5 m) depended on a coil of green algae, which provided air in return for him urinating on the plants each day. Meals came in through a manhole in the capsule and he rode a bicycle to generate electricity, which recharged his waterproof laptop computer.

NASAL DRINKER!

A drink is not to be sniffed at for this performer in Hefei, China, in May 2007. He can drink the liquid by inhaling it through his nose!

STEEL SWALLOWER

This Chinese performer can swallow a stack of steel bars—without suffering any adverse effects.

ONTARIO SUPERMAN

For five minutes, Rick Ellis of Chatham-Kent, Ontario, Canada, hung suspended in midair from a piece of wood by eight steel hooks that had been inserted into his skin. The hooks—six in his back and one in each calf—had made the 36-year-old scream in agony as they were sunk into his skin, but once suspended he felt fine: "I wasn't in any pain then," he said. "I was at peace with myself. There was a lightness like there was nothing around me. It was like I was flying."

AQUA GOLF

A marine life aquarium in Fuzhou, China, staged what is thought to be the world's first underwater golf tournament. Five players overcame problems presented by fish, mammals, buoyancy, and water currents to play golf in a tank that was 50 ft (15 m) deep. The result was decided on how long it took to complete the hole rather than the number of strokes taken. The winner sunk the ball in 1 minute 20 seconds.

RAPID ESCAPE

Tied with chains and thrown underwater, Akash, a magician from Hyderabad, India, managed to escape from his shackles in a mere 15 seconds!

WET HAIR

Jurijus Levčenkovas of Vilnius, Lithuania, performed an underwater haircut in six minutes at an aquarium in July 2006.

BARREL ORDEAL

Apart from the occasional toilet break, Dutch philosopher Eric Hoekstra spent an entire week in April 2007 living in a 6-ft (2-m) wine barrel at Leeuwarden University.

STRONGMAN STUART

Stuart Burrell of Essex, England, lifted a 48½-lb (22-kg) weight 522 times in one hour!

ROUND OF APPLAUSE

Paramjit Singh of India, can clap his hands more than 11,600 times in just one hour!

BRA BUSTER

Thomas Vogel of Germany can unhook 56 women's brassieres in just one minute—using only one hand!

QUICK ESCAPE

An officer in the U.S. Navy took just 20 seconds to escape from a straitjacket—that's less time than it takes for a garage door to open and close. Performing as "Danger Nate" and wearing star-spangled running tights, Jonathan Edmiston freed himself from the regulation straitjacket at Yokosuka Naval Base's 2007 Fourth of July celebration.

KEYBOARD MARATHON

A Hollywood actor put himself in the spotlight in 2007 by continuously typing on a computer keyboard for five consecutive days (with a five-minute bathroom break per hour) in the front window of a Manhattan business center. Norman Perez said he stayed awake by chatting with strangers online and even received a marriage proposal.

Romanian circus gymnast Ioan-Veniamin Oprea is able to contort his body into all manner of weird and wonderful shapes inside a colored plastic tube. With the aid of an assistant, he can even create a stunning octopus dance routine.

Oprea and his assistant in the slinky.

NOSE BLOW

Not content with blowing up a hot-w[...] bottle with his mouth, 52-year-old Z[...] Zhenghui, of Liling, China, has done [...] his nose! After three years of practice [...] him just two minutes to blow up the [...] and make it burst. He has also used [...] to inflate the inner tube of a truck tire [...] ten minutes, defeating competition [...] young men with bicycle pumps!

WRITE ON!

Subhash Chandra Agrawal and his w[...] Madhu, from New Delhi, India, are n[...] lost for words. Between them they h[...] had more than 18,000 "letters to the [...] published in newspapers and magaz[...]

CHECK MATES

On October 23, 2006, 13,446 people [...] gathered to play chess simultaneous[...] Mexico City's Zocalo Square.

Oprea's colorful plastic [...]

BACKWARD RACE

On August 20, 2006, a 7-mi (11-km) backward running race was held on the slopes of the Stanserhorn mountain in the Swiss Alps.

LONG SPEECH

Never pausing for more than 30 seconds at a time, India's Jayasimha Ravirala delivered a speech that lasted for 111 hours. His lecture on Personality Development Concepts ran for six days and five nights.

BRIDGE HOP

Six hundred people bouncing along on children's Spacehopper toys took part in a simultaneous hop on London's Millennium Bridge in April 2007. The bridge was chosen for the challenge because it wobbled alarmingly when it was first opened to the public in 2000.

LIQUID LUNCH

Five hundred people sampled a lavish dinner party in September 2007—underwater. The feast took place at the bottom of a swimming pool in London, England, but because of the difficulties of eating underwater, each of the three courses consisted of just one mouthful of food.

GLASS ROOM

Ye Fu and Hairong Tiantian lived in a single glass room on a sidewalk in Beijing, China, for a whole month. They were separated by a transparent wall in what they say is a metaphor for the gap in modern family relationships in China.

UNDERWATER HOCKEY

Eight international teams braved the freezing temperatures of an Austrian lake in February 2007 to take part in the first-ever World Underwater Ice-Hockey Championship. Competing under 12 in (30 cm) of ice, the players, wearing wetsuits, masks, and flippers, chased a Styrofoam puck around a "rink" that was 20 ft (6 m) wide and 26 ft (8 m) long. As they had no oxygen tanks, the players resurfaced every 30 seconds for air.

WOOL RUSH

In 40 hours, Garry Hebberman of Jamestown, Australia, sheared 1,054 sheep—that's one sheep every 2 minutes 17 seconds!

CROWDED WAVE

Timing things to perfection, 84 surfers simultaneously rode the same wave at Quebra Mar, Santos, Brazil, in 2007.

LET'S ROCK!

On January 27, 2007, Pat Callan of LaCrosse, Wisconsin, headbanged for more than 35 minutes straight at a rock concert.

HEADSTRONG

Appearing on a German TV show in 2007, Kevin Shelley of Carmel, Indiana, broke 46 wooden toilet seat lids in 60 seconds— with his head! It is not the first time he has used his head for entertainment—he has previously smashed ten pine boards with his head in just over seven seconds.

YOUNG SWIMMER

Leah Robbins of Norfolk, England, swam 164 ft (50 m) in May 2007—even though she was only two years old! She swam the distance backstroke, which is normally tackled by children three times her age.

SPEED-SKIPPER

Olga Berberich, a 23-year-old German fitness coach, completed 251 skips with a rope in one minute in Cologne in September 2007.

ROLLER-COASTER RIDE

Richard Rodriguez certainly experienced the ups and downs of life in 2007. The 48-year-old American roller-coaster enthusiast spent 17 consecutive days riding the Pepsi Max Big One at Blackpool Pleasure Beach in northern England.

He got a five-minute break every hour he was on the ride, and could save these up for longer breaks if he preferred. Eating, drinking, and sleeping on the roller coaster, Rodriguez completed nearly 8,000 rides and covered over 6,300 mi (10,140 km)—almost as far as the return journey from Blackpool to his hometown of Brooklyn, New York.

Ripley's ask

"When did you start riding roller coasters, and why? Initially, I was afraid of roller coasters and only rode my first white-knuckle coaster at the age of 16. As a child, Charles Lindbergh was my hero, and 1977 was the 50th anniversary of his solo nonstop flight across the Atlantic. He had previously ridden the Cyclone so, as a tribute to him, I did my first roller-coaster marathon.

Did you ever feel sick while on the Big One? I haven't been sick yet. The main thing that bothers me is the wind pressure against my skin. It's like sticking your head out of a car window for x amount of hours at 80 mph!

Did you get bored? Yes, but I find boredom less of an issue during the day because the general public can ride on the coaster with me. One little boy asked me if the park knew I was doing a roller-coaster marathon or was it a big secret!

Did you get a sore backside? I probably would—if I didn't sit on foam. I am quite particular about foam, it has to be a certain type (industrial packing foam) and cut to fit exactly (bottom size).

When you stepped off the roller coaster to have a break, did you feel unbalanced? I did get the odd wobble, yes. After a while it feels more normal to be on the roller coaster than on the ground.

Did you sleep on the roller coaster? Yes, but sporadically, and the first night is always very hard. However, I didn't sleep on the Big One, I slept on the nearby Big Dipper. The Big One isn't allowed to run at night because of noise pollution, so it was a quick change-over every evening.

Is there a particular roller coaster that you want to ride on? I'd like to do a coaster challenge in an exotic place like Japan or India."

Richard gets ready to bed down for the night on the Big Dipper surrounded by his protective foam padding.

The Big One rises majestically above the beach at Blackpool.

PLEASURE BEACH

PLEASURE BEACH BLACKPOOL

BUS RIDE
Bill Kazmaier of Burlington, Wisconsin, can pull a bus—full of schoolchildren! Three times crowned the world's strongest man, he can also lift a boy off the ground by means of a rope attached to just his little finger.

HELD BREATH
Freediver Dave Mullins from New Zealand swam 740 ft (226 m) in a Wellington swimming pool in 2007—on a single breath. He held his breath for 3 minutes 42 seconds.

PREVENTED TAKEOFF
In Superior, Minnesota, in 2007, Chad Netherland used his body strength to hold back two Cessna 206 airplanes from taking off in opposite directions for 60 seconds!

ROLL WITH IT
A toilet roll measuring more than 11 mi (18 km) long was unraveled at London's Wembley Stadium in July 2007. The toilet roll, which was 4 ft 10 in (1.5 m) wide and weighed 1,440 lb (653 kg), was almost as long as the Victoria Line in the English capital's subway system.

BIG CATCH
Over the past 25 years, fervent fisherman Dave Romeo of Mount Joy Township, Pennsylvania, has caught more than 25,000 bass! What's more, he keeps a journal detailing every bass he has ever hooked.

ONE FINGER
Ji Fengshan of Harbin city, China, can pull four taxis with just one finger! He has been building up the strength in the middle finger of his right hand for more than 40 years by using it to carry a bucket of water each day.

VERTICAL EGGS
To mark the summer solstice on June 21 in 2005, at 12 noon residents of Chiayi County, Taiwan, made 1,972 eggs stand on end simultaneously.

UP AND DOWN
Mark Anglesey of Yorkshire, England, lifted the back end of a car, weighing 450 lb (204 kg), at least 12 in (30 cm) off the ground 580 times in an hour.

STONE-SKIPPER
Russ Byars of Venango County, Pennsylvania, can skip a stone across water 51 times—reaching distances of up to 250 ft (76 m). He started stone-skipping eight years ago for something to do while out walking his dog. He favors smooth, rounded stones about 3–4 in (7–10 cm) across, grips them between his thumb and forefinger and, for maximum distance, adds spin and follow through.

PENNY LINE
In 2007, 80 penny-layers, mostly under the age of ten, set out 2,879 ft (878 m) of pennies in a parking lot at Hancock, Maine, in only 2 hours 26 minutes.

DIZZY HIPS

Many people can't run a mile in under eight minutes, but Paul Blair, aka Dizzy Hips, of San Francisco, California, can—and while twirling a hula hoop! He can also hula hoop while skating, skiing, or snow boarding and has performed a routine with a hula hoop measuring 43 ft (13 m) in circumference!

REVERSE GEAR

Germany's Isabella Wagner can complete the 100 meters running race in less than 17 seconds—while running backward!

SIMULATED KISS

A total of 3,249 residents of Taipei, Taiwan, simultaneously administered the kiss-of-life in September 2007. Ranging in age from a four-year-old girl to a 97-year-old grandmother, the volunteers gave simulated CPR (cardiopulmonary resuscitation) to plastic mannequins.

Hypnotic POWER

Canadian hypnotist Ian Stewart is a firm believer in mind over matter. He shows the extreme power of the mind in a demonstration of self-hypnosis in which he endures the shock of more than 100 firecrackers taped to his chest going off with a bang!

TATTOO PARADE

In June 2005, people with tattooed backs paraded on the beach at Zandvoort, the Netherlands, forming a line measuring more than 3 mi (5 km) long.

GRAND REUNION

When Stadium High School at Tacoma, Washington, held its 100th anniversary reunion in 2007, no fewer than 3,299 former pupils showed up!

COLD FEET

Nico Surings, of Eindhoven, the Netherlands, braved the cold to run the 100 meters barefoot on ice, in 17.35 seconds in December 2006.

HUGE SLEEPOVER

Some 35,000 children from all over the U.K. staged a mass sleepover in June 2007. Nearly 1,000 different sleepovers occurred in schools and scout groups across the country.

TEA PARTY

Nearly 15,000 people took part in a mass tea party at Nishio, Aichi, Japan, in October 2006. Almost a mile of red carpet was used for the participants to sit or kneel on while they drank powdered green tea.

MARATHON DRIBBLE

In February 2006, Joseph Odhiambo, a 41-year-old schoolteacher from Phoenix, Arizona, dribbled a basketball through the streets of Houston, Texas, for a total of 26 hours 40 minutes. During that period he also managed to bounce the ball an estimated 140,000 times!

TOUGH GUY

York, Pennsylvania, strongman Chris Rider can perform amazing feats of strength. He can tear two car license plates in half simultaneously, break a baseball bat over his knee, bend an 8-in (20-cm) adjustable wrench, bend a metal horseshoe into the shape of a heart in just seven seconds, and break a 20-oz (567-g) hammer in two.

SNOW ANGELS

In February 2007 in Bismarck, North Dakota, 8,962 people waved their arms simultaneously while lying in the snow to create a multitude of snow angels.

CAN COLLECTION

Schools across South Africa collected nearly two million tin cans for recycling in just one month in 2007.

STITCH IN TIME

While running the 2007 London Marathon, 49-year-old Susie Hewer of Sussex, England, knitted a 4-ft-long (1.2-m) scarf! Susie, who describes herself as an "extreme knitter," still managed to complete the course in under six hours.

NOODLE KING!

From just 2 lb 3 oz (1 kg) of flour, Li Enhai, of China, can make more than 2,090,000 strings of noodles. The noodles he creates are so fine that 39 can pass through the eye of one needle!

HELICOPTER PULL

Lasha Pataraia pulled a 17,050-lb (7,734-kg) military helicopter for a staggering 86 ft 4 in (26.3 m) with only his ear at an airfield near Tbilisi, Georgia. One end of a rope was attached to his ear while the other was tied to the front wheel of the helicopter.

BOUNCE-JUGGLER

Tim Nolan of Virginia Beach, Virginia, can bounce-juggle 11 balls simultaneously. Bounce-juggling is the art of bouncing objects off the ground while juggling them.

BURSTING WITH PRIDE

John Cassidy of Philadelphia, Pennsylvania, created 747 balloon animals in one hour in 2007. His creations included dogs, turtles, snails, and fish. Afterward, he said his secret was "keep your cheeks in, blow hard, and think pure thoughts."

RECORD YEAR

Canadian singer/songwriter Kevin Bath recorded an album a week for an entire year—and with eight tracks per album, that came to 416 songs in 365 days. Working in his home studio, he adopted a strict schedule whereby he completed tracks on a Thursday and mixed them over the weekend for Sunday release. To save valuable time on shaving, he grew a beard for a while.

FLORAL RIBBON

To raise awareness for breast cancer, a Dubai healthcare group created a pink ribbon symbol measuring 95 ft (29 m) in length and made up of 105,000 carnations.

GIRL HERCULES

At age 13, Varya Akulova from Krivoy Rog, Ukraine, can lift 772 lb (350 kg)—nearly ten times her body weight. Known as "Girl Hercules," she is an accomplished arm wrestler and could carry three children on her shoulders at age ten.

HUGE GATHERING

A total of 3,500 priests took part in a single religious ceremony at Jaipur, India, in 2007. The ceremony, named Bhoomi Poojan, was held to worship a piece of land before it is put to use, and all of the participating priests dug the earth with pickaxes and hoes.

HAY RIDE

Organized by Bill Buckelew and an army of volunteers, a hay ride on a 500-ft-long (150-m) line of trucks and trailers carried 1,042 people at the 2007 Farm Day celebrations in DeFuniak Springs, Florida.

SUMO SQUATS

At the age of nearly 40, Dr. Thienna, a Vietnamese-born female fitness expert, performed 5,135 sumo squats in one hour in San Francisco, California, in December 2007.

STATESIDE RUN

In 2007, 36-year-old Reza Baluchi from Boulder, Colorado, spent six months running around the perimeter of the United States—a jog of over 11,000 mi (17,700 km). He started and finished in New York City, running an average of 55 mi (90 km) a day.

SHOW STOPPER

Instead of reaching for the off switch, Germany's Marco Boehm can stop a rotating electric fan with his tongue! He demonstrated his astounding art on a German TV show filmed in Mallorca, Spain, in June 2007.

FLAT OUT

With his legs split, chest bent forward, and chin almost skimming the ground, six-year-old Aniket Chindak of Belgaum, India, is so flexible that he can roller-skate under parked cars. Aniket is a leading exponent of the sport of limbo-skating and can also limbo under poles set just 8 in (20 cm) off the ground. Of his car-skating he says: "It took three months before I could get my body in the right position. The hardest thing is to go fast enough before I bend down, because that's how you can skate under the car and come out the other side."

Aniket shows off his incredible skill by limbo-skating under a car that sits just 9½ in (24 cm) off the ground.

EIGHT-LIMBED GIRL

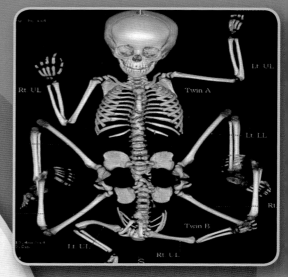

A girl born in India with four arms and four legs had the extra limbs removed in a groundbreaking 27-hour operation. Shortly afterward, she was able to stand up and walk for the first time in her life.

Lakshmi Tatma was born a conjoined twin in the impoverished northern state of Bihar. In a rare condition called isciopagus, her twin had stopped developing in the mother's womb and the surviving fetus had absorbed the parasitic twin's limbs, kidneys, and other body parts. Although the twin had a torso and limbs, it had no head and its body was joined to Lakshmi's at the pelvis.

So Lakshmi, who was named after the four-armed Hindu goddess of wealth, was born with two spines, four kidneys, entangled nerves, two stomach cavities, two chest cavities, four arms, and four legs. Many local people revered her as a goddess and lined up for a blessing from the child, but her father, Shambhu, was forced to keep her in hiding after a circus tried to buy her.

In November 2007, the two-year-old underwent an operation at a hospital in Bangalore. As well as removing the surplus limbs, surgeons transplanted a kidney from Lakshmi's twin into her own body, moved her bowels and intestines into a more central position, and amputated the headless twin altogether.

Afterward, when Lakshmi was able to stand up to reach her favorite toy, her mother, Poonam, said: "I had tears in my eyes, it was a dream I thought would never happen."

CHAIR ATTACK

An X ray shows a metal chair leg lodged in Shafique el-Fahkri's left eye socket following a fight outside a nightclub in Melbourne, Australia. When the chair was thrown at el-Fahkri, the leg penetrated his eye socket, moving his eyeball to the side, and speared down into his neck. Incredibly, he has recovered 95 percent of his vision, although the incident has left him with a raspy voice.

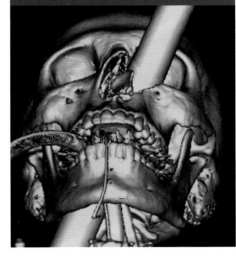

ROBOTIC LEGS
Peng Shulin of China lost his lower body in a 1995 truck accident, but 12 years later doctors in Beijing gave him robotic legs.

REATTACHED LIMB
Israel Sarrio of Valencia, Spain, had his arm severed during an accident in January 2004 and doctors sewed it to his leg to keep it alive until they could reattach it properly.

TIMELY RECOVERY
Carlos Camejo of Venezuela was declared dead following a car accident in September 2007, but awoke during his autopsy as the coroner began to cut him!

INTERNAL DECAPITATION
Shannon Malloy survived a car crash in which her skull was separated from her spine—a condition called internal decapitation. At a special surgical unit in Denver, Colorado, doctors drilled five screws into her neck and four into her head to reattach it. Then she was fitted with a metal halo—which consists of rods and a circular bar—to keep her head stabilized, but even during the fitting of the halo her unattached head kept slipping off her neck.

SCISSORS FOUND
In November 2006, doctors found surgical scissors in the abdomen of a woman from Thenpattinam, India. The scissors had been there for 12 years—ever since a previous operation on the woman in 1994.

BROKEN NECK
Fourteen-year-old sports fanatic Alfie Tyson-Brown of Dorset, England, led an active life for 10 years—unaware that he had a broken neck that could have killed him at any time. He played rugby, surfed, went mountain biking, and rode roller coasters before doctors finally discovered his life-threatening injury.

IMPALEMENT HORROR
Ezra Bias of Spokane, Washington, miraculously survived after being impaled through the head by a 2-ft-long (60-cm) piece of steel bar. He was delivering pizza when a car drove over the bar as it lay in the road, flipping it up into the air, from where if flew through Bias' windshield and into his head.

PROSTHETIC ARMS
Jesse Sullivan of Dayton, Tennessee, has a pair of amazing prosthetic arms that he is able to move merely by thinking about their movement!

HIDDEN GLASS
Xiao Zhu of China wondered why he always kept crying from one eye—until doctors found that he had had a 1⅓-in-long (3.5-cm) piece of glass buried under his right eye for the past six years. The eye had been injured in a fight, but the operation to repair the injury had missed the shard of glass.

MIRACLE CURE
Frazer Simpson of Northumberland, England, was accidentally splashed in the face with a corrosive chemical and, rather than hurting his eyes, it miraculously improved his eyesight to the point where he no longer needed glasses to drive.

MASSIVE TUMOR

A medical technician at a hospital in Belgrade, Serbia, holds a huge tumor removed from the abdomen of a 54-year-old woman. The benign tumor weighed 86 lb (39 kg)—that's the weight of an average 11-year-old! Amazingly, the woman survived.

BRIEF AWAKENING

A woman awoke from a six-year coma—but only for three days. Christa Lilly had been in a coma in Colorado Springs, Colorado, since suffering a heart attack and stroke in late 2000. Then, in 2007, she suddenly woke up and started talking to doctors and family, although she believed it was 1986. However, three days later she mysteriously lapsed back into a vegetative state.

SWEET TASTE

Humans with a particularly acute sense of taste are able to detect sweetness in a solution that is one part sugar to 200 parts water. In comparison, certain moths and butterflies can detect sweetness when the ratio is one part sugar to 300,000 parts water.

LANGUAGE CONFUSION

After being knocked unconscious in a speedway race in Glasgow, Scotland, Czech driver Matej Kus came round and started talking perfect English—even though he could barely speak the language before he had the accident! His newfound language skills did not last, however, and when he had recovered he could once again speak only broken English.

NO PULSE

Gerard Langevin of Quebec, Canada, was fitted with a new heart but now he has no pulse!

SECOND LIVER

Jenna Hopkins of Crab Orchard, Kentucky, was born with a second liver growing in her right lung.

PHONE LIGHT

As a result of a power failure, surgeons at a hospital in Villa Mercedes, Argentina, had to finish an operation using the light emitted by cell phones.

CELL NUMBERS

Our galaxy has more than 100 billion stars, but a human body has about 100 trillion cells.

POWERFUL PUMP

The human heart creates enough pressure when it pumps blood out into the body to squirt blood a distance of 30 ft (9 m).

MOSQUITO SWARM

It would take approximately 1.2 million mosquitoes to drain an average human being of all of their blood.

RARE BLOOD

The rarest blood group in the world is a type of Bombay blood known as H-H. It was first discovered in Bombay in 1950, and it is thought that only 57 people in the whole of India have it.

BRICK BITE

The muscles on the sides of a human mouth allow you to bite into things with a force of 160 lb (72.5 kg)—equivalent to the weight of 35 house bricks.

HUGE HAIRBALL

An 18-year-old from Chicago, Illinois, had a huge hairball weighing 10 lb (4.5 kg) and measuring 15 in (38 cm) long removed from her stomach in 2007. The teenager, who had a habit of eating her hair, complained to doctors of pains in her stomach—where they later found a mass of black, curly hair.

BACTERIA MASS

There are 516,000 bacteria per square inch in a human armpit.

THE BLUE MAN

A man from California has skin that is permanently blue. Paul Karason of Madera developed the condition 15 years ago after using a homemade silver remedy to treat dermatitis on his face. Despite the unfortunate side effect, he swears by its powers and has even got used to his nickname of Papa Smurf.

Ripley's research

Suffering from stress-related dermatitis after his father's death, Paul Karason decided to treat it with his own mixture of colloidal silver, a medicine widely used before the discovery of penicillin. However, silver has been banned in U.S. medicines since 1999 because it causes argyria, a condition that turns the skin blue. He probably exacerbated the problem by rubbing the silver into the peeling skin on his face as well as taking it orally.

MIRACLE WALKER

Born with spina bifida, by the age of 34 Mark Chenoweth was resigned to spending the rest of his life in a wheelchair. Doctors told him he would never walk again.

Then, on holiday in Menorca in 1998, against the advice of his doctor, he persuaded a dive center to let him go scuba diving for the first time. He plunged to a depth of 55 ft (17 m)—and when he emerged from the water he found that he could walk again.

"It was just unbelievable," says Mark. "I came out and I could feel my legs like I had never felt them before. They were actually working. The instructor couldn't believe it. He'd seen me arrive in my wheelchair, and now I didn't need it."

Three days later his legs became lifeless again, but back home in Staffordshire, England, he quickly booked his next diving holiday. Since then he has found that the deeper he dives, the longer he can walk for afterward. As a result he now needs his wheelchair only twice a year.

DEPTH DIVED	WALKING PERIOD AFTERWARD
55 ft (17 m)	3–4 days
100 ft (30 m)	2–3 months
130 ft (40 m)	4 months
165 ft (50 m)	8 months

Ripley's research

The deeper divers go, the richer the mix of oxygen that they take in from their aqualungs, and one theory is that this extra oxygen is affecting the nerve cells damaged by Mark's spina bifida and is making them temporarily work.

SPOON SURGERY

In 1942, Wheeler Lipes, a 23-year-old crewman in the U.S. Navy, performed an emergency appendectomy on another crew member using only spoons as retractors and a scalpel blade with no handle. Lipes was not even a doctor—he was a pharmacist's mate—and he carried out the successful operation on a submarine that was cruising 120 ft (36 m) under the South China Sea!

IRON RESOURCE

If all the iron in the human body were gathered together, there would be enough to make a medium-sized nail.

PREMATURE BABY

Born at Miami, Florida, in October 2006, little Amillia Sonja Taylor survived despite a gestation period of fewer than 22 weeks. She spent 21 weeks 6 days in the womb (full-term births are between 37 and 40 weeks) and at birth weighed less than 10 oz (284 g) and measured just 9½ in (24 cm) long—that's only slightly longer than a ballpoint pen.

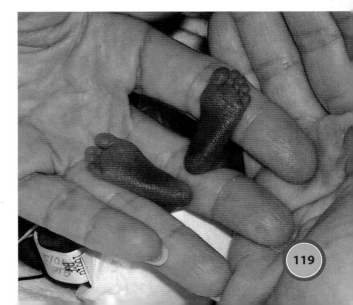

COCKROACH TEA

In Louisiana in the 1800s, a tea made using cockroaches was a remedy for tetanus, while cockroaches fried in oil with garlic were used as a cure for indigestion.

STONE DOCTOR

A statue that was covered with magical inscriptions was used for centuries by the ancient Egyptians as a cure for snakebite and scorpion stings. The patient would pour water over the statue and then drink it.

HAIR SANDWICH

To cure a cough in medieval England, a hair from the cougher's head was placed in a bread-and-butter sandwich and fed to a dog.

PROLONGED PREGNANCY

An X ray on a 90-year-old woman in Sichuan, China, revealed that she had been pregnant for 58 years. When doctors examined the old lady, they found a dead, distorted fetus in her uterus, dating back to 1949 when she had a still birth.

LUCKY LOOK

Women in China undergo cosmetic surgery to look lucky. They ask for less prominent cheekbones, which are said to bring bad luck to their husbands, or to have small blemishes removed from around the eyes or mouth because they, too, are considered unlucky.

WORM TEA

Chong Cha, a Chinese black tea made from the droppings of certain caterpillars, is drunk to prevent heatstroke. Popularly known as worm tea, it is also claimed to help with diarrhea, nosebleeds, and hemorrhoids.

BEAUTY TREATMENT

Drinking the saliva of small birds called swiftlets is said to promote beautiful skin for women in China. The saliva is collected from the binding material of the birds' nests, which are then cleaned and cooked in water.

WIZARD LIZARD

The spiny-tailed iguana is eaten in the Sierra Madre Mountains of Mexico as a cure for depression.

EGG REMEDY

An American cure for lowering fever is to soak two cloths in egg whites and put them on the soles of the feet. The egg whites immediately start to draw the temperature down from the brain to the feet.

Scorpions!

Dead scorpions and slices of ginger are laid on a patient's face in China in an attempt to cure facial paralysis.

SOME AGE-OLD CURES

➤ Passing a child three times under the belly of a donkey cures whooping cough.

➤ Extracting the tooth of a live mole and wearing it cures toothache.

➤ Binding the temples with a rope with which a man has been hanged relieves a headache.

➤ Urinating in an open grave is a remedy for incontinence.

➤ Carrying a dead shrew in your pocket wards off rheumatism.

➤ To cure tuberculosis, put your head into the carcass of a freshly slaughtered cow while the body is still steaming, draw the folds of flesh around your neck, and inhale.

TOOTHBRUSH TREE

Instead of brushing their teeth, some African tribes in Chad and the Sudan chew on sticks carved from the wood of the *Salvadora persica*, or "toothbrush tree." The wood releases a bacteria-fighting liquid that helps prevent infection and tooth decay.

SWALLOW PLEASE!

A cure for dizziness in 16th-century England was to take a young swallow from its nest during a crescent moon, cut off the bird's head, allowing the blood to run into a vessel containing frankincense, and give the potion to the patient when the moon was waning.

WART REMEDY

A popular cure for warts was once to put a piece of silver and some rocks in a small sack by the side of the road, in the belief that whoever took the sack would also take the warts. Another wart remedy was to steal a steak and bury it where three roads crossed.

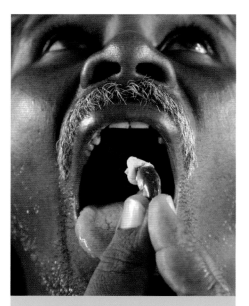

OPEN WIDE!

Live fish dipped in medicinal paste are claimed to be a cure for asthma in parts of India.

PEE POWER
In many parts of Asia, people believe that drinking your own urine cures a variety of ailments—including snakebites, heart disease, chicken pox, infertility, and baldness. Some Japanese women even bathe in their own urine as part of their beauty regime—to improve their skin.

SHEEP'S EYE
In Outer Mongolia, a cure for a hangover consists of eating a pickled sheep's eye in a glass of tomato juice.

ASTHMA CURE
The Chinese believe that eating dried seahorses will cure impotence and asthma. Two tonnes of seahorses are used each year in the Chinese medicine trade.

BUFFALO DRIVE
The cure for any plague that besets the Bhar tribesmen of India is to drive a black water buffalo out of their village—in the belief that it will carry away the disease.

DANCE ROUTINE
The cure for any illness among the Betsileo tribesmen of Madagascar is to put the patient into a trance and then order him to rise from his bed and dance. After a week of this treatment the patient is usually cured—or dead!

MIXED SOUP
A soup made from herbs and Taiwanese tree lizards is believed to be good for asthma and colds. The cure is apparently most effective when one male and one female lizard are used in the soup.

COW TEA
An unusual cold remedy in the southern states of the U.S.A. is to drink tea made from dried cow manure.

SWEEPING DIAGNOSIS
Nigerians believe that a man hit with a broom will become impotent unless he retaliates by hitting the hitter seven times with the same broom.

ORANGE CURE
Sara Jane Trout of Aspinwall, Pennsylvania, ate 3,248 oranges in 1938 as a cure for diabetes.

BITTER LESSON
Some people insist that putting earwax in your mouth can help to ease toothache —apparently it numbs the area that is hurting.

FROGS ALIVE!
Jiang Musheng from China has been eating live frogs to cure his coughs for 40 years.

SAND REMEDY

Patients in Thailand travel from far and wide to be buried up to their necks in hot sand and then stood on by a doctor. They flock to the northeastern province of Buriram to be treated by witch doctor Pan Rerngprasarn, who believes ancient Cambodian healing can cure anything from cancer to mental illness.

HALF BRAIN

A 39-year-old woman from Wuhan, China, has lived a normal life despite having only half a brain. Although scans showed no gray matter on the left side—the part of the brain that controls language—she has no problem communicating with people.

STRETCHED EARS

The witch doctor of the Kuria tribe in Tanzania, Africa, used to stretch his ear lobes until they were so large that a child could be passed through them—an act believed to cure the children of their ailments.

HEART STOPPING

Three-time New York City Marathon champion Alberto Salazar survived a heart attack at Beaverton, Oregon, in 2007—even though his heart stopped beating for a whopping 16 minutes.

BEAR NECESSITY

In 16th-century Europe, a cure for fainting was to take fur from the belly of a live bear, boil it in alcohol, and place it on the soles of the ailing person's feet.

HEALING GRAVE

Locals say that graves in a churchyard at Launceston, England, can cure a stiff neck if, on May 1, 2, or 3, the ailing person applies dew from a newly dug grave to their neck.

CANCER CURE

In 1588, Jean Nicot, France's ambassador to Portugal, sent tobacco plants to his homeland in the belief that tobacco was a cure for cancer.

WRONG LEG

Surgeons in China trying to correct the limp of a five-year-old boy accidentally lengthened the wrong leg. They said the mistake was due to the boy being anesthetized on his back but then operated on while lying on his stomach. As a result, he had to undergo two more operations—one to extend his right leg, the other to shorten his wrongly extended left leg.

TWO WOMBS

At a hospital in Bristol, England, in December 2006, Hannah Kersey gave birth to three children from two different wombs. Identical twins Ruby and Tilly were delivered from one womb and a single baby, Grace, was delivered from the other. Kersey was born with an unusual condition called uterus didelphus, which leads to the abnormal development of the reproductive organs.

MISTAKEN IDENTITY

In October 2007, after overseeing the cremation of a man she thought was her son, a woman was shocked when he turned up alive the next day. Gina Partington had identified a body found in Manchester, England, as her 39-year-old son Thomas Dennison, but 24 hours later he was found alive and well 85 mi (137 km) away in Nottingham.

SNAKE BITE

Matt Wilkinson of Portland, Oregon, spent three days in a coma in 2007 after putting his 20-in (51-cm) pet diamondback rattlesnake into his mouth. He made it to the hospital just in time, as his airway had nearly swollen shut from the venomous bites.

FIERY TREATMENT

Walnuts and ignited dry moxa leaves are placed on a patient's eyes in Jinan, China, as treatment for eye disease. Taken from the plant *Artemisia chinensis*, burned moxa leaves are a staple ingredient of Traditional Chinese Medicine.

IMPALED ON SPIKE

A five-year-old boy from Sydney, Australia, survived after being speared through the throat by an iron-fence spike in July 2007. The spike plunged 2 in (5 cm) into the throat of Hugo Borbilas, narrowly missing his carotid artery, esophagus, windpipe, all the major nerves in his neck and throat, and stopping just short of his brain. The injury could have killed Hugo instantly, but he managed to pull himself off the spike and yell for help.

VODKA DRIP

Doctors in the city of Brisbane in Queensland, Australia, attached a poisoned Italian tourist to a vodka drip in 2007 after running out of supplies of the medicinal alcohol they normally use.

RABID RECOVERY

Teenager Jeanna Giese of Fond Du Lac, Wisconsin, had to relearn how to walk, talk, and function after catching rabies from a bat bite in September 2004. It took more than a year for her to be able to walk unaided, but she still graduated highschool with honors in 2007. Jeanna is thought to be the only person ever to have survived the deadly disease, which attacks the nervous system, without having had a vaccination.

HOLY SNAIL

The Church of St. Leonard in the medieval town of Guingamp, France, was visited for centuries by people from Brittany in the belief they could cure a fever by finding a snail in a cavity in the church walls and carrying it in a pouch.

DINOSAUR MEDICINE

Villagers in China have spent decades digging up dinosaur bones for use in medicine. The calcium-rich bones are boiled with other ingredients and fed to children to treat dizziness and leg cramps. They are also ground into a paste and then applied directly to wounds to help heal bone fractures.

FROG IN THE THROAT

Ancient Romans would cure toothache by holding a frog boiled in water and vinegar inside the mouth of the patient.

NEW GRADUATE

Maurice Yankow of Valhalla, New York, enrolled in medical school at age 63—and became a practising licensed physician at 70 years of age.

MUDDY BEAUTY

Visitors to a resort in China's Sichuan Province cover themselves from head to toe in black mud. The mineral-rich mud is said to be beneficial to the skin.

WOBBLY WORLD

San Francisco may be expecting an earthquake some day soon, but this shaky city is ridiculous!

Liz Hickok has re-created San Francisco in Jell-O, constructing a whole scale model first and then using it to make molds for the Jell-O. She adds painted backdrops, model trees, and lights the Jell-O from underneath or behind. Then she snaps a photo before it decays and all her work becomes a sloppy mess.

Ripley's ask

How long did the Jell-O city take to make? I've made several different pieces over time. Each image represents, in general, a different piece. And each scene usually takes about three months to complete.

How long does it last? Each piece will last about a week before it starts to decay.

Where did you make and store all that Jell-O? As I do one scene at a time, it's not so much to store. I make it in my studio and usually leave it set up until I have to throw it away.

ACTUAL **1:1** SIZE!

This awesome overhead view of San Francisco, looking toward downtown, is made entirely from Jell-O and covers an area of approximately 32 sq ft (3 sq m).

Hung with fairy lights, Liz's Bay Bridge is a gravity-defying work of Jell-O.

unusual art

EAT MY SHORTS!
Los Angeles artist Kasey McMahon has designed a pair of meat shorts, in which pieces of dried meat are glued or sewn on to an ordinary pair of shorts.

BUTTER POTTER
Harry Potter was magically carved from butter for the 2007 Iowa State Fair in Des Moines. The butter model, the work of sculptor Sarah Pratt, even had Potter's trademark glasses and wand.

EDIBLE CAR
A team of British bakers cooked up a cake in the shape of a full-sized Skoda car using 180 eggs, 125 jars of jam, and 220 lb (100 kg) of sugar. The tires were chocolate frosting, the rear lights were jello, the wipers were licorice, and the engine was filled with syrup.

CHOCOLATE JESUS
Canadian artist Cosimo Cavallaro created a 6-ft (1.8-m) sculpture of Jesus made entirely from 200 lb (90 kg) of milk chocolate.

BIG CHEESES
Troy Landwehr carved a sculpture of Mount Rushmore from a 700-lb (320-kg) block of Wisconsin cheddar cheese. It took him four days to carve the replicas of U.S. presidents George Washington, Thomas Jefferson, Teddy Roosevelt, and Abraham Lincoln.

BREAD MODEL
A British artist baked a life-size model of herself out of bread and then invited visitors to the exhibition to eat it.

GUM ART

Street artists in London, England, use a variety of media to express themselves, including these paintings on discarded pieces of chewing gum. With an estimated 300,000 pieces of gum stuck to Oxford Street alone, the artists will never be short of materials.

TINY BOOK
Teeny Ted From Turnip Town, a book produced by the nanotechnology laboratory at Simon Frasier University, British Columbia, Canada, is so small that 20 copies of it can fit on the head a of a pin!

PAPER DRESSES
Thanks to Ed Livingston of Boston Harbor, Washington, women can read what they wear. That's because he makes women's dresses from newsprint!

POST-IT PORTRAIT
David Alvarez, 19, of Leavenworth, Washington, spent three months creating a three-dimensional portrait of Ray Charles that stood 10 ft (3 m) high from more than 2,000 colored Post-it® notes.

ALL CHANGE
It took six years for Mike and Annie Moore to cover every flat area in their McKittrick, California, bar with pennies—there were more than a million of them, glued to the walls, floors, ceiling, and furniture.

TONGUE TWISTER

A Chinese man has discovered that he can write with his tongue. Zhang Yongyang, of Xi'an City, found that he could touch his nose with his tongue and decided to use that dexterity in his hobby of calligraphy. So now he dips his tongue in ink and writes Chinese characters.

TRENDY TRASH

Justin Gignac has made trash trendy. He collects garbage from the streets of New York City, puts it in a box, labels it, and then sells it for up to $100!

COSTLY BLOW

Casino mogul Steve Wynn accidentally put his elbow through a Pablo Picasso painting shortly after he had agreed to sell it for a record $139 million. Wynn was showing the painting, called *Le Reve* ("The Dream"), to guests in his office at Las Vegas, Nevada, in 2006 when he caught the painting with his right elbow, causing a hole in the canvas the size of a silver dollar.

COBRA GUARD

In September 2007, Harrods Department Store in London, England, used live cobras to guard a $120,000 pair of shoes encrusted with diamonds, rubies, and sapphires.

HAIR DRESS

A model appeared on a catwalk in Zagreb, Croatia, in 2007 wearing a dress made entirely from human hair. Designers at the Artidjana company used 165 ft (50 m) of blonde hair in the dress.

LONG PAINTING

In 2007, some 3,500 people in Wakayama, Japan, combined their talents to create a painting that is 15,154 ft (4,663 m) long! It took them more than a month to complete.

DISNEY COLLECTION

In 2007, Disney unveiled a range of bridal dresses inspired by their fairytale films, including *Sleeping Beauty* and *Beauty and the Beast*. Created by L.A. designer Kirstie Kelly, the dresses cost from $1,500 each.

ART IN MOTION

In October 2006, German artist Carsten Hoeller installed five huge spiraling slides—the tallest being 180 ft (55 m) in height—as part of an exhibit at the art gallery Tate Modern in London, England.

COLOR-BLIND

Florida artist Jay Lonewolf Morales paints beautifully vivid pictures despite suffering from monochromacy—complete color blindness. He can see in only black and white and shades of gray, yet all his paintings are done with vibrant colors. He says: "I cry every time I paint, because I cannot enjoy the pigments of my labor."

TAB BELT

Sean Taylor of Stratford, New Jersey, has designed a belt—out of soda can tabs!

STOLEN KISS

Police charged a woman in Avignon, France, after she was caught kissing a $2-million painting by American abstract artist Cy Twombly. She was apparently so overcome with passion in front of the work that she just could not stop herself.

LONG SARI

A team of skilled weavers in India worked tirelessly for 14 days in 2007 to create a spectacular green-and-yellow sari that measured an amazing 2,226 ft (685 m) in length.

NAIL PAINTER

Instead of using a brush to create his paintings, Indian artist Nangaji Bhati simply grows his fingernails. By applying paint to the tip of his 4-in (10-cm) thumbnail, he is able to produce striking artworks on canvas.

BRICK ART

Dubbed the Picasso of LEGO® bricks, Wall Street lawyer-turned-artist Nathan Sawaya creates astonishing masterpieces from the small building blocks beloved by children the world over. Requiring hours of painstaking work, each of his pieces can use more than 250,000 LEGO® bricks in total.

Sawaya was bestowed with the honor of becoming a Master Model Builder by LEGOLAND® California in 2004. The pieces shown here were displayed at Nathan's first solo art exhibition, The Art of the Brick, at the Lancaster Museum of Art in Philadelphia, Pennsylvania, in 2007.

Body

LEGO® SWIMMER

A giant plastic figure resembling a smiling LEGO® minifigure was fished out of the sea off the coast of Holland in August 2007. The 8-ft (2.4-m) model with a yellow head and blue body was found by workers in the Dutch resort of Zandvoort. Its origins were shrouded in mystery, but it was believed to have floated from the direction of England.

CHOCOLATE CHESS

An English artist has designed a chess set in which you can eat your opponent. Prudence Emma Staite from Gloucestershire, creates chocolate sculptures, and has made a chess set with playing pieces in white and milk chocolate arranged on a solid chocolate board. She also used more than 440 lb (200 kg) of Belgian chocolate to make a life-sized chocolate bed (complete with chocolate duvet and pillow) for England's Alton Towers theme park.

SIX FACES

A keen gardener has created replicas of the famous Moai statues on Easter Island in his hedge. Retired banker Michael Geiger used shears to clip six faces into the 12-ft (3.6-m) conifer hedge in his front garden in Billericay, England.

TOY CAR

An actual-size replica of a Volvo XC90 unveiled at the 2004 New York Auto Show was built from more than 200,000 LEGO® bricks. The car took a team of five builders two months to construct.

ACTUAL 1:1 SIZE!

Hey, Baby!

Artist Camille Allen from Powell River, British Columbia, applies her knowledge of doll-making and sculpture to create these tiny, highly detailed babies made from polymer clays. Allen, who started this artistic venture when she had some leftover materials from a larger project, uses tiny dentist tools to sculpt the babies' fine features and even applies fine mohair, a strand at a time, to imitate real baby hair.

TALL TOWER
In May 2007, visitors to LEGOLAND®, California, used 465,000 LEGO® bricks to build a tower an incredible 94 ft 4 in (28.7 m) tall.

SOIL TRIBUTE
Thousands of students from China's Zhongyuan University of Technology spent a day in March 2007 digging 96 faces out of the soil on the college campus to pay tribute to the country's farmers.

HEDGE MONSTER
John Dobson from Sussex, England, has spent 17 years creating a topiary model of the Loch Ness Monster in his garden hedge. He regularly trims the head, humps, and tail into the 15-ft-high (4.5-m) hedge. He is now growing another monster for his neighbor.

FAMOUS SCENES
Using the alias "Udronotto," Italian artist Marco Pece has re-created Leonardo da Vinci's painting of *The Last Supper* using LEGO® figures. He has also re-created the *Mona Lisa*, and movie scenes from *The Blues Brothers* and *The Graduate*.

POSTCARD CREATIONS
British artist David Mach creates works of art from postcards. In 2007, he used 8,000 identical postcards of Dubai's Jumeirah Emirates Towers to create a picture of a racehorse that measured 12 x 9 ft (3.6 x 2.7 m).

STILL LIFE
Discovering that his former hometown of Teococuilco, Mexico, had turned into a ghost town over the past 30 years, sculptor Alejandro Santiago decided to repopulate the area with 2,501 clay statues.

DISTINCTIVE DESK
Designer Eric Harshbarger has built a full-sized office desk from 35,000 LEGO® bricks for a company in Seattle. The desk weighs around 120 lb (55 kg) and has seven working drawers. After creating the prototype, he had to take it apart and then glue each piece back together to make the desk stronger.

SCULPTURE RISES
A prolonged drought in Utah's Great Salt Lake resulted in a sculpture that had been buried for over 30 years suddenly emerging above the surface. In 1970, artist Robert Smithson used 6,650 tons of black basalt and earth to create "Spiral Jetty," a structure measuring 1,500 ft (460 m) in length that coiled around in the water. For three decades it was visible only from the air until lack of rainfall exposed it to a wider audience.

WOOLEN HOUSE
Five-hundred women from across the world—including the U.S.A., Canada, and Europe—knitted for thousands of hours to create a 140-sq-ft (13-sq-m) woolen house. The brainchild of British knitter Alison Murray, the multi-colored "Gingerbread House," displayed in Devon, England, in 2007, was made from millions of stitches. It had 1,000 knitted roof tiles and was surrounded by a knitted garden, with knitted flowers and knitted trees 12 ft (3.6 m) tall.

129

Miniature Knitting

Imagine a cardigan that is smaller than a dime—or a pair of gloves so tiny that a grain of rice would fit neatly into each finger. These, and other miniature marvels, are the creations of nano-knitter Althea Crome Merback.

Althea, from Bloomington, Indiana, knits cardigans, sweaters, and jackets on a 1:144 scale and gloves on a 1:12 scale by using fine silk sewing thread, as well as needles made from stainless steel medical wire that is just 0.001 in (0.03 mm) thick. With this method she is able to create garments that have up to 80 stitches per inch.

It is not only the size of her "bug-knit" clothing that amazes people, but also the patterns on them. Her love of art has encouraged her to knit a tiny cardigan bearing a reproduction of a Picasso painting (right), a sweater with the design of an ancient Grecian urn, and a 2¼ x 1¼-in (5.7 x 3.2-cm) cardigan inspired by the treasures of King Tutankhamun's tomb. She has also knitted a pair of miniature "City-Country" socks—one sock featuring a pattern of the Chicago skyline, the other a country landscape—which sold for $750.

Since 2000, she has created countless items for dollhouse collectors and has had her work featured in the Radical Lace and Subversive Knitting exhibit at the Museum of Arts and Design in New York.

Of her miniature creations she says: "I really enjoy making clothes that don't have to fit and I love tricking the brain into thinking that things aren't miniature. Also, I don't spend a fortune on yarns—a little goes a long way."

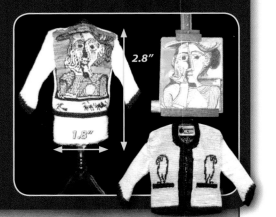

2.8"

1.8"

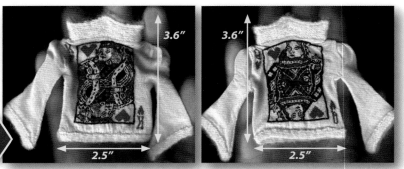

ACTUAL 1:1 SIZE!

"I believe that these tiny cardigans may be among the smallest cardigans in the world!"

"These City-Country socks represent my move from Chicago, Illinois, to Bloomington, Indiana."

"This sweater has the King of Hearts on one side and the Queen of Hearts on the other. The knitting's so fine that the sweaters are see-through!"

3.6"

2.5"

3.6"

2.5"

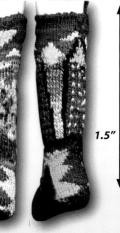

1.5"

"*The front panels of my tiny Egyptian cardigan show the goddess Nut greeting King Tutankhamun; the back panel is an Egyptian amulet design.*"

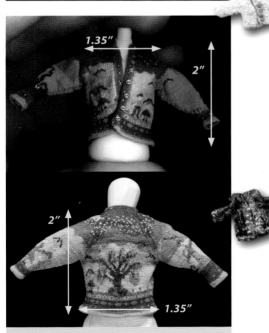

"*The Earth to Sky cardigan takes the viewer on a journey extending deep into the earth's strata and far above the heavens—it's a cosmic landscape.*"

Ripley's ask

Why did you start knitting miniature clothes? I started by knitting adult-sized clothes, making sweaters for my family. Then I had children and I enjoyed making things that were a little smaller. Next, still hungry for more of a challenge, I decided to design a pair of gloves for my mom and I found that I LOVED it. Then, in 2000, I decided to build a dollhouse. I used to shop online for my supplies, and one day I came across a tiny knitted jumper. It was very simple but it was a lightbulb moment for me. I thought 'Hey, I bet I could do that.' So I found the smallest needles (probably a 0) and some baby yarn—it wasn't even that fine—and I knitted a man's cardigan that night. It was intoxicating and I was hooked from that point onward.

Do you use special knitting needles, and are they miniature? Yes, I have to make my own needles. I order 6-foot lengths of medical grade stainless steel, and cut and polish them to my desired length (usually 4, 5, or 6 inches long). They are very thin—some down to only 0.009 inches for the very tiniest sweaters. They are also very strong and have a high tensile strength so they can take a lot of bending and abuse without breaking.

What kind of wool do you use? I use mostly silk sewing threads—either 50 or 100 weight—but I have also used some very thin wools and cottons. I have a wool that isn't made any more that has about 25,000 feet to the pound so it is extremely thin.

How long does it take to knit a detailed miniature jumper? The longest it has ever taken was six months, the shortest was about six weeks.

Do you follow knitting patterns or do you make them up? I design all my own patterns. Usually I will have a vision of an image that I want to knit and then I will spend time designing the garment around that vision. I try to design everything with a very complete concept. For example, the ancient Greek sweater is shaped like a Greek vase, with a neck and foot and arms like a vase. The design elements on those parts of the sweater are designs found on Greek vases.

Can you explain what 'bug-knit' scale means? 'Bug-knit' scale simply means on a very small scale. However, most of the pieces I make are 1:12 scale which is a standard dollhouse scale. Some pieces are in 1:44 scale and on a very few occasions I have made 1:144 scale pieces.

What kind of reactions do you get to your work? Amazement. Really, people have been so generous with their praise and encouragement and it tickles me. I get so many emails from people just telling me 'Thank you for the eye candy.' I like that.

Is there anything you would like to knit that you haven't already? So much! I have a million ideas—I would like to knit a Roman relief, Japanese cranes, more artist-based sweaters like the Picasso and the Warhol. Hopefully my hands, eyes, and mind will hold out long enough to get just a fraction of them made.

ICE WORLD

Every January, part of the northeastern Chinese city of Harbin is transformed into a beautiful ice kingdom. Teams of local and international ice sculptors create a fairytale setting of buildings, people, animals, cartoon characters, and deities using compacted snow and blocks of ice.

Snow and ice sculpting in the region dates back 1,400 years, but the Harbin Snow and Ice Festival originated in 1985. For the 2007 festival, more than 2,000 ice sculptures were crafted from more than 4 million cubic ft (120,000 cubic m) of ice and more than 3 million cubic ft (90,000 cubic m) of snow.

Each year, five million people from across the world converge on the city, drawn by the spectacular ice structures and night illuminations. Most of the sculptures are fitted with colored lights, and at night they glow red, yellow, pink, and blue.

Many of the 2007 exhibits had a Canadian theme, in honor of Canadian doctor Norman Bethune, who went to China in 1938 and is credited with introducing modern medicine into the country. There was a large ice likeness of Dr. Bethune, a model of the Chateau Frontenac in Quebec City, a snow sculpture depicting Niagara Falls that was 800 ft (244 m) long and 90 ft (27 m) high, and the Crossing of the Bering Strait built from some 460,000 cubic ft (13,000 cubic m) of snow.

Previous year's sculptures have included re-creations of the Great Wall of China and Paris's Arc de Triomphe.

Visitors to the festival can also climb a wall of solid ice, dine in a restaurant constructed from ice, and enjoy a drink in an ice bar.

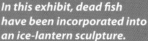
In this exhibit, dead fish have been incorporated into an ice-lantern sculpture.

An ice sculpture of a girl on a swing formed part of an ice-lantern exhibition on the theme of "The World's Fairy Tales."

Ripley's research

How do they do it?

The snow and ice used in the festival are quarried from the Songhua River, where the ice can be several yards thick. Chainsaws cut through the ice and reduce it to blocks. Each team— and participants come from as far away as Canada, France, South Africa, and Russia—starts with a 10-ft (3-m) cube of packed snow and begins carving. These blocks are then fused together to make the larger sculptures.

Ordinarily, there is no danger of the creations suddenly melting, because average winter temperatures in Harbin range between –28°F (–31°C) and 5°F (–15°C). In fact, people leave stored food outside on balconies to freeze. However, as temperatures rose unexpectedly in February 2007, heads started to topple from statues, and 2,000 workers were brought in to carry out repairs.

Sculptors labored for hundreds of hours to create these superb ice replicas.

Harbin's famous St. Sophia church was one of the centerpieces of the festival.

CASH SNATCH

During an art exhibition in Norway, artist Jan Christensen had his work, *Relative Value*, made out of 100,000 kroner ($16,300) worth of bank notes, stolen out of its frame by bandits in a gallery robbery.

FINGER FUN

Eighteen hundred people, ranging from two-year-old children to senior citizens, created a 20,000-sq-ft (1,858-sq-m) finger painting in just one day at New Paltz, New York, in September 2007.

PAINTED PIGS

Art students in China have been painting live pigs to create colorful images as the animals roam in a field. The students from Sichuan Fine Arts Institute chose pigs because they represent harmony and happiness.

CRAYON SCULPTURE

No school bag ever housed a set of crayons like these, but U.S. sculptor Pete Goldlust has turned art on its head by carving intricate designs into ordinary wax crayons.

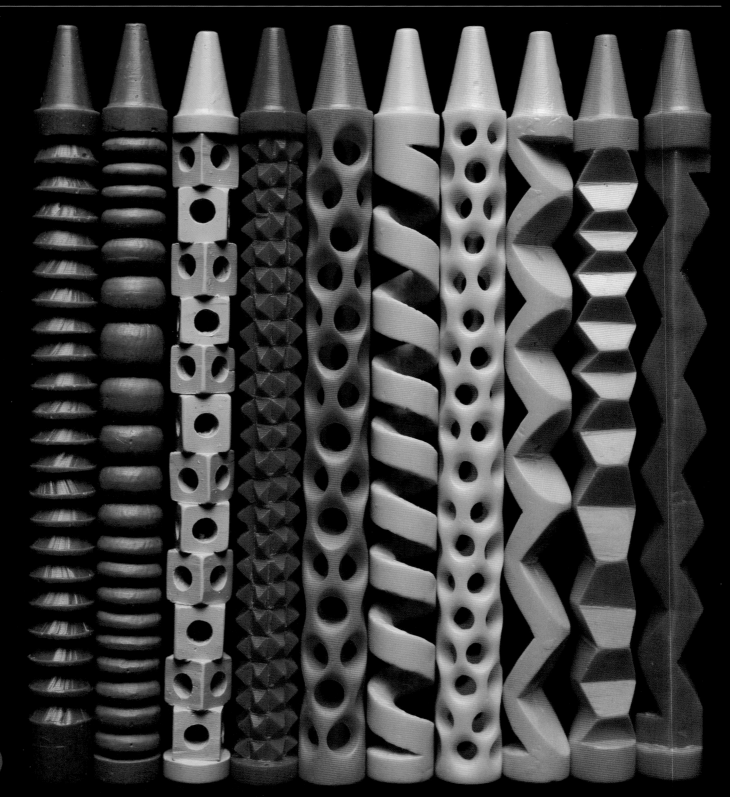

NAKED SHOOT
More than 600 naked people were photographed as a living sculpture on a Swiss glacier in 2007. The photo shoot was arranged by New York artist Spencer Tunick to raise awareness of the effect of climate change on shrinking Swiss glaciers.

FRIDGEHENGE FALLS
In Santa Fe, New Mexico, artist Adam Horowitz created a replica of Stonehenge from more than 100 old refrigerators. The refrigerators, stacked and arranged in a ring like the famous English landmark, became a popular tourist attraction. They stood for nearly a decade until, in 2007, the 80-ft (24-m) structure was demolished by a mixture of high winds and the city council.

FACE-PAINTERS
In June 2006, a team of five face-painters painted a total of 989 faces in four hours at Longleat House, Wiltshire, England.

DORMANT TALENT
Sleepwalker Lee Hadwin of Henllan, North Wales, is a talented artist when he is asleep— but when awake he struggles to draw at all! Wandering around the house in his sleep, he draws anywhere—even on walls and tables—but experts are baffled as to why he cannot re-create these works of art when he wakes up.

FIELD ART
In a clover field at the Thomas Bull Memorial Park in New York, artist Roger Baker mowed an image of a Purple Heart medal, which is given to U.S. servicemen who are killed or wounded in action, that measured an astonishing 850,000 sq ft (79,000 sq m).

SPILT MILK
An artist from Devon, England, did not cry over 1,300 gal (5,000 l) of spilled milk. Instead, Martin White poured it into a huge dish, 30 ft (9 m) in diameter, and left it to turn sour as a work of art. Entitled *Spilt Milk*, it was designed to highlight the pressures faced by dairy farmers.

SCRABBLE® BLING
Boise, Idaho, artist Millie Hilgert creates jewelry from discarded items. Vinyl records are made into necklaces, earrings, and rings; game pieces from dominoes or Scrabble® are converted into bracelets; bottle caps are turned into necklaces; and jar lids become belt buckles.

CHOC STAR
In 2005, Madame Tussauds created a life-size model of musical supremo Sir Elton John—in chocolate. Made to the singer's measurements, it was built from 227 lb (103 kg) of chocolate and took more than 1,000 hours to create. The finished product was displayed at the London, England, tourist attraction in a special air-conditioned tent to stop it from melting.

OLD HEART
Jennifer Sutton was able to view a unique exhibit at an art gallery in London, England, in 2007—her old heart! The 23-year-old science graduate from Hampshire had her diseased heart removed in a transplant operation earlier in the year and agreed to allow it to be displayed in a jar as part of an exhibition that explored the historical significance of the human heart in art, literature, and medicine.

DUAL PURPOSE
Gala Contemplating the Mediterranean Sea Which at Twenty Meters Becomes a Portrait of Abraham Lincoln, painted by Spanish artist Salvador Dali in 1976, is both a painting of his wife and a pixilated portrait of U.S. President Abraham Lincoln!

R.A.P. ARTIST
Portuguese artist Leonel Moura has built a Robotic Action Painter—a robot that creates its own art. He has also constructed "the first zoo for artificial life," filled with 45 robots (each representing a different creature) housed in cages and enclosures.

RELIGIOUS SIGN?
Visitors flocked to the home of Eric Nathaniel in Port Blair, Andaman Islands, India, in 2007, after two of his paintings of Jesus began to drip red fluid. Experts suggested it was more likely to be red paint from the pictures melting in the humidity, than blood.

ICE QUEEN
In 2007, sculptors Ivo Piazza and Rainer Kasslatter created a huge sculpture of Marilyn Monroe—from ice. It earned them first prize an annual ice-sculpture contest in Austria.

BRICK DRAGON
A model dragon at the LEGOLAND® Windsor theme park in England has been built from nearly one million LEGO® bricks. The "Ice Dragon" measures 30 ft (9 m) in length, weighs nearly 3 tons, and took 2,200 hours to build. It is so big that it had to be built in nine sections before being hoisted into place.

Crystal Curiosities

Dutch artist Hans van Bentem makes beautiful crystal chandeliers in the most amazing, avant-garde designs—ranging from a champagne bottle to a skull and crossbones. Abandoning the traditional chandelier shape, he has also created chandeliers in the design of a globe, a spider, an easel and brushes, a heraldic lion, a fighter plane, a seahorse, a violin, a pipe, and even a gun. He says he finds his inspiration in art history, comic strips, and the world of modern communication. Each piece takes up to two months to create and sells from $16,000.

SHAKESPEARE RECITAL

In February 2004, more than 150 members of the Wellesley College, Massachusetts, Shakespeare Society read aloud the complete works of Shakespeare (a total of 39 plays, 154 sonnets and poetry) in 22 hours 5 minutes.

LATE RETURN

Robert Nuranen of Hancock, Michigan, paid $171 in late fees when he returned a library book 47 years after he had borrowed it.

Ripley's research

The Last Supper took Mark Beekman a year to make. He began by buying up all the Lite-Brite pegs he could find—both direct from the manufacturer Hasbro and local suppliers—and constructing a frame out of lightweight aluminum pipes. He used perforated sheet metal as backing and employed computer printouts of the original painting to help him work out where the different-colored plastic pegs should go. The pegs were then attached to the metal backing with eight layers of glue. He painted the frame antique gold and backlit his creation with high-tech electroluminescent panels.

LITE SUPPER

Artist Mark Beekman from Charlestown, Pennsylvania, used more than 125,000 Lite-Brite pegs to create a 1:9-scale version of Leonardo da Vinci's painting *The Last Supper* that measured 5 ft (1.5 m) tall by 10 ft (3 m) wide.

PROLIFIC AUTHOR
At her most prolific, British romantic author Barbara Cartland completed a novel every two weeks. Altogether, she published 723 novels in her 70-year career!

TINY SUN
Using a new nanoprinting technique, Swiss computer experts have created an image of the Sun that is just 80 microns wide—less than one-tenth the size of a pinhead!

GUITAR GATHERING
In June 2007, Kansas City radio station KYYS (99.7FM) assembled a ballpark full of 1,721 guitarists—ages ranging from five to 60—to play Deep Purple's song "Smoke on the Water" simultaneously.

TOP BRASS
A band of German musicians staged a concert on a Bolivian mountain top in 2007. They played instruments at the summit of the Acotango Volcano for 30 minutes at an altitude of 19,855 ft (6,052 m).

BABOON'S BUTT
Matthew Roby from Lancashire, England, creates characters from old bits of machinery and scrap metal. Nothing goes to waste—he even used the bright orange ballcocks from a toilet system for a baboon's butt!

ONE-NOTE GIG
The White Stripes finished their 2007 Candian tour by playing a show just one note long. Jack and Meg White took to the stage in St. John's, Newfoundland, played a C-sharp accompanied by a bang of the cymbals, announced that they had now officially played in every province and territory in Canada, and left the stage. Fans had been warned that the show would be just one-note long, but still hundreds turned up. Later, the band played a full-length set elsewhere in the city. Previous venues on their quirky tour had included a bowling alley in Saskatoon and a Winnipeg Transit bus.

YODEL-AY!
More than 1,000 American yodelers converge on Salt Lake City, Utah, each June for the Swiss Singing and Yodeling Festival.

CURTAIN CALLS
Italian opera star Luciano Pavarotti, who died in 2007, once received an astonishing 165 curtain calls at the end of a stage show.

WOODEN HORSE
Saimir Strati of Albania, has created a mosaic of a leaping horse that is 13 ft (4 m) long—from more than half a million toothpicks. It took him 40 days to construct, working 13 hours a day.

TINY SCISSORS
In 2003, Chen Yu Pei of China, designed a pair of stainless steel scissors that measured just 0.068 in (1.75 mm) long and 0.054 in (1.38 mm) wide—and they actually worked!

SLEEPING STATUE
A 1,365-ft-long (415-m) sleeping Buddha statue has been carved into the side of a mountain in Yiyang, Jiangxi, China.

INSURED EYES
Cross-eyed silent movie star Ben Turpin was insured for $500,000 against the possibility of his eyes ever becoming normal again.

ROOT CARVER
Micro-artist Shelvaraj from Nagapattinam, India, carves tiny ornate figures from the roots of trees. Shelvaraj, who has been pursuing his art since his teens, specializes in religious figures and has carved a row of elephants, ranging in size from a minute speck to 3/8 in (1 cm) tall.

COCONUT ORCHESTRA
The cast and creators of the Monty Python musical *Spamalot* led 5,567 people in a mass coconut orchestra as they clip-clopped in time to "Always Look on the Bright Side of Life" in Trafalgar Square in London, England, in April 2007.

QUICK ON THE DRAW

Leonardo da Vinci's Mona Lisa, by Jeff Gagliardi

MAGIC *Etch A Sketch* SCREEN

Some artists work in oils, others choose watercolors, but Jeff Gagliardi of Boulder, Colorado, prefers a different artistic medium—the Etch A Sketch® drawing toy. Using this much-loved children's toy of the 1960s, Gagliardi has been able to create wonderful works of art. He has had exhibitions at some of the U.S.A.'s leading galleries and his Etch A Sketch® version of Leonardo da Vinci's *Mona Lisa* has been valued at $10,000!

Amazingly, Gagliardi never had an Etch A Sketch® as a child but developed an interest while playing with his nephew's. He first tried it out seriously while at art college in New York in the early 1970s. He says: "I did a drawing of the Taj Mahal, complete with reflecting pools. Quite frankly, I didn't think it was a big deal, but my family wouldn't let me erase it. From that point on it became apparent that I had some sort of gift for drawing on this little toy. People would walk past the serious work I was doing as a painter and want to see the Etch A Sketch® drawings."

Ripley's ask

How do you create your works of art? Each sketch takes a lot of planning as to how I'll start and where I'll end, but I also need to plan how to interpret a painted piece into a line drawing—how to render the subtle shading, for example.

How long does it take? Because each piece is only one unbroken line, much of the work is in retracing lines to get back and forth between areas. Also, in the case of the 'Mona Lisa,' I do what I think will be the most difficult areas first (her face and smile) and then I do the rest. Typically, this can take from five to 20 hours—in the case of 'Mona Lisa,' closer to 20.

Which is your favorite? I like 'Mona Lisa' the best. Partly because of her sweetly subtle smile and the fact that she's drawn sidewise in order to get her in portrait mode. I am also very fond of my 'Vitruvian Man' tribute, as it is done with an economy of lines (true to da Vinci's style!).

Vincent van Gogh's Starry Night, *in* Etch A Sketch®.

Since then he has re-created details from Michelangelo's Sistine Chapel and copied paintings by Van Gogh.

His work requires enormous patience. Pictures are drawn by twiddling two knobs, which operate a stylus across the underside of the glass, scraping a line in the aluminum coating. The toy's system operates horizontally, which means that to create a vertical portrait—as in the Mona Lisa—Gagliardi has to draw sidewise!

Jeff's sketch of Grant Wood's American Gothic.

Vitruvian Man, *originally drawn by* Leonardo da Vinci c.1492.

Enter the Vault

PEN-KNIFE SCULPTURE ▶

Displaying 1,936 blades in 1936, the "Year Knife" was the creation of cutlery makers Joseph Rodgers & Sons of Sheffield, England. The company started assembling their creation in 1822, with 1,822 blades, and added a new blade every year thereafter.

BOTTLE CAP INN

The Bottle Cap Inn was the appropriate name for this bar in Miami, Florida, that was decorated with more than 300,000 bottle caps in the 1930s.

ROBERT RIPLEY

Seen here in the 1940s drawing one of his famous cartoons, Robert Ripley used to receive thousands of letters from devoted fans every week, all hoping to have their unbelievable facts included in his cartoon strip.

◀ LINE ART

The famous portrait of George Washington that graces the front of every $1 bill and Emanual Leutze's well-known painting, "Washington Crossing the Delaware," are both re-created here in a 1932 drawing by Forest Ages McGinn—drawn in a single continuous line without lifting the pencil from the page!

CARTOON CAPERS

Clarence Thorpe of Riverside, California, could simultaneously draw cartoons with his hands and feet. Thorpe first appeared at Ripley's Dallas Odditorium in 1936.

BELIEVE ◀ IT OR NOT! BLOUSES

Blouses featuring Ripley's Believe It or Not! cartoons were sold at the Ripley's New York City Odditorium in 1939. During the 1930s, the worldwide-syndicated Ripley cartoons had more than 80 million readers daily.

BLIND SCULPTOR

Mark Shoesmith of New York, seen here with his model, sculpted this bust of Robert Ripley in 1938. Remarkably, Shoesmith was blind and achieved Ripley's likeness purely by touching his face.

BIBLICAL ART

This drawing of a praying child is made entirely from the words of the New Testament. It was created by Korean artist Gwang Hyuk Rhee in the 1950s.

COMPUTER CASTLE

A teacher from Shandong Industrial Arts College, China, created a sculpture of a castle from the parts of an old computer. The piece, titled *Fossil*, was exhibited at Shandong Museum in 2007.

SKIN BINDING

A 300-year-old book discovered in the center of Leeds, Yorkshire, England, in 2006 is thought to have been bound in human skin. The book was written mainly in French and was published at a time when accounts of murder trials were sometimes bound in the killer's skin.

ODD TITLES

A book titled *The Stray Shopping Carts of Eastern North America: A Guide to Field Identification* was named the oddest book title for 2007 in an annual competition. Its author, Julian Montague, beat off stiff competition from *Tattooed Mountain Women and Spoon Boxes of Dagestan*, *How Green Were the Nazis?*, and *Better Never to Have Been: The Harm of Coming Into Existence*.

BIKE LINE

Rod Pasold of Blue River, Wisconsin, has created a work of art consisting of a line of 30 old motorcycles chained to posts and adorned by approximately 200 different colored crash helmets. To give the bikes a distinctive look, many of them have been customized with add-ons, such as a set of antlers and an animal skull.

HARD FRIES

British sculptor Keith Tyson made models of every item on a KFC menu, even down to the fries—in lead. His other weird and wonderful works have included pouring a thimble full of paint from a skyscraper and attaching 366 chopping boards to a wall.

BARGAIN BUY

Michael Sparks of Nashville, Tennessee, bought a 184-year-old print of the American Declaration of Independence for $2.48 at a thrift store. Appraisers estimate that it is worth at least 100,000 times that price!

LONG OVERDUE

In 1650, the Bishop of Winchester, England, borrowed a book from Somerset County Records office but it was not returned to Somerset County Library until 1985—335 years later—by which time it had accrued $6,000 in unpaid fees. The title of the overdue book? *The Book of Fines*!

TXT BK

The Last Messages, a novel by Hannu Luntiala of Finland, consists exclusively of text messages exchanged between the main character and his friends and relatives.

SENIOR SINGERS

A new band made an assault on the U.K. and U.S. charts in 2007—even though they had a combined age of more than 3,000 years! The Zimmers were a group of 40 British seniors who became a surprise Internet hit with their version of The Who's "My Generation," complete with its inappropriate line "I hope I die before I get old."

SAND TEMPLE

Indian sculptor Sudarsan Patnaik created a lifelike replica of the Taj Mahal—in sand. It took him 56 working hours to complete the model, which stood 15 ft (4.5 m) high.

STAMP PORTRAITS

Artist Pete Mason, from Hednesford, Staffordshire, England, creates amazing portraits of famous people from thousands of used postage stamps. He sketches each portrait on to a grid before painstakingly cutting the individual stamps to size and sticking them in place. In 2007, he completed a 12,000-stamp tribute to Princess Diana, which measured 7 x 7 ft (2.1 x 2.1 m), to mark the tenth anniversary of her death. His previous works have included prime ministers Winston Churchill and Tony Blair, soccer star David Beckham, and Queen Elizabeth II.

MANILOW SENTENCE

People who break the noise laws in Fort Lupton, Colorado, are given an unusual sentence—they are forced to listen to Barry Manilow music for an hour! The punishment is the idea of Judge Paul Sacco, who claims that offenders who go through the Manilow treatment rarely re-offend. Also on his punishment playlist are The Carpenters, Dolly Parton, and Barney the Dinosaur.

BABY BOOMERANG

In 1997, Sadir Kattan of Australia, created a boomerang smaller than the palm of his hand that could be thrown 65½ ft (20 m) and returned accurately.

HAIR SCULPTURE

For a 2007 exhibition, Chinese artist Wenda Gu created a sculpture using more than 7 mi (11 km) of braided human hair.

SMALL IS BEAUTIFUL

A pinhead-sized replica of the Lloyd's of London building sold for $180,000 at an auction in 2007. The model, which was an exact replica of the famous building, took English micro-sculptor Willard Wigan four months to create, using white gold and platinum. The sculpture can be viewed only through a microscope. Wigan, whose previous works include re-creating the Statue of Liberty inside the eye of a needle, said that the Lloyd's of London building was the most difficult piece he has ever made.

OUTSIZE ALBUM

A photo album unveiled in Orlando, Florida, in 2007 was so big that it needed two adults to turn each of its 20 pages. Created for the launch of the 2008 Dodge Grand Caravan, it measured 9 ft (3 m) wide by 12 ft (4 m) tall.

Disk Dragon

Sculptors in China built a huge dragon-shaped lamp from hundreds of used computer disks for a 2007 carnival at Beijing International Sculpture Park.

SMALL WORLD

Mysterious tiny figures have been appearing all over the city of London, England. They are the work of British artist Slinkachu, who has been painting the small plastic people used in architects' models and planting them in streets and on benches across the capital. His "Little People" were inspired by the idea of a hidden world existing right in front of our eyes.

NO VERBS

In 2004, a French author writing under the pseudonym Michel Thaler wrote a 233-page novel, *Le Train de Nulle Part*, without the use of a single verb.

SCRAP ELEPHANTS

Jim Powers of Gage, Oklahoma, has created giant insects, life-size elephants, and dinosaurs out of scrap metal from cars.

TOOTHPICK MODELS

Chicago, Illinois, artist Wayne Kusy spent eight years building a 25-ft-long (7.5-m) model of the ocean liner *Queen Mary* from 814,000 toothpicks. A specialist in toothpick ships, he has also made replicas of the English tea clipper *Cutty Sark*, and the ill-fated liners *Titanic* and *Lusitania*.

TWISTED TREES

The tree circus of Gilroy Gardens features one-of-a-kind tree sculptures—with various grafts, twists, and bends—all grown over 30 years by a farmer in California.

SKEWER CITY

Edgar Gata of Las Pinas City, Philippines, used more than 30,000 wooden barbecue skewers to assemble a model town with dozens of buildings, vehicles, and landmarks from around the world.

THE SMALL TOP 〜〜〜

Sculpting nearly 400 characters from clay, Sonny King of Los Angeles, California, has created a miniature circus. Each diorama took three months to make, and the model is based on his father Mervyn's adventures as a circus-owner in the 1940s and 1950s. Models include his father in the lion's cage, and veteran strong man Johnny Zelinsky, who could hold aloft a trapeze artist using only his teeth when he was in his eighties!

LONG NOTE 〜〜〜

In September 2007, saxophonist Aaron Bing of Jacksonville, Florida, held a single, continuous low G note on his saxophone for 39 minutes 40 seconds while standing on a windy New York City street.

GUN PLAY 〜〜〜

Colombian musician and anti-violence advocate Cesar Lopez creates and plays guitars built from guns.

THE HILLS ARE ALIVE 〜〜〜

The city of Salzburg, Austria, has a cable channel that plays the movie *The Sound of Music* 24 hours a day, every day of the year!

CYMBAL OF COURAGE 〜〜〜

Despite being born without lower arms and a badly deformed leg, which was later amputated, 15-year-old Cornel Hrisca-Munn of Whittington, England, beat 420 able-bodied youngsters to take second place in a national drumming competition. He uses straps to attach the drumsticks to his upper arms and a false leg so that he can operate the bass pedal.

CHAMBER MUSIC 〜〜〜

Police in Bolzano, Italy, seized a toilet from an art gallery because it played Italy's national anthem while flushing.

NONSTOP ELVIS 〜〜〜

Elvis impersonator Gaétan Lalonde of St.-Jérôme, Quebec, Canada, sang numbers by the King nonstop for two days in June 2007. The singer, also known as Scotty Davis, performed a rotation of 44 tunes over the course of 46 hours 30 minutes.

KERMIT FAN 〜〜〜

A man claiming to have a bomb took over a radio station in Wanganui, New Zealand, in 1995 and demanded to hear the song "Rainbow Connection" by Kermit the Frog!

BURSTING WITH PRIDE

Canadian artist Sean Rooney makes amazing sculptures from balloons— flowers, creatures, even costumes. In June 2007, he built a 20-ft (6-m) pyramid sculpture out of hundreds of balloons for a children's festival in Sarajevo, Bosnia.

MIXED MESSAGE 〜〜〜

Mourners at a funeral service in Kent, England, were startled when the church PA system accidentally played Rod Stewart's 1978 hit "Do Ya Think I'm Sexy," which includes the inappropriate line "If you want my body... "!

STONE COOKIES 〜〜〜

Artist Robin Antar from Brooklyn, New York, can create everyday objects from stone. Even though Robin is blind in one eye, she carves lifelike stone sculptures of iconic American items, such as a pair of Diesel jeans, a bag of Milano cookies, a Skechers' logger boot, a bag of M&M's®, and a giant Heinz Ketchup bottle. She usually works on her sculptures at night and spends up to six months on each piece. Her sculptures are so realistic that they have to be roped off to stop exhibit visitors trying to help themselves to a stone cookie or an M&M®!

PLASTIC FANTASTIC 〜〜〜

Luis Torres, a Metropolitan Transit Authority worker who lives in New York City, crafts sculptures from the transit credit cards that he collects during his day-job.

EXTRA LARGE

It took Wu Shujun of Handan, China, nearly four years to make this sweater—not surprising as it is 16 ft (5 m) long, 8 ft (2.5 m) high and weighs 22 lb (10 kg). The logo on the front of the sweater was designed to herald the 2008 Beijing Olympics.

PRIZE PUMPKINS

Like thousands of American youngsters, Scott Cummins used to carve out a pumpkin to make a jack-o-lantern for Halloween. But whereas others mastered just the basic eyes, nose, and mouth, Cummins has gone on to create amazingly intricate works of art from the fruit.

The junior high school teacher from Perryton, Texas, has been carving pumpkins since he was 16. His extensive portfolio includes portraits of Leonard Nimoy, Albert Einstein, and George W. Bush; characters such as Gollum from *The Lord of the Rings* and Winnie-the-Pooh; lifelike animal heads; expressive faces born of his own imagination; the Statue of Liberty; and a beautiful baby in the womb. Each carving takes him just a couple of hours.

Sometimes the shape of the pumpkin dictates the face; at other times he has an idea of what he wants to create and looks for a pumpkin of appropriate form and size. He begins by scraping away the inside of the pumpkin and the tough orange skin. For the actual carving, he uses a variety of implements—sharpened spoons, ice-cream scoops, knives, drill bits, and even saw blades—and is always on the lookout for new tools.

Finally, he lights many of the carved pumpkins with a 30-watt bulb, and, as the light shines through the thinner areas of the rind, his fantastic creations acquire an eerie, almost mystical appearance.

Ripley's ask

How do you choose what to sculpt and do you take requests? I just find myself overcome with the feeling that some particular character or expression really NEEDS to be captured in pumpkin rind. The shape of the pumpkin also affects my decision. I take "suggestions" once in a while. Not too many requests though.

What is your favorite and why? I don't really have a favorite. I guess I can say that I'm very fond of the Albert Einstein carving... probably because the image is so iconic.

How long does each sculpture take? Eleven months of planning and anticipation and about an hour or two of actual carving.

To date, what is your total number of pumpkin carvings? I'd say about a wagon load. Somewhere over one hundred, I suppose. Since I began photographing them, most are on my online gallery.

Do you like pumpkin pie? It's delicious.

What do you do with the pumpkins once you have finished carving? I display them, take a picture or two, and then I allow them to decompose with quiet dignity.

What will you do next? I'll probably keep on carving. I'd like to do more Tiki faces and maybe a zombie or two. Or I could retire to an exotic location and get fat off the enormous wealth from my pumpkin-carving empire!

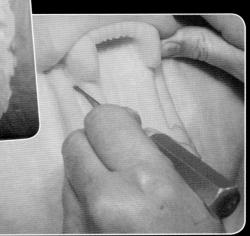

Scott breathes life into his pumpkins using a selection of instruments and his considerable carving skills.

LAND SWIMMER

An over-sized sculpture of a man swimming through grass was unveiled on the banks of the Thames River in London, England, in 2007. The piece was commissioned to promote a reality TV show by Louis Molloy.

FIREARM ART

Peace art project artists in Cambodia created original sculptures and furniture from decommissioned pistols and assault rifles.

TIN PANTS

A pair of jeans 16 ft (5 m) tall made from 3,000 soft drinks cans was on display at a shopping mall in Xiamen City, China, in October 2007.

TAPING DAVE

Judy Carter of Seymour, Indiana, created a sculpture of TV host David Letterman using duct tape!

FILMED FLIGHT

In 2005, Francisco Gutierrez flew with a swarm of Monarch butterflies to film the flight of their 4,375-mi (7,040 km) migration from Canada to Mexico. Gutierrez flew among the thousands of insects in a small ultralight plane.

TRASH PEOPLE

A thousand trash people—molded from tin cans, computer parts, and crushed plastic—have appeared in some of the world's most famous locations. The work of German artist H.A. Schult, the garbage army has been arranged on the Great Wall of China, near the Egyptian Pyramids, in Moscow's Red Square, at the base of the Matterhorn mountain in Switzerland, and in front of Cologne Cathedral in Germany.

HOMEMADE BANJO

Dean Clemmer of Bolivar, Missouri, has been in a band since 1999 playing a five-string banjo made from a car's hubcap!

TV GLUT

The average U.S. home has more television sets than it has people, and believe it or not, one in four Americans have actually appeared on TV!

GAME HOST

A Swedish TV presenter became a hit on the Internet site YouTube after she vomited live on air. Eva Nazemson was hosting a late-night phone-in game show when she suddenly felt ill. As a caller tried to solve a puzzle, she quickly turned her head to one side and vomited before bravely carrying on with the program.

BURNING AMBITION

In June 2006, a man from Beijing, China, fled a burning house with only his television set... which he immediately plugged in elsewhere so that he could continue to watch a World Cup soccer match!

EDIBLE MOZART

Japan's Junko Terashima prepared an amazing likeness of the composer Wolfgang Amadeus Mozart—from food! Terashima is an expert in Bento Art—the Japanese craft of lunch sculpture—whereby incredible edible images are created from fruit, vegetables, and other foodstuffs.

TITANIC TIME

Watchmaker Romain Jerome of Geneva, Switzerland, has created a line of watches that use steel and coal that has been taken from the wreck of the R.M.S. Titanic. Incorporating steel from the stricken ship's hull and coal from the wreck site, the watches sell for anything between $8,000 and $175,000.

OPTICAL ILLUSION

American street artist Kurt Wenner adds the finishing touches to a 3-D work of art at Waterloo Station in London, England. The classically inspired Wenner has pioneered an art form known as anamorphic, in which a street painting creates an optical illusion by popping up in 3-D when viewed from a certain angle. Here he appears to sit obliviously on a sofa while a taxi crashes through the walls of the house.

STARTLING ART

FLOUR POWER

Other people see a tortilla as a tasty snack, but Joe Bravo sees it as a canvas on which to create incredible works of art. The Los Angeles artist has earned such a reputation that some of his tortilla paintings sell for more than $3,000. Among those who have bought a Bravo creation is Flea, the bassist with the Red Hot Chili Peppers.

As an art student in the early 1970s, Bravo could not afford canvas, so he chose tortillas instead, reasoning that a staple Hispanic food was the ideal medium for displaying Hispanic imagery. He made a mobile of hanging tortillas—all hand-painted—but it blew apart in the Santa Ana winds. Then, nearly a decade ago, somebody reminded him about it and he started painting on tortillas again.

In his early days he used corn tortillas, but now he uses 26-in (66-cm) flour tortillas, custom-made by a Los Angeles company. He says: "An audience sees a painting on a little regular tortilla, they might go, 'OK.'

But to see a really, really big tortilla? That gets their attention."

His ideas are inspired by the individual texture, burn marks, and appearance of each toasted tortilla. He has re-created such diverse icons as Marilyn Monroe, Che Guevara, Ronald McDonald, and La Virgin de Guadalupe. For an exhibition in Hong Kong he chose Oriental themes, including dragons, pandas, and koi fish. He has also designed a tortilla mask and costume adorned with kernels of corn. "You're working with the environment of the tortilla," he explains. "The tortilla is almost like a collaborator."

" THE BRAVO CODE FOR TORTILLA PAINTING

Tortilla painting is more a collaboration between the artist and nature. It is not only about the artist painting on a tortilla, it is also about the tortilla suggesting themes for the artist to paint.

Visualize, contemplate, and imagine what the tortilla is conveying with its texture, burn marks, and appearance. Consider the tortilla as you would the smooth lines on a beautiful piece of natural wood, the veins of a marble stone, or the clouds in a bright blue sky. Use what you see on the tortilla as a starting point for your painting.

STEP 1: Let the tortilla dry either naturally (about 2–3 days) or in the oven (monitor carefully).

STEP 2: Cook the tortilla over an open flame on the stove top to get some interesting texture and color surfaces.

STEP 3: Varnish the tortilla on both sides, allowing each side to dry overnight.

STEP 4: Look at the tortilla and let it suggest something to you. Do you see people, a landscape, animals, stars, or other objects? Then paint what you see on the tortilla and have fun with it.

STEP 5: Once you finish painting, add several coats of varnish to the tortilla for further protection.

STEP 6: When dry, mount the tortilla in a shallow box frame or on some type of strong backing, such as a plastic plate, to display.

151

◀ PRICE OF LOVE

A Japanese chocolate made for Valentine's Day 2006 was encrusted with 2,006 diamonds and priced at 500 million yen ($4.4 million). The chocolate was designed in the shape of the continent of Africa.

TINY SUSHI

Sushi on single tiny grains of rice is served at the Omoroi Sushiya Kajiki Sushi Restaurant in Fukuoka, Japan.

LARGE SLAB

In May 2007, the Northwest Fudge Factory of Levack, Ontario, Canada, produced a slab of fudge that measured 45½ ft (13.9 m) long, 6½ ft (2 m) wide, and 4 in (10 cm) thick, and weighed 5,038 lb (2,285 kg).

SCOTCH GEORGE

George Washington, the first president of the U.S.A., also ran one of the largest whiskey distilleries in North America.

COLOR CHANGE

The first orange carrot was bred by Dutch farmers to honor their royal family, the House of Orange. Prior to that, most carrots were purple, yellow, or white.

EXPENSIVE TASTE

A hamburger on the menu at the Ritz-Carlton Hotel in Tokyo, Japan, costs 13,450 yen ($112)—that's more than 40 times the price of a McDonald's burger. The beef in the burger comes from Wagyu cattle, which are specially bred for the flavor, juiciness, and tenderness of their meat. ▼

LUXURY BAGEL ▲

Frank Tujague, executive chef of the Westin New York Hotel in Times Square, prepared a $1,000 bagel in 2007. Topped with white truffle cream-cheese and goji berry-infused Riesling jelly with golden leaves, the luxury bagel was so pricey because white truffle is the second most expensive food in the world, next to premium caviar.

GIANT OMELETTE

Sixty thousand eggs were poured into a specially built 44-ft (13.4-m) pan to make a giant omelette weighing 6,510 lb (2,950 kg) at Brockville, Ontario, Canada in 2002.

CAKE CATHEDRAL

George D'Aubney built a 4-ft-tall (1.2-m) replica of the famous landmark St. Paul's Cathedral in London, England. The replica was complete with lights, music, moving parts—and made primarily from fruitcake.

BANANA SPLITS

There are more than 300 banana-related accidents a year in Britain, most involving people slipping on skins.

RICH DESSERT

A restaurant in the Sri Lankan resort of Galle is charging $14,500 for a dessert, which comes with a chocolate sculpture and a large gemstone. The Fortress Stilt Fisherman Indulgence consists of cassata, mango, pomegranate, champagne, and an 80-carat aquamarine stone.

SOUND OF THE SEA

At his restaurant in Berkshire, England, chef Heston Blumenthal serves a dish that comes with an iPod Nano in a clamshell—so that customers can listen to the sea as they eat their seafood.

GOLDEN DESSERT △

In 2007, a New York City restaurant unveiled a chocolate dessert costing a cool $25,000. Stephen Bruce, owner of Serendipity 3, revealed that the expensive sundae contained a blend of 28 rare cocoas from 14 countries, topped with cream and sprinkled with 23-carat edible gold dust and an exotic truffle. In addition to the food, the customer got to take home the gold-and-diamond goblet in which it was served, the 18-carat gold spoon used to eat it, and a ladies' gold bracelet.

POPCORN BALL

A popcorn ball that measured 8 ft (2.4 m) in diameter and 24½ ft (7.5 m) in circumference and weighed 3,415 lb (1,150 kg) was manufactured at Lake Forest, Illinois, in October 2006.

COFFEE SENTENCE

King Gustav III, who ruled Sweden in the 18th century, was so convinced that coffee was poisonous that he ordered a convicted criminal to drink himself to death with it. However, the condemned man eventually died of old age instead.

POTATO FIGHT

In 2007, a woman in Nicholson, Georgia, knocked out her husband with a potato! She picked up the potato and threw it at him during a row and it hit him square on the nose. He decided not to press charges.

Prized Lychee

Known as the "king of fruit," the lychee has always been popular in China. Few, however, have been sold for anything like the price of this one, which went for a huge 555,000 yuan ($67,000) at auction in Zengcheng City, China, in 2002. It came from a 400-year-old tree, named Xiyuangualu, which yields only a few dozen lychees each year.

VANILLA ICE

Using an extra-large spoon of his own invention, Ed "Cookie" Jarvis of New York City, ate a whopping 1 gal 9 oz (4 l) of vanilla ice cream in only 12 minutes. He says he avoided the dreaded brain freeze by eating his ice cream with the spoon facing downward toward his tongue, rather than the roof of his mouth.

THE VERMONSTER

Ian Hickman from Sterling, Virginia, has tamed The Vermonster—a 6-lb-15-oz (3.1-kg) Ben & Jerry's ice cream sundae. Although the dessert—which contains 20 scoops of ice cream, four bananas, three cookies, a brownie, hot fudge, whipped cream, and 18 teaspoons of topping—is designed to be eaten by a group of people, Hickman devoured it single-handedly in just 9 minutes 22 seconds.

CHESTNUT CHAMP

In 2007, Joey Chestnut of San Jose, California, ate 182 chicken wings in 30 minutes to win the "Wing Bowl 15" eating contest in Philadelphia. He also consumed 8 lb 10 oz (3.9 kg) of asparagus spears in 10 minutes for a third straight win at the World Deep-fried Asparagus Eating Championship at Stockton, California.

THE BIG BITE

Staff at Wild Woody's Chill In Grill in Roseville, Michigan, made a corned beef sandwich in 2005 that weighed a staggering 5,672 lb (1,210 kg). Measuring 12 x 16 ft (3.6 x 4.8 m) and being 17 in (43 cm) thick, the sandwich had a filling made up of 1,131 lb (513 kg) of corned beef, 150 lb (68 kg) of mustard, 260 lb (118 kg) of white American cheese, 531 lb (240 kg) of lettuce, and an amazing 3,600 lb (1,635 kg) of white bread.

PIE FACE

Winner Craig Bernston from Gloucester, Rhode Island, powers ahead during his assault on the pie-eating contest at the state's Washington County Fair held in the town of Richmond.

BIG BREAKFAST

The proud winner of Britain's first All You Can Eat Breakfast Eating Championships is seen here with one of the 5½ breakfasts he ate in just 12 minutes at the contest held in London in July 2007. Each breakfast consisted of a delicious pile of eggs, bacon, sausages, mushrooms, and croissants.

FAST FOOD ▽

Champion competitive eaters' average consumption per minute:

55.2	Oysters	Sonya Thomas, U.S.A.
45.6	Russian dumplings	Dale Boone, U.S.A.
27.5	Crawfish	Chris Hendrix, U.S.A.
16	Chicken nuggets	Sonya Thomas, U.S.A.
13.4	Chicken wings	Sonya Thomas, U.S.A.
11.3	Chinese dumplings	Cookie Jarvis, U.S.A.
9.8	Hard-boiled eggs	Sonya Thomas, U.S.A.
7.5	Conch fritters	Joe Menchetti, U.S.A.
6.1	Donuts	Eric Booker, U.S.A.
5.8	Sausages	Takeru Kobayashi, Japan
4.7	Grilled cheese sandwiches	Joey Chestnut, U.S.A.
4.5	Nathan's famous hot dogs & buns	Takeru Kobayashi, Japan
4.3	Soft chicken tacos	Sonya Thomas, U.S.A.
3.9	Matzo balls	Eric Booker, U.S.A.
3.8	Cow brains	Takeru Kobayashi, Japan
3.6	Maine lobsters	Sonya Thomas, U.S.A.
3.5	Cannoli	Cookie Jarvis, U.S.A.
3.3	Crab cakes	Sonya Thomas, U.S.A.
2.8	Ears of sweet corn	Crazy Legs Conti, U.S.A.

SUPER BOWL

Pupils at a school in Warwickshire, England, cooked a bowl of porridge that was big enough to feed 300 people. The porridge was made from 44 lb (20 kg) of oats and 13 gal (50 l) of milk and, when it was made, weighed 145 kg (66 kg).

CHOCOLATE SIGN

A giant chocolate billboard in London, England, took a team of ten people 300 hours to build—but it took lucky shoppers in London's busy Covent Garden just three hours to eat. The sign measured 14½ x 9½ ft (4.4 x 2.9 m) and was made of ten chocolate bunnies, 72 large chocolate Easter eggs, and 128 chocolate panels, each of which weighed more than 4 lb (1.8 kg).

SENSATIONAL SAUSAGE!

Butchers put the finishing touches to a mammoth sausage that is the star of the show at the annual Sausage Festival in the Serbian village of Turija. The sausage was created by 12 butchers and measured a whopping 6,627 ft (2,020 m) in length. It was made from the following impressive list of ingredients: pork from 28 pigs, 110 lb (50 kg) of salt, 4 lb 6 oz (2 kg) of pepper, 88 lb (40 kg) of paprika, and 11 lb (5 kg) of garlic.

FROG FEAST

Dr. Matt Allen, a chemistry professor at Wayne State University, Detroit, Michigan, ate 1 lb 10 oz (740 g) of frogs' legs in only five minutes to win the first-ever World Frog Leg Eating Championship held at Madison, Wisconsin.

PIZZA POWER

Patrick Bertoletti just loves pizza—so much so that the Chicago man ate 19 slices in 10 minutes at the 2006 Three Brothers World Pizza Eating Championship in Annapolis, Maryland.

ROYAL MEAL

In 1999, chef Rick Royal and students from the Art Institute of Los Angeles School of Culinary Arts created a crème brulée with a diameter of 23½ ft (7 m). It was made from no fewer than 3,600 egg yolks.

BIRTHDAY CAKE

To celebrate the 230th birthday of the U.S.A., caterers in Fayetteville, Arkansas, baked a 230-layer cake for the Fourth of July, 2006. The cake, which stood 2 ft (60 cm) high and weighed more than 100 lb (45 kg), took 21 hours to bake.

HOT STUFF

Mark "The Human Vacuum" Lyle ate 8 lb 5 oz (3.75 kg) of chili in five minutes at the 2007 Midwest Chili Eating Championship in Canton, Ohio.

STIR-FRY CRAZY

Helped by 20 assistants, chef Nancy Lam made a stir-fry weighing 1,543 lb (700 kg) in London, England, in 2004. The stir-fry was made from 153 lb (69 kg) of green cabbage, 489 lb (222 kg) of Chinese cabbage, 449 lb (204 kg) of white cabbage, 413 lb (187 kg) of carrots, and 21 lb (9.5 kg) of baby corn.

FROG REMEDY

Jiang Musheng, 66, of China, has eaten a diet of live tree frogs and rats for the past 40 years. As a young man, he had suffered abdominal pains and coughing until an elderly villager prescribed the unusual remedy. After just one month of eating live frogs, the pains and coughing disappeared.

NORWEGIAN DELICACY

The local delicacy in the Norwegian town of Voss is smoked sheep's head. Nothing goes to waste except the bare bones of the skull as residents tuck in to the flesh of the entire head, including the sheep's eyeballs, tongue, and ears.

PRESERVED GIFT

A circle of friends has been handing around an old fruitcake as a Christmas present for more than 20 years. Christopher Linton-Smith, Steve Glum, and Tim Arnheim were friends at Stetson University, Florida, and started sending each other the $2.99 world-famous Claxton, Georgia, fruitcake as a joke in 1986. Each Christmas it is passed on to one of the group—even though none of them actually likes fruitcake.

ATE LENSES

Stopped by police for a breath test in 2007, a 19-year-old man from Ontario, Canada, took out his contact lenses and ate them—and then tried to eat his shirt and socks too.

DOG FOOD

Two students from the town of Swindon in Wiltshire, England, sat in a paddling pool in 2005 and ate dog food while fellow students pledged money to charity in return for covering them in baked beans, baking flour, and cornflakes.

ORGANIC RESTAURANT

Guolizhuang is China's first speciality penis restaurant. Every item on the menu at the Beijing diner is an animal's organ—yak, donkey, horse, dog, goat, deer, and ox. The luxury dish is Canadian seal's penis at $440. It has to be ordered in advance.

DESERT DIET

Eighty-year-old Ram Rati of Lucknow, India, eats 1 lb (450 g) of sand every day. She has been eating sand before each meal for the past 40 years and says it helps her to fight old age and stomach problems.

EDIBLE HEIRLOOM

A hot cross bun has been kept in a family for more than 100 years! Ever since 13-year-old Ada Herbert of Ipswich, England, died holding the bun in 1899, it has been passed down the family's generations. Amazingly, it has never gone moldy and the original cross is still visible.

STRANGE COMBINATION

Danny Partner of Los Angeles, California, used to eat 12 iceberg lettuces covered in chocolate sauce every day!

CARDBOARD BUNS

Steamed buns sold in a neighborhood of Beijing, China, are being made from cardboard! Although its use is illegal in foodstuffs, chopped cardboard, softened in caustic soda and enhanced with pork flavoring, is sometimes the main ingredient of the baozi buns.

ANTIQUE HAM

The same slab of ham has been on display at the Mecca restaurant in Raleigh, North Carolina, since 1937. The 25-lb (11-kg) ham was first acquired by the grandfather of the restaurant's current owner, Paul Dombalis, more than 70 years ago and has remained an uneaten favorite with customers ever since.

GRASS EATER

Gangaram, a man in Kanpur, India, has been eating more than 2 lb (900 g) of grass a day for many years. He says it gives him energy and that, although he can do without food, he cannot live without grass.

STEAMING RATS

Piping hot, cooked field rats are one of the dishes on offer at a wild game restaurant in Guangzhou, southern China.

BRAIN FOOD

This unusual-looking sandwich makes a regular appearance on the menu at the Hilltop Inn in Evansville, Indiana, even though it is made from deep-fried cow brains! Its origins are said to date back to a time when German and Dutch immigrants to southern Indiana wasted precious little of anything, especially when it came to animals slaughtered for food. Ketchup anyone?

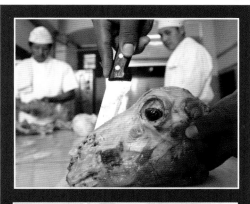

SHEEP SUPPER

Boiled sheep's head served on a bed of rice is the speciality of the Solar de las Cabecitas (House of the Little Heads), a restaurant in the Bolivian capital, La Paz. The dish originates from the Andean mining city of Oruro, where the salty highland pasture gives the lamb its particular flavor.

COSTLY COCKTAIL

Visitors to a nightclub in London, England, can buy a cocktail costing $70,000. The Flawless cocktail, which has to be ordered in advance, consists of a large measure of Louis XII cognac, half a bottle of Cristal Rose champagne, brown sugar, Angostura bitters, and a few flakes of 24-carat edible gold leaf. But what really makes the drink so expensive is at the bottom of the glass where, once you have supped the whole drink, there is a beautiful 11-carat white diamond ring.

CHOCOLATE FINGER

A man in Mainz, Germany, found part of a human finger in his chocolate bar. The fingertip, complete with nail, was right in the middle of the bar. A police officer said: "I suppose it went unnoticed because there were nuts in the chocolate and it was hard to tell the difference."

DINING TOMB

At the Lucky Hotel Restaurant in Ahmedabad, India, guests dine among the 22 tombs that remain from an ancient burial ground.

CHOC ART

Australian artist Sid Chidiac, who now lives in the Lebanon, paints with chocolate. He uses fine Belgian chocolate and food dye on an edible canvas to create portraits of, among others, John F. Kennedy, Oprah Winfrey, and Abraham Lincoln. Each painting takes him up to three days to complete and can last for several years if it is kept in the right conditions.

PAWS FOR THOUGHT

Chinese chef Wang Wei Min presents a plate of barbecued dogs' paws at a Chinese restaurant in Tokyo, Japan, in 2006. Apparently, Japanese diners are generally unaware that dog is served in Chinese restaurants in their country, but this dish would leave them in little doubt!

157

SCORPION SKEWERS

Conveniently served on wooden skewers, fried scorpions and centipedes were two of the delicacies on offer at one of the food stalls at the Nanjing Food Fest in China.

SCORPION SCALOPPINE

Ingredients:

8 frozen desert hairy scorpions (*Hadrurus arizonensis*) or similar species, thawed

1 pint low-fat milk

1 cup white cornmeal

2 tablespoons unsalted butter

1 tablespoon fresh lemon juice

2 tablespoons fresh parsley, chopped

Using a sharp knife, remove and discard stingers and venom glands from the tips of the scorpions' tails.

Pour milk into a medium-sized bowl; add scorpions and set aside while preparing the rest of the ingredients.

In a 12-in (30-cm) skillet, melt the butter. Remove scorpions from the milk mixture, allowing excess to drain off. Dredge the scorpions through the cornmeal, one at a time. Shake off excess flour.

Place the scorpions in the hot butter and cook until golden brown (about 2 minutes), then turn scorpions over and cook until done (about 1 minute).

Drain on paper toweling and sprinkle with lemon juice and chopped parsley.

The Eat-a-Bug Cookbook by David George Gordon, in which the above recipe appears, offers adventurous cooks "33 ways to cook grasshoppers, ants, water bugs, spiders, centipedes, and their kin."

THAT'S CRACKERS!

A factory in the Japanese town of Omachi is the proud producer of rice crackers that contain the added protein of digger wasps. The "jibachi senbei" or "digger wasp rice cracker" is a delicacy that has been specially commissioned by a Japanese fan club for wasps. Fan club members say that the extra ingredient adds a waspish note to the traditional flavor of the crackers.

SNAKE SNACK

Shyam Atulkar from Nagpur, India, catches snakes and sometimes eats them alive! "I like the taste of snakes," he says, "especially the tail end, which tastes like raw mutton. The head and neck taste somewhat bitter because of the poison."

COCKROACH CONTEST

With his hands tied behind his back, Shai Pariente ate 13 oven-cooked cockroaches in New York in 2004 to win an iPod in a contest.

ANT COOKIES

Cookies made with *bachaco*, a type of large ant, were served during a demonstration by Venezuelan chef Nelson Mendez at a food fair in Caracas in 2007.

SCORPION ADDICT

Hasip Kaya of Turkey has become addicted to eating live scorpions. The father-of-two has been eating them since childhood and enjoys them so much that villagers search under rocks to find him fresh supplies.

BEATING HEART

A delicacy in Japanese restaurants is the still beating heart of a freshly-killed frog! The dish is said to be particularly tasty if accompanied by lizard sake.

TASTY TARANTULA

A Cambodian woman munches on a tasty fried spider as she passes through the town of Skuon, which is also known as Spider Town to the locals. The spiders, which are collected from the surrounding countryside, are deep fried in salt and garlic. Customers wash the meal down with a bowl of medicinal tarantula wine, which is served with the rotting spiders' bodies still lying in the bottom of the bowl, with the fangs intact to prevent the medicine from losing its power.

FIRST AUCTION

A bottle of 81-year-old scotch was sold for $54,000 in 2007—in New York State's first liquor auction since Prohibition. Although Prohibition ended in 1933, the state continued to ban the auctioning of spirits until recently.

COFFEE GUM

People in Japan can buy coffee-flavored chewing gum that leaves their breath coffee-fresh.

INSECT TREAT

For centuries, farmers in Santander, Colombia, have harvested queen ants as a tasty treat for local consumption. They now export the ants abroad as gourmet delights.

CHEESE BRIBE

Four police officers in the Campagnia region of Italy were arrested in 2007 for demanding mozzarella bribes from motorists. They were said to have stopped cheese delivery trucks and forced the drivers to hand over the contents or face a large fine.

WORM MAN

Wayne Fauser, alias The Worm Man, from Sydney, Australia, eats live earthworms, either in sandwiches or just plain.

CHOCOLATE SIN

Two hundred years ago chocolate was considered to be a temptation of the devil. In some Central American mountain villages, no one under the age of 60 was allowed to taste it and churchgoers who defied the ruling were threatened with excommunication.

HOT STUFF

A two-year-old boy in Assam, India, has become addicted to Bhut Jolakia, the world's hottest chili. Young Jayanta Lahan has eagerly devoured the chilies ever since he first tried them while his mother was cooking when he was eight months old. He can eat about 50 of these chilies in three hours without suffering any ill effects—they are so hot that they would make most of us cry involuntarily and suffer a burning sensation in the stomach. The Bhut Jolokia is one hundred times hotter than a Jalapeno pepper and has half the potency of weapon-grade pepper spray!

RATTLESNAKE TACO

The Mexican town of Santiago de Anaya hosted a gastronomic festival featuring more than a thousand dishes made from all kinds of local flora and fauna in April 2007. This local resident is seen enjoying a taco made from rattlesnake meat.

Enter the Vault

◀ SHARP APPETITE

Professor Leo Kongee of Pittsburgh, Pennsylvania, ate with a hatpin stuck through his cheeks to prevent him from eating too fast!

PILES OF PASTA

A marathon spaghetti-eater works his way through mountains of pasta at Ripley's New York City Odditorium in 1939. Giuseppe Ricore ate a mammoth 1½ mi (2.4 km) of spaghetti in three hours.

SKINNY DINER

This slender eatery in 1940s Miami, Florida, was a mere 50 in (130 cm) wide. It stretched back 52 ft (16 m), however, so it could accommodate a long line of hungry diners.

BEER BONANZA

The strong, steady hands of Bavarian waiter Clemens Pichl could carry 35 beer steins, full of beer, at the same time in Old Heidelberg, Pittsford, New York in 1935.

COLOSSAL CAKE ▶

This giant wedding cake measured 15½ ft (4.7 m) tall, and was baked for the county fair in Ferndale, California, in the 1950s. The cake served no fewer than 10,500 people!

OYSTER LOVER

During the 1930s, Joseph A. Cohen of Douglas, Arizona, could eat 120 fried oysters at a single sitting, and did so on many occasions.

BIG BEAN

Backyard gardener C.W. Forschner of Cleveland, Ohio, grew a butter bean that measured 27½ in (70 cm) in length and 20½ in (52 cm) in diameter.

CORN-UCOPIA

Champion sweet-corn eater Ed Kottwitz of Ortonville, Minnesota, once ate 50 large ears of corn in one mammoth corn-eating session in the 1930s.

◄ BRAVE BAKER

In 1935, in a feat of finger-tingling dexterity, George Gotsis of Chicago, Illinois, cut a 16-in (40-cm) loaf of bread into perfect slices in 40 seconds, while wearing a blindfold!

PIE-MAKER ► EXTRAORDINAIRE

Mrs W. E. Updegraff of Vinita, Oklahoma, made 60 pies in just 45 minutes, every weekday for a period of no less than 23 years. During this time she baked more than an astonishing 380,000 pies!

LATTE ART

Visitors to a café in Melbourne, Australia, often find a face, a flower, or a butterfly staring back at them from the cup. The artistic frothy designs are all the rage among the city's baristas who use the coffee cup as a canvas and even take part in special latte art competitions. The patterns are created either by manipulating the flow of milk from a jug into an espresso or by etching, using stencils, powders, and milk foam.

GIANT KEBAB
Using 3.8 tons of chicken meat, 250 students in Cyberjaya, Malaysia, created a kebab that was more than 1¼ mi (2 km) long.

LUXURY PIZZA
Domenico Crolla, a chef from Glasgow, Scotland, creates a specialty pizza with a $4,000 price tag. It includes champagne-soaked caviar, cognac-marinated lobster, smoked salmon, venison, and 24-carat edible gold shavings. It is named the Pizza Royale 007 after James Bond.

TEA BAG
In 2006, a German company made a tea bag that was 11 x 8½ ft (3.4 x 2.6 m). It contained more than 22 lb (10 kg) of tea.

ULTIMATE TAKEOUT
An Indian restaurant in Belfast, Northern Ireland, delivered the ultimate takeout meal in 2006—to Manhattan. Steve Francis, a New York dance music producer, ordered the $16,000 transatlantic takeout—complete with fish flown in specially from Bangladesh—after Arif Ahmed's Indie Spice restaurant had served him delicious food at a festival in England.

SUPER SOUP
Cooks in Caracas, Venezuela, prepared a 3,963-gal (15,000-l) pot of soup in September 2007 that was big enough to feed 70,000 people. The soup contained 6,615 lb (3,000 kg) of chicken, 4,410 lb (2,000 kg) of beef, and literally tons of vegetables.

SUNDAE BEST
In 1988, Mike Rogiani of Edmonton, Alberta, Canada, created an ice cream sundae that weighed a staggering 54,917 lb (24,910 kg). The ingredients—which included 63 different flavors of ice cream—cost about $7,000 and had to be mixed in an empty swimming pool.

BANANA BUNCH
A bunch of bananas harvested in Holguin, Cuba, in 2007, contained more than 300 bananas. The bunch was 3 ft 10 in (1.2 m) high and weighed 125 lb (57 kg). Amazingly, the plant was growing in a clay soil to which no fertilizers had been added—apparently, water was the only catalyst needed for such enormous growth.

STARBUCKS ADVENTURER

Poughkeepsie, NY

Seekonk, MA

Freeport, NY

Carmel, NY

Incline Village, NV

DRIP FEED

At a hospital-themed restaurant in Taipei, Taiwan, customers drink from intravenous tubes suspended from the ceiling. The waitresses are dressed as nurses, crutches hang from the walls, a wheelchair is parked in the lobby, and the sign for the bathrooms is marked "emergency room."

CHOCOLATE IGLOO

Marco Fanti and his co-workers created a 9,200-lb (4,173-kg) igloo totally out of edible chocolate for the Eurochocolate Fair in Perugia, Italy, in 2006.

CREAM CAKE

In Alanya, Turkey, 285 cooks baked a cream cake 8,840 ft (2,720 m) long, using 159,000 eggs, 12,150 lb (5,512 kg) of sugar, 12,150 lb (5,512 kg) of flour, 1,400 gal (5,300 l) of milk, 5,840 lb (2,650 kg) of bananas, 700 gal (2,650 l) of water, and 1,750 lb (795 kg) of carbonate and baking additives.

GOOD KARMA

Hoping to bring some good karma to his establishment, a restaurant owner in Guangdong, China, paid $75,000 for a single "lucky" fish in April 2007.

COLOSSAL CAKE

To celebrate the centennial of Las Vegas in May 2005, a giant birthday cake was baked that measured 102 ft (31 m) long, 52 ft (16 m) wide and 20 in (50 cm) high. It weighed 130,000 lb (59,000 kg), had 34,000 lb (15,420 kg) of icing, and contained 23 million calories!

MASSIVE MUG

In April 2007, a Panama coffee producer brewed a 750-gal (2,840-l) cup of coffee. Café Duran took four hours and used 300 lb (135 kg) of coffee to fill a 9-ft (2.7-m) tall mug.

DAIRY DELIGHT

Stew Leonard's, a family-owned foodstore with outlets in Connecticut and New York, has the world's largest in-store dairy plant, packaging more than 10 million half-gallon (2 l) cartons per year. That's enough milk to fill a straw reaching from Earth to the Moon and halfway back!

CHEESY HIT

More than 1.5 million people have logged on to an Internet site to watch a round of Cheddar cheese as it slowly matures in a storeroom in western England.

FROG FEAST

Visitors to the annual four-day Fellsmere Frog Leg Festival in Florida routinely eat around 6,000 lb (2,720 kg) of crispy fried frogs' legs.

For more than ten years, a contract computer programmer named Winter has been on a mission to drink a cup of coffee in every Starbucks store in the world. The idea originated in 1997 at his local Starbucks in Plano, Texas, and by October 2007 he had visited 7,103 stores in the U.S.A. (92.7 per cent of the total) and 457 international stores, from Montreal to Madrid and Paris to Hong Kong. Winter, whose travels are documented in the movie "Starbucking," started out averaging around ten stores a day, although in 1999 he managed 28 in one day at Portland, Oregon. The only problem is that Starbucks continues to open new stores every week around the world and has no plans to slow down!

Foodscapes

Photographer Carl Warner creates beautiful, realistic landscapes with a secret ingredient—they're all made of food.

He makes forests from broccoli, clouds from cauliflower or mozzarella cheese, mountains from bread, and buildings from Parmesan cheese. What appears to be a natural view of a sunlit fishing boat at sea turns out to be a pea pod "boat" resting on a "sea" of smoked salmon, bordered by pebbles made from soda bread and potatoes, and a beach of brown sugar.

Carl from Kent, England, has been perfecting his amazing artworks—called "Foodscapes"—for the past few years. He says: "I begin by drawing a conventional landscape using classic compositional techniques, as I need to fool the viewer into thinking it is a real scene." He plans each image carefully, scouring supermarkets for ingredients. Finding the right shaped broccoli to use for a tree is crucial to his art.

With the help of model-makers, he then creates the set on a table top that measures 8 ft (2.4 m) wide. Each set takes up to three days to build and photograph. The various foodstuffs are either glued or pinned in place. Next, the scenes are photographed in separate layers, from foreground to background and sky, to stop the food wilting under the lights. Then the individual layers are put together on a computer to achieve the final image.

"My favorite scene has to be the broccoli forest," he says, "because it was the first one that went from my head to my sketch book to the finished image as a smooth process. It also raised the bar on how realistic I could make them look. It is the realization of what the real ingredients are that brings a smile, and for me that's the best part."

A smoked salmon and soda bread sunset scene looks good enough to eat.

This idyllic scene of a small village set in rolling countryside is made of dozens of different foodstuffs.

GIANT CALZONE
In 2007, a restaurant in Madison, Wisconsin, created a huge calzone pizza measuring 19 ft 4 in x 2 ft 5 in (5.9 x 0.74 m) and weighing more than 100 lb (45 kg).

LARGE TIP
A family who were regulars at a Pizza Hut restaurant in Angola, Indiana, were so impressed by their waitress that they gave her a $10,000 tip. After 20-year-old waitress Jessica Osborne had told them she had twice been forced to drop out of college because of lack of money, they returned a few days later with the surprise check.

GOING POP
More than 500 Canadian boy scouts popped over 1,200 cubic ft (34 cubic m) of popcorn in just eight hours in 2007. Using two giant, homemade machines, the scouts popped at an average rate of two cubic ft per minute into a large bucket at Calgary Zoo, Alberta.

POPPADUM PILE
Richard Bradbury and Kris Browcott took four hours to stack a pile of around 1,000 poppadums to a height of nearly 5 ft (1.5 m) at an Indian restaurant in London, England.

SQUIRREL PANCAKES
A hotel in Cumbria, England, served up free gray squirrel pancakes. The squirrels were all caught in the grounds of the Famous Wild Boar Hotel at Crook and served in Peking duck-style wraps. Customers said the squirrel meat tasted like rabbit.

SOLO FEAST
A Thanksgiving meal for ten people was devoured by just one person in 15 minutes in 2007. Competitive eater Tim Janus from New York City consumed a 10-lb (4.5-kg) turkey, 4 lb (1.8 kg) of mashed potatoes, 3 lb (1.4 kg) of cranberry sauce, and 2½ lb (1.1 kg) of beans... and still had room for dessert—an entire pumpkin pie.

COSTLY TRUFFLE
A white truffle weighing 1 lb 10 oz (750 g) from Alba, Italy, was sold to a Hong Kong resident for $210,000 in 2007. Italian truffles were more expensive than usual in 2007 following a dry summer.

CHOPSTICK EXPERT
In November 2007, Rob Beaton of Asbury Park, New Jersey, used chopsticks to eat 78 single grains of rice in three minutes.

TEA DRINKER
Levi Johnson of Tea, South Dakota, drank 5½ oz (165 ml) of hot Tabasco® sauce—that's nearly three bottles—in just 30 seconds in 2007.

FISH HOOK
A man eating fish at a restaurant in Shanghai, China, got a fish hook stuck in his tongue. At first he thought it was a bone, but when he discovered blood all over his mouth, he was taken to hospital where the hook was removed.

DIRT SODA
For its contract to supply soda to Qwest Field, home of the Seattle Seahawks football team, Jones Soda Co. came up with new flavors, such as Perspiration, Dirt, Sports Cream, and Natural Field Turf.

BIG BIRD
As part of an annual contest with his sister Andra to see who can cook the biggest Thanksgiving turkey, Rich Portnoy, of Minneapolis, Minnesota, basted a bird weighing 72 lb (33 kg). The giant turkey needed 15 hours of roasting in a 36-in-wide (90-cm) oven.

GINGERBREAD HOUSES

Some of the most beautiful buildings in the world are displayed each year at the Grove Park Inn, Asheville, North Carolina—and they're all made out of gingerbread. First staged in 1993, the National Gingerbread House Competition draws sugar-and-spice creations from all over the U.S.A.

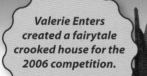

Valerie Enters created a fairytale crooked house for the 2006 competition.

Trish MacCallister took third prize with a festive gingerbread house in 2005.

Patricia Howard of Winter Springs, Florida, won the coveted Grand Prize with this snowy scene at the 2006 National Gingerbread Competition. She retained her title in 2007.

NICE ICE!

An ice-cream parlor in Nice, France, sells tomato-flavored sorbet. Fenocchio offers 70 beautifully presented flavors of ice cream and sorbet, including such wacky tastes as tomato and basil, black olive, rhubarb, lavender, and gingerbread.

Top Ten Unusual Ice Cream Flavors

Tomato & basil	Thyme
Black olive	Lavender
Licorice	Chewing gum
Beer	Violet
Rosemary	Rose

An enchanting gingerbread church won Virginia Pilarz third place in 2006.

A bejewelled gingerbread model of St. Basil's Cathedral in Moscow earned Nancy Kyzer first place at the 2005 contest.

Monkey Buffet

Monkeys are invited to dinner in Thailand. The annual Monkey Buffet Festival at the Pra Prang Sam Yot temple in Lopburi provides food and drink for the local monkey population, which numbers more than 2,000. The monkeys feast on over 4,400 lb (2,000 kg) of fruit and vegetables that are artfully presented in the deliciously edible displays.

BODY PAIN

The Hindu festival of Thaipusam in Malaysia is celebrated with devotees piercing their bodies with a variety of objects—from pins to swordfish bills.

GRAVY WRESTLING

The first-ever World Gravy Wrestling Championships were held in Lancashire, England, in 2007. Eight teams took part, wrestling each other in a swimming pool filled with lukewarm gravy!

FURNITURE RACE

Couches, chairs, toilets, baby cribs, trash cans, and even coffins are fixed to skis or snowboards and driven at breakneck speed down a snow-covered mountain in the annual Big Mountain Furniture Race. Held every April since 1970, the event at Whitefish, Montana, marks the end of the skiing season. As well as appearance and speed, points are also awarded for accuracy, as there is a target at the end of the run and competitors are scored by how close to it they can stop without actually hitting it.

SCISSORS DANCE

This competitor at a national scissors dance contest in Lima, Peru, has livened up his act by dancing with two crates attached to hooks pierced through his skin. Other dancers perform with nails hammered into their tongue or metal wires driven through their cheeks in a true test of courage and agility. Contestants perform each dance to the accompaniment of a pair of scissors, made from two 10-in (25-cm) pieces of metal.

BURNING WHEELS

On Easter Sunday night throughout Germany, giant oak wheels—7 ft (2.1 m) in diameter and weighing 800 lb (363 kg)—are stuffed with straw, set alight, and rolled down hillsides into the valleys below. It is believed to be a good omen if the wheels are still burning when they reach the valley.

BUN SNATCH

At the Cheung Chau Bun Festival in Hong Kong, China, contestants climb a 33-ft (10-m) tower stacked with plastic buns and try to grab as many as possible in three minutes. Local belief says that the buns make sure there will be a smooth sailing and a good catch for fishing boats.

POKER RUN

Thousands of motorbike enthusiasts take part in the annual Key West Poker Run, held in Florida every September. The riders collect their playing cards at five stops between Miami and Key West before playing their hand at the final destination.

BURRY MAN

Every August, a resident of Queensferry, Scotland, dressed in white flannels and covered from head to toe with the Velcro-like burrs of the burdock plant, parades 7 mi (11 km) through the town. During the journey he drinks whisky through a straw. The Burry Man is believed to date back to a shipwreck victim who, having no clothes, dressed himself in burrs.

SHOVEL RACE

The World Snow Shovel Racing Championships were staged at Angelfire, New Mexico, for 30 years until they were cancelled in 2005 on safety grounds. Competitors sat on a snow shovel and sped for 1,000 ft (305 m) down a snow-covered mountain at speeds that exceeded 75 mph (120 km/h).

COWBOY CONVENTION

For more than 20 years, cowboys from all over the U.S.A. and abroad have assembled in Elko, Nevada, each January to read poems and tell stories as part of the National Cowboy Poetry Gathering.

CARCASS CONTEST

In the Central Asian sport of *buzkashi*, two teams of horsemen compete to grab a livestock carcass and carry it into their opponent's circle to score points.

RAIN PRAYERS

For the Tohetohe festival in Nagasaki, Japan, people wearing conical bamboo hats and straw raincoats visit dozens of homes where residents promptly drench them with water! The festival is held each January to pray for rain during the rice-planting season.

FIRE ANT FESTIVAL

The October Fire Ant Festival, at Marshall, Texas, is a celebration of all things related to the humble fire ant—including a parade where people dress up as the insects.

DONKEY CLIMB

Runners and donkeys team up for the most arduous pack-burro race in the world, run over a rocky 29-mi (47-km) course at Fairplay, Colorado, with a climb of 3,000 ft (915 m). Each donkey must carry a miner's pack containing a pick, a shovel, and a gold pan, plus any rocks required to achieve a total weight of at least 33 lb (15 kg). A 15-ft (4.5-m) rope connects each runner and donkey.

HAMMER BLOW

Participants in Portugal's So Joo Festival express their attraction to members of the opposite sex by hitting them over the head with a large plastic hammer!

SKUNKFEST

North Ridgeville, Ohio, is home to an annual Skunk Festival that features pet skunk beauty and costume contests.

CHAINSAW CARVING

A sculptor wielding a chainsaw carves a bald eagle at the annual Woodsmen's Field Days festival in New York State. The chainsaw carvers are given 45 minutes to create a sculpture, at the end of which the artworks go to auction. The winner is the sculpture that attracts the highest bid.

EXPLODING ANVILS

Steel anvils are blasted up to 400 ft (120 m) through the air at Laurel, Mississippi, every April during the National Anvil Shooting Contest. Each anvil must weigh at least 100 lb (45 kg) and no more than 2 lb (1 kg) of explosives can be used to blow them up. The contest has its origins in the American Civil War when Yankee troops raided the region, blowing up anvils to destroy weapon-making facilities.

SHEEP MARCH

Bringing traffic to a standstill once a year, farmers lead some 700 sheep through the center of the Spanish capital, Madrid. The November sheep march is designed to protect Spain's 78,000 mi (125,500 km) of paths that are used for the seasonal movement of livestock.

HAIRY CONTEST

Staged at Fairbanks, Alaska, in July, the Hairy Chest, Hairy Legs, and Beard Contest sets out to find the hairiest men in the U.S.A.

CAT LAUNCH

At the annual Flying Cat Ceremony in Verviers, Belgium, a toy cat attached to a small balloon is launched from the tower of the Church of St. Remacle. The ceremony is supposedly based on fact—in 1641 an apothecary conducted an experiment in aerodynamics by launching a live cat attached to inflated pigs' bladders from the same tower. The cat is said to have landed on its feet and run off unharmed.

MOSQUITO CALLING

The Great Texas Mosquito Festival at Clute features a mosquito-calling contest, where people are judged by their interpretations of a mosquito call, and a mosquito legs contest for the men and women with the skinniest legs. The festival is presided over by Willie Man-Chew, a 25 ft (7.6 m) mosquito in cowboy hat and boots.

MISS FATTY

A Russian youth-oriented newspaper organizes an annual beauty contest with a difference. At the Miss Fatty contest in Moscow, large ladies try to impress with their skills at such disciplines as skipping.

WORM RACE

At Banner Elk, North Carolina, each October woolly worms (a variety of furry caterpillar) crawl up a piece of string for a first prize of $1,000. The race derives from the belief that we can forecast the weather depending on the worm's ability to climb the string.

MAKING A SPLASH

In the National Cannonball Championships at Toronto, Ontario, Canada, heavyweight divers leap feet-first from a 16½-ft (5-m) tower into a swimming pool with the goal of making as big a splash as possible. Burly men plummet into the pool in a variety of costumes—including Michael Jackson, a Viking, and Princess Leia from *Star Wars*. Competitors are judged on splash, flair, and the ability to tuck.

WATER BATTLE

To cleanse the community in readiness for the Buddhist New Year, each April, around 100,000 residents of Chiang Mai, Thailand, soak each other with water pistols in a giant battle as part of the Songkran Festival.

BETTY PICNIC

An annual Betty Picnic takes place at Grants Pass, Oregon, in June to celebrate people all over the world who are called Betty or who display Betty-like characteristics!

BATHTUB REGATTA

At the International Regatta of Bathtubs—held in August on the River Meuse at Dinant, Belgium—each craft must have at least one bathtub as part of its design.

MAGIC TOUCH

In the depths of the Japanese winter, a man wearing nothing but a cotton loincloth wanders through the streets of Inazawa City, while those who try to touch him are doused by "guards" with icy water. Since 767 BC, the Naked Man has been making the journey to a local shrine, supposedly absorbing all the evil and bad luck of the people who touch him. So, every January, at a festival called Hadaka Matsuri, some 10,000 men, equally scantily clad, jostle to touch the naked man as he makes his way through the city.

CARDBOARD SLEDGES

The annual Colorado Cardboard Classic features sleds made from cardboard and glue. The 2007 event attracted 75 teams and sleds in all different shapes.

FLYING PUMPKINS

At the Punkin' Chunkin' Championship staged at Nassau, Delaware, each November, enthusiasts build catapults and mini cannons to launch their pumpkins as far as possible into the sky.

TYPEWRITER TOSS

At the annual Typewriter Toss held each April in Springfield, Missouri, contestants stand on an elevated platform and hurl their old typewriters from a height of 50 ft (15 m) at a target on the tarmac below.

FIRECRACKER TRAIL

On the last day of Chinese New Year in 2007, festival organizers in Tainan, Taiwan, lit a string of firecrackers over 8 mi (13 km) long!

SUICIDE RACE

The Suicide Race at Omak, Washington, is probably the most dangerous horse race in the world. Riders career down the steep, 33-degree Suicide Hill at breakneck speed and into the Okanogan River.

RECKLESS ROCKETS

The Yenshui Beehive Rockets Festival in Taiwan is so dangerous that spectators wear protective clothing and crash helmets. Even so, each year, dozens of people suffer eye injuries and burns as thousands of small rockets are fired into the air and explode in a cloud of sparks and flames. The spectacular fireworks display is supposed to scare away evil spirits for the start of the Chinese New Year.

AMAZONIAN MAN

Dodging pirates, piranhas, whirlpools, sharks, and crocodiles, Martin Strel swam the mighty Amazon River in just 66 days.

On April 7, 2007, Martin, a 53-year-old from Slovenia, completed his colossal 3,274-mi (5,268-km) swim. From the Amazon's near-source in dense jungle around Atalaya in Peru across the vast width of Brazil to Bélem on the Atlantic coast, he swam a jaw-dropping average 50 mi (80 km), 10 hours a day, emerging from the water on the final afternoon exhausted and delirious, with blood pressure at near heart attack levels. He staggered to the ambulance still wearing the wet suit that had protected him from the snakes, spiders, and carnivorous fish that had chewed at his body during his remarkable adventure.

Throughout the mammoth journey, support crews in a boat beside him had tipped vast bucketloads of pig and chicken blood into the water in an attempt to lure the predators away. To work, the blood had to be old and the stench was revolting. The theory wasn't always successful—Martin was once pulled from the water yelling in agony, as a piranha gnawed into his leg. Other obstacles were women wielding machetes, murderous drug smugglers, and almost constant diarrhea (which had to be released into the said wetsuit and attracted more pests, including parasitic fish). But Strel was happy to add the Amazon to his list of conquests, and even happier to be on dry land!

Martin wore a pillowcase mask to help protect against sunburn.

Martin's incredible journey was the equivalent of swimming some 105,500 lengths of a 50-m (165-ft) pool.

Martin starts his swim weighing 253 lb (115 kg).

Start

Grease is liberally applied at the beginning of the swim.

Martin receives extra oxygen at the end of a particularly hard day's swim.

Many of the perils faced by Martin were hidden in the murky water.

River Racer

Martin Strel taught himself to swim when he was six years old. Since then he's set the pace for distance swimming.

Danube River, June 25–August 23, 2000 First person to swim the river from source to estuary—1,867 mi (3,004 km)—passing through ten European countries in 58 days.

Danube River, July 2001 First to swim 313 mi (504 km) non-stop in 84 hours 10 minutes, the furthest distance ever swum without rest.

Mississippi River, July 4–September 9, 2002 Swam the whole length of the river—2,360 mi (3,797 km)—in 68 days, breaking his own previous record.

Paraná River, Argentina, November 15–December 8, 2003 Swam from the Iguazu Falls to the center of Buenos Aires (1,200 mi/1,930 km).

Yangtze River, June 10–July 30, 2004 Beat his achievements along the Mississippi by swimming 2,488 mi (4,003 km) of the longest Chinese river in 50 days.

Ripley's ask

How do you prepare for a swim? I train two times a day for three to five hours, in the pool or in the sea or lakes. I do this at least 400 times. I also do cross-country skiing, hiking, and gymnastics. During the swim, I eat lots of soup, pasta, and carbohydrates, and drink at least 10 liters of fluid a day—water, one cup of beer, and maybe a bottle of wine!

Why was the Amazon the most difficult river you have swum yet? The Amazon was recently confirmed as the longest river in the world, longer than the Nile. It is very special. Every hour of every day, there was one question: how to stay alive, just for that day. The water is muddy and you can't see anything, none of the dangers.

How did you stay alive? In my team, on a boat alongside me, I had two armed guards with Kalashnikovs [assault rifles] in case the pirates attacked. And they had buckets of blood and flesh ready to throw in the water to distract the piranhas. They had to be ready in seconds. If they had fallen asleep I would have died.

And what kept you going mentally? I knew I had to swim around 12 hours a day and cover 50 miles—it didn't matter if I was tired or sick. So I would talk to myself. I would go into a kind of trance, and sometimes even hallucinate. I had to be stronger than the Amazon.

What will you do next? I need half a year to recover—I will swim just 45 minutes a day. But then comes the next challenge. I won't swim the Nile—it's just a creek compared to the Amazon—but maybe a lake or sea.

Martin says that he swims "for peace, friendship, and clean water," and "to raise awareness of global warming."

Start: **Atalaya** February 1, 2007

Finish: **Bélem** April 7, 2007

PERU

BRAZIL

Not all of the creatures that Martin encountered were bad for his health!

Exhausted but triumphant, and 36 lb (16 kg) lighter, at the end of the swim.

Finish

bull shark

parasitic fish

piranha

whirlpool

pirates

smugglers

RUNS IN FAMILY

Thirteen sons and daughters of Janet Weisse of Oshkosh, Wisconsin—aged between 33 and 54—took part in the 2007 Fox Cities Marathon at Appleton. All 13 completed the course.

SPEEDY SOFA

A gardener from London, England, hit speeds of 92 mph (148 km/h) in May 2007—driving a sofa! Marek Turowski demonstrated the go-faster furniture at an airfield in Leicestershire. The rear-engined, street legal, high-speed sofa was built by Edd China, who has also designed an 87 mph (140 km/h) office desk.

MARATHON EFFORT

Richard Takata of Toronto, Ontario, Canada, ran a marathon on seven different continents in just under 30 days in 2007. He took part in marathons in New Zealand, U.S.A., Egypt, Spain, Antarctica, Argentina, and Cyprus. Before his first race he had more than a foot of hair cut off that had taken him four years to grow.

WATERFALL PLUNGE

Tyler Bradt, 21, of Missoula, Montana, successfully paddled his kayak over a thunderous 107-ft (33-m) waterfall in September 2007. He made the daring drop at the Alexandra Falls on the Hay River in Canada's Northwest Territories—and landed at the bottom without flipping, even though part of the cockpit of his kayak exploded on impact.

CLIMBING FANATIC

Cheered on by 200 supporters, an Indian man scaled a 2,100-ft (640-m) hill 101 times in the space of 20 hours in August 2007. Bank employee Girish Kulkarni from Pune has been practicing running up hills for five years.

MOUNTAIN DASH

Austria's Marcus Stoeckl, aged 33, reached a speed of 130.7 mph (210 km/h) while traveling down a snow-covered mountain in Chile—on a mountain bike—in September 2007. His icy dash made him the fastest man on two wheels without an engine.

NONSTOP RIDE

George Hood, of Aurora, Illinois, rode a stationary bike nonstop for nearly five days in 2007. He finally stopped pedaling at 111 hours 11 minutes 11 seconds because the time was easy to remember. He said that he started having hallucinations about eating donuts toward the end of his multi-marathon ride.

SUBWAY SPRINT

Armed only with beef jerky and water, college friends Don Badaczewski and Matt Green rode the entire New York subway system nonstop in just over 24 hours in August 2006. They set off from Queens and finished in the Bronx after passing through all 468 stations on the city's 26 lines... with no bathroom breaks. Don had the idea for the underground adventure after reading about riding the subway on the Internet.

EPIC ADVENTURE

Using only human power, Colin Angus of Vancouver Island, British Columbia, Canada, circumnavigated the world in 720 days between 2004 and 2006. Starting and finishing in Vancouver, he cycled, skied, canoed, walked, and rowed through 17 countries, going through around 4,000 chocolate bars, 550 lb (250 kg) of freeze-dried foods, and 72 bicycle inner tubes. He hiked 3,125 mi (5,000 km) across Siberia, was blown 375 miles (600 km) off course while traversing the treacherous Bering Strait and, together with his fiancée Julie Wafaei, rowed for five months across the Atlantic Ocean.

ISLAND SWIM

Skip Storch from New York City spent nearly a day and a half in the water swimming around Manhattan Island in August 2007. He eventually completed three laps of the island in just under 33 hours. Once out of New York's Hudson River, Storch was taken to hospital to be treated for hypothermia.

WORLD TOUR

From 2001 to 2005, Alastair Humphreys of Yorkshire, England, peddled the world on his bike, riding 45,000 mi (72,420 km) through 60 countries on five continents.

COAST TO COAST

New Yorker Alexander Roy drove the 2,794 mi (4,496 km) from New York City to Los Angeles in October 2006 in just 31 hours 4 minutes. He averaged 90 mph (145 km/h) in his BMW M5, occasionally hitting top speeds of 150 mph (240 km/h).

UNICYCLE MARATHON

Sam Wakeling, a 22-year-old student at Aberystwyth University in Wales, traveled 282 mi (455 km) on a unicycle in a single day in September 2007. The computer science undergraduate was so at home riding his customized unicycle, with 36-in (90-cm) wheels around the university's running track that he covered the first 105 mi (170 km) without dismounting. He eventually completed 1,141 laps at an average speed of nearly 13 mph (21 km/h). In 2005, he had ridden a one-wheeler from the most southwesterly point of England (Land's End) to the northeastern tip of Scotland (John O'Groats)—a distance of 874 mi (1,406 km).

Tuk to the Road

Two British women drove a little pink tuk-tuk (a three-wheeled motorized taxi, popular in Thailand) 12,000 mi (19,000 km) through 12 countries from Thailand to England in 2006. Antonia Bolingbroke-Kent and Jo Huxster, both 27, took three months to complete the journey in their tuk-tuk.

Raising money for charity, they traveled through Thailand, Laos, China, Kazakhstan, Russia, Ukraine, Poland, the Czech Republic, Germany, Belgium, and France before finally reaching England. En route they passed such sights as the Great Wall of China and the Gobi Desert.

Although they had to repair two snapped accelerator cables and a failed suspension, the three-wheeler, with a top speed of 70 mph (115 km/h), stood up well to the test and averaged 150 mi (240 km) a day.

Huxster had thought up the idea for the adventure four years earlier during a visit to Thailand. "I was just driving around Bangkok with two friends, and the tuk-tuk driver let me sit in the front to pretend I was driving. I thought, 'One day I will drive one of these back to England.' And that's how it happened."

"We stopped at a salt lake in Xinjiang, northwest China, for a few hours of relaxation—the salty water making us look like this!"

Wandering sheep were just one of the problems the women had to deal with on their drive across Asia.

Antonia (left) and Jo back in England with their trusty tuk-tuk which they named Ting Tong.

MOSHI MOSHI

Enter the Vault

SUPERBABY

In 1950, strong and supple baby Philip Dellagrotti of Berwick, Pennsylvania, could swing impressively on his father's hands and hold himself out horizontally!

ANTONIO

Inflates a balloon with his ears

EXTRAORDINARY EARS

Cuban Antonio Galindo performed with the Ringling Circus in 1931—his specialty was using his ears to blow out candles and inflate balloons.

◄ MUSICAL MAYHEM ►

F.G. Holt of Nashville, Arkansas, used to demonstrate his ability to control every facial muscle by attaching bells to his eyebrows and playing some well-known tunes. And H.C. Harris, of Jackson, Mississippi, could play the harmonica and whistle at the same time!

◀ TOUGH TEETH

Joe Ponder of Love Valley, North Carolina, was a well-known strongman who performed lifts using his teeth. Here he is seen lifting a 500-lb (230-kg) mule with his champion choppers.

YOUNG AT HEART

In 1934, A.T. Brown of Grand Junction, Colorado, could slide head-first down 40-ft (12-m) telegraph poles at the grand old age of 80!

PICK-UP KING

In the 1930s, Julius Schuster of Jeannette, Pennsylvania, could pick up ten billiard balls in one hand, from a flat surface and without the aid of his other hand.

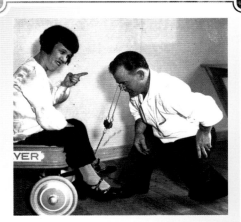

THE EYES HAVE IT

Performing at Ripley's Chicago Odditorium in 1933, Harry McGregor of Philadelphia, Pennsylvania, could pull his wife Lillian around in a wagon—a load of 150 lb (68 kg)—with his eyelids!

PLAYING PIGGYBACK

Jack Trimbledon (bottom) led a novelty orchestra in the 1930s and 1940s. Here, two bandmates play while riding piggyback on Jack's back.

Eurasian Trek

In September 2007, Australian Tim Cope completed a 3½-year, 6,200-mi (10,000-km), solo trek across some of the harshest terrain on the planet, from Mongolia to Hungary, following in the footsteps of the 13th-century Mongolian warlord Genghis Khan.

En route he endured temperatures ranging from –54°F (–52°C) to 130°F (54°C), had his horses and his dog stolen, and survived a night surrounded by howling wolves hungry for their next meal.

The inspiration for this epic journey was a desire to understand what life is like for the nomadic people who populate the steppes of Asia and Central Europe. When Tim from Gippsland, Victoria, set off in June 2004, he expected his journey to take 18 months,

but unforeseen delays, including extreme weather, long border hold-ups, and the death of his father, meant that Tim's epic journey took much longer.

Throughout the trek, Tim traveled with three horses—one to carry him and two to carry food and supplies—even though at the start he could barely ride a horse. He needed 13 horses in total to complete his marathon adventure, and in Kazakhstan he also used a camel to combat the intense heat. At other times he had to ride headlong into fierce blizzards, guided only by a compass.

The animals were his lifeline, so he was devastated when just five days into his travels, two of his horses were stolen in the dead of night. With the help of a Mongolian herdsman, they were returned the next day and Tim quickly came to appreciate the value of striking up friendships on the

steppes. Around 160 families welcomed the stranger into their homes. "They were the real heroes of my journey," he said.

In Kazakhstan, Tim kept predatory wolves at bay by throwing firecrackers—a tip he picked up from the local people. Describing his fear of these animals, he said: "When you hear that howl alone at night in the forest, it's one of the most frightening sounds you'll ever hear."

On eventually reaching his destination, the Hungarian town of Opusztaszer on the river Danube, he admitted: "Sometimes I didn't think I would ever arrive." However, his joy at achieving his goal was tempered by having to let the animals go. "I'm feeling a bit panicky," he said, "because I can't imagine saying goodbye to the horses. A lot has happened in my life during this journey."

Tim with Tigon, which means "hawk" in Kazakh, in the Carpathian Mountains.

Pausing in the Harhiraa Mountains of western Mongolia in September 2004.

Tim Cope's faithful companion on his travels was Tigon, a black Kazakh hunting dog given to him by villagers in Kazakhstan. After Tigon was snatched by rustlers, a villager found the dog nearly frozen to death, locked inside an ice-filled mine shaft. He nursed Tigon back to health by putting him in a hot sauna and feeding him a diet of raw eggs and vodka. Nevertheless, it was three weeks before Tigon was fit enough to resume the journey.

Tim and his leading horse, Taskonir, taking a dip in the Black Sea in the Ukraine.

In Kazakhstan with his three horses, Tim heads into his first winter of the trip.

Ripley's ask

How did you plan for the journey? The majority of the planning was done by reading and getting help from the Long Riders' Guild, who are a group of experienced equestrian explorers who thought my journey was historically important. I knew that I would need at least three horses—one for equipment, one for grain, and one for myself. Looking after them was also important, so I met with an equine vet who was always ready to help me, even via satellite phone when I was in the saddle. I also trained in Australia with some packhorse tour leaders.

What was the hardest part of the journey? There were many hard parts. The winter of 2004–05 when I was stuck in winter storms on the betpak dala ("starving steppe") was particularly bad. My horse developed an abscess, my tent ripped, my sleeping bag froze, and the only place we found for shelter was with some alcoholics in a gold-mining village, who served up boiled street pigeon for Christmas lunch. I was stuck there for almost three months. The temperature that year in Kazakhstan dropped as low as –54°F (–52°C).

What inspired you to carry on? Whenever it was really hard, I only had to think about the nomads. They had to deal with these problems and hardships all their lives. I was inspired by their strength to carry on.

What kind of things did you eat? I drank fermented mares' milk daily, and carried dried mutton with me called "borts." This dried meat is so compact that Mongolians say you can carry a whole sheep in your pocket! The first sight of a camel, horse, or lamb's head on the table was a bit of a shock!

What kind of places did you sleep in? I mostly slept in my own tent, family yurt tents, or village homes that ranged from underground mud huts to large mudbrick and wooden homes.

What was the most vital piece of equipment you took with you? I would have to say my pen and diary! I love writing and getting all my thoughts, feelings, and impressions down.

BAT MAN

A British climber has discovered a new method of tackling tough cliff faces—he hangs upside down like a bat for two minutes while more than 100 ft (30 m) up in the air. Steve McClure from Yorkshire practices the "bat hang" to shake fresh blood back into his arms, thereby ridding them of the crippling lactic acid that builds up during climbs. He created the technique to conquer the treacherous overhang on the 300-ft (90-m) limestone cliff at Malham Cove—one of England's hardest climbs—and after three years and dozens of attempts, "Bat Man" finally reached the top in 2007.

SOLO CROSSING

Michael Perham of Hertfordshire, England, sailed solo across the Atlantic Ocean when he was just 14 years old. The schoolboy set off from Gibraltar in his 28-ft (8.5-m) yacht *Cheeky Monkey* on November 18, 2006, and arrived six and a half weeks later in Antigua in the West Indies on January 3, 2007. During the 3,500-mi (5,635-km) voyage, he had to contend with sharks, technical problems, and ferocious storms.

NAKED AMBITION

In 2007, a couple from Bedfordshire, England, climbed 15 Scottish mountains, each more than 3,000 ft (915 m) in height—naked. The naturists, known only as Stuart and Karla, commemorated each climb with a nude photo of themselves on the summit. There are 284 peaks in Scotland over 3,000 ft—known as the Munros—and Stuart and Karla intend to climb every one.

MULTIPLE JUMPS

In 2006, Jay Stokes of Yuma, Arizona, celebrated his 50th birthday by jumping out of an airplane—640 times. Despite injuring a muscle around the 200th leap, he completed the jumps in 24 hours—averaging out at one jump every 2 minutes 15 seconds.

BLIND ACE

Despite being blinded by diabetes more than 25 years ago, golfer Sheila Drummond hit a hole-in-one at Mahoning Valley Country Club, Lehighton, Pennsylvania, in 2007. The odds of an amateur golfer getting a hole-in-one are 1 in 12,750—for a blind amateur golfer it must be a shot in a million.

CYCLING PHENOMENON

Born with a deformed right leg, Emmanuel Ofosu Yeboah peddled his bike 379 mi (610 km) across Ghana in 2001 using only his left foot in order to challenge stereotypes about the disabled people of his country.

TIGHTROPE WALKER

It took Abudusataer Dujiabudula of China only 11 minutes 22 seconds to walk a half-mile (800-m) tightrope across the Han River in Seoul, South Korea.

JASON'S JOURNEY

British adventurer Jason Lewis completed a 46,000-mi (74,000-km), 13-year journey around the world. Between 1994 and 2007 he walked, cycled, roller-bladed, kayaked, swam, and pedaled across five continents, two oceans, and one sea. En route he was chased by a saltwater crocodile in Australia, questioned as a spy in North Africa, and suffered two fractured legs after being hit by a car in Colorado as he roller-bladed across the U.S.A. To help pay for his adventure, he worked as a cattle drover in North America and in a funeral parlor in Australia.

CROC BAIT

Wearing only a swimming costume, Kerry Shaw was secured inside a reinforced steel cage and plunged into a pool full of 14-ft-long (4-m) crocodiles. She was lowered by crane into position at a wildlife park in Oudtshoom, South Africa, in 2007, and warned that under no circumstances should she reach through the bars!

EXTRA TIME

Two soccer teams at Exeter, Ontario, Canada, played against one another continuously for 30 hours 30 minutes in May 2007. The final score was Stratford Enterprise 138, Exeter Fury 105. Players' injuries included a dislocated shoulder and a broken foot.

HOT WORK

Queensland shearers Dave Grant and Laurie Bateman shaved 709 Merino sheep in just eight hours at Hughenden, Australia, in October 2007. The pair trained for 12 months to build up the stamina necessary for the challenge, during which their bodies perspired up to 135 fl oz (4 l) of sweat every two hours.

UNDERWATER SURVIVOR

Hungarian escape artist David Merlini spent 10 minutes 17 seconds chained and handcuffed underwater in 2007, without air. His hands were tied by five sets of police handcuffs and he was bound by 60 lb (27 kg) of chains before being padlocked in a metal cage and lowered into a transparent tank of water in Hollywood, California.

CAN DO!

In June 2007, three men from Queensland, Australia, sailed nearly 50 mi (80 km) down the Brisbane River in a boat made from beer cans.

TIRE CRAFT

Cheng Yanhua traveled more than 1,500 mi (2,400 km) down China's Yangtze River in 2007—on a tire inner tube. Using two small bamboo paddles, and with a basin in the tire for his feet, he took 43 days to get from his home in Jinzhou City to Shanghai.

BIKING MARATHON

In a three-month journey in 2007, British actor Ewan McGregor and his friend Charley Boorman rode their motorcycles 15,000 mi (24,000 km) from the most northerly point of Scotland to the southern tip of South Africa. Three years earlier, they rode their bikes from London, England, to New York via central Europe and Asia—20,000 mi (32,000 km).

SLOW ROUTE

Choosing not to fly for environmental reasons, Barbara Haddrill spent six months traveling by bus, train, and cargo ship on a 9,770-mi (15,725-km) journey from Powys, Wales, to attend her best friend's wedding in Brisbane, Australia.

MARATHON SWIM

In September 2007, Firas al Mualla swam 68 mi (110 km) nonstop across the Mediterranean Sea in 42 hours from Cyprus to his native Syria.

ROUND THE WORLD

Jamaican-born Barrington Irving of Miami, Florida, flew solo around the world in 2007—at just 23 years of age. His epic flight in a single-engine plane took three months, and on the way he encountered snowstorms, sandstorms, thunderstorms, monsoons, 100-mph (160-km/h) winds, and freezing fog. He named his plane "Inspiration" because, he said, "that's what I wanted my historic venture to be for young people."

BUMPY RIDE

Two British students travelled a distance of 9,500-mi (15,300-km) through 14 countries, three mountain ranges, and two deserts—in a car designed 60 years ago. George Vlasto and Max Benitz drove from the University of Calcutta, India, to London, England, in an Ambassador car that was held together by two rolls of duct tape.

HIGH NOTES

Six British and U.S. musicians played a rock concert at a height of 18,540 ft (5,650 m) on Mount Everest in October 2007. The six were Mike Peters of The Alarm, Slim Jim Phantom of the Stray Cats, Cy Curnin and Jamie West-Oram of the Fixx, and Glenn Tilbrook and Nick Harper of Squeeze.

UNICYCLE TEAM

A dozen cyclists rode 560 mi (900 km) across New Zealand's South Island in 15 days in 2007—on unicycles.

DESERT RUN

Charlie Engle (U.S.A.), Ray Zahab (Canada), and Kevin Lin (Taiwan) ran the equivalent of two marathons a day for 111 days to cross the entire 4,000-mi (6,440-km) Sahara Desert on foot in 2007. They ran through six countries—Senegal, Mauritania, Mali, Niger, Libya, and Egypt—and had to cope with temperatures over 100°F (38°C) by day, but sometimes below freezing at night.

HISTORICAL VOYAGE

Taking the same route as his ancestor Christopher Columbus had 508 years earlier, Scottish stockbroker Leven Brown rowed single-handed across the Atlantic from Cadiz, Spain, to the port of Scarborough in Trinidad and Tobago. Rowing up to 18 hours each day, Brown completed the 4,278-mi (6,885-km) voyage in five months. Apart from storms, his biggest problem came from whales that wanted to use his 23-ft (7-m) boat as a scratching post!

WEARY LEGS

In 2007, Greg Kolodziejzyk of Calgary, Alberta, Canada, traveled 107 mi (172 km) by pedal boat in 24 hours around the city's Glenmore Reservoir.

> "Two days into the nine-month journey, 350 mi (560 km) from civilization, on the North Slope Brooks Mountain Range, Alaska."

> "No water, 6 mi (9.5 km) to next water source, 100°F (38°C) heat."

AMERICAN ODYSSEY

Starting in May 2007, Quinn Baumberger of Stevens Point, Wisconsin, cycled for nine months and traveled more than 19,000 mi (30,600 km) the length of the Americas from Deadhorse, Alaska, to Ushuaia, Argentina. Along the way, he fixed 50 flat tires, was robbed twice, and sprained his ankle in Nicaragua, which put him out of action for two weeks. He replaced his old, worn shirts with those he found on the road.

TRACTOR TREK

Tractor fan Wolfgang Mueller drove his 44-year-old tractor 700 mi (1,130 km) from Stuttgart, Germany, to Coventry, England, in 2007. He towed a caravan through Luxembourg and France, boarded a ferry at Calais, and drove the tractor sedately through English country lanes. He wanted to visit the place where his beloved Massey Ferguson MF35 had been built—only to find that the factory had been demolished.

CHICKEN WING HUNT

In August 2007, Matt Reynolds led a team of fellow food enthusiasts on a 2,627-mi (4,230-km) trek through New York State in search of the best chicken wings. The Great Chicken Wing Hunt began in Manhattan and ended in Buffalo at the National Wing Festival. Reynolds and his team eventually crowned chef Columbus Grady, of Abigail's Restaurant in Seneca Falls, maker of the best wings in the whole of New York state.

ICY SWIM

In 2004, Lynne Cox of Southern California, completed a 25-minute, 1.2-mi (1.9-km) swim through the polar ice water along the Antarctic shoreline, in water temperatures that would have given most people hypothermia in just five minutes.

DOUBLE FIRST

In July 2006, 15-year-old Jenna Lambert from Kingston, Ontario, Canada, became the first disabled person to swim across Lake Ontario. Jenna has cerebral palsy, and could use only her upper body—not her legs—to swim, but despite strong winds and waves, she completed the 21-mi (34-km) swim in 32 hours. Then, a year later, her 14-year-old sister Natalie became the youngest person to swim the lake when she made a 32½-mi (52-km) crossing from Sackets Harbor, New York, to Kingston in under 24 hours.

SIMPLY BREATHTAKING

In August 2007, German diver Tom Sietas managed to hold his breath underwater for 15 minutes 2 seconds—without surfacing once. He breathed in oxygen from a tank for 20 minutes beforehand to help prepare his body for the feat.

BALLPARK TOUR

Brothers Brigham and Todd Shearon from Windsor, Ontario, Canada, visited all 30 major-league baseball stadiums in 28 days in 2007—a journey of 14,500 mi (23,000 km).

BIKE TRAVELS

Gregory Frazier of Fort Smith, Montana, has ridden around the world on a motorcycle five times—four solo and the fifth, in 2005, with a 63-year-old grandmother of six on the back of the bike. He has traveled more than one million miles (1.6 million km), riding from Alaska to Tierra del Fuego, and Norway to the tip of South Africa. In the course of his adventures, he has been imprisoned, bitten by snakes, run over by bulls, had his bike stolen, and been held up at gunpoint by a Mexican bandit.

TUXEDO TRAVELERS

Doug and Heath modeling their special tuxedos made at a tailor in Bangkok, Thailand.

Posing with people dressed in traditional costume in Yangshuo, China.

Two men completed a five-month, 6,214-mi (10,000-km) trek from Hong Kong to London—dressed the entire way in tuxedos.

Briton Heath Buck and American Doug Campbell dreamed up their bizarre charity adventure in a Hong Kong bar in 2005 despite having known each other for only a few days. Before setting off on April Fool's Day 2007, the pair—who promoted themselves as "two fools, one adventure, no idea"—trashed their ordinary clothes and donned the tuxedos, which had been specially made for them in Bangkok, Thailand, from extra-resilient fabric and fitted with hidden pockets for valuables.

Apart from sleeping and showering, they wore their dinner dress every step of the way on a journey that took them through remote regions of China, Vietnam, Tibet, Nepal, India, Pakistan, and Kyrgyzstan—among other places.

In Vietnam, they plowed rice paddies, weeded corn crops, and built a wall—still wearing their black suits and bow ties. "It was quite a surreal experience," admitted Campbell. "At the end we brought a few of the local tribal women to tears when we donated fertilizer for the year's crop. In return they made us honorary tribe members."

The pair also went wrestling in India and had to deal with temperatures of over 120°F (50°C), but the tuxedos survived to the finish. Not surprisingly, the two men got some odd looks along the way. "Everyone asked if they could take a picture of us," said Buck. "They often asked us if we were getting married!"

Heath gives a rickshaw rider a much needed break in Kathmandu.

Doug with a Tibetan man while in Shangri La in China's Yunnan Province.

Doug and a member of the Dao Hill Tribe in Vietnam.

The guys stayed with the Dao Hill Tribe and helped them with buffalo plowing.

The two men were made honorary members of the tribe on their departure.

Heath hosted an English tea party at Everest Base camp.

Heath jumping the Taj Mahal in India.

While staying in freezing conditions at an altitude of 9,800 ft (3,000 m) in Kyrgyzstan, Heath and Doug's tuxedos provided much-needed warmth.

Wearing Kyrgyzstani robes gave their tuxedos a local feel in Kyrgyzstan.

Approaching England's famous white cliffs of Dover at the end of their journey.

Ripley's ask

"

How did you meet? DOUG: We met randomly in Hong Kong at a street party. HEATH: We exchanged e-mails after making a pact to save the world! Doug was committed to not being outdone by me, whatever my imagination could come up with.

Why decide to travel in tuxedos? DOUG: Heath came up with the tuxedo idea. I said I'd join only if we could add a charitable angle—so we weren't just being idiots, but idiots on a quest! And so the planning began… .

Was there a point at which you really wished you weren't wearing tuxedos? DOUG: India, India, India!! It was so hot and also the early part of the monsoon season so very humid and wet. I also had giardia [a parasite in the small intestine] and was pretty upset about the whole situation. We were close to calling the trip off, but settled our differences and Heath's classic English resolve pulled us through!

How did people react to you? DOUG: As far as the tuxedos went—people thought we were going to a marriage, or that we were Western businessmen, professional snooker players, religious missionaries, jazz musicians, magicians, or otherwise just complete nut-jobs!

What was your biggest achievement during the tuxedo challenge? DOUG: Besides successfully completing the mission (a feat many thought we would fail at), I believe we showed our audience that the world is a friendly place. People were often surprised that we survived, but I usually joke that I've felt more scared in downtown L.A. than anywhere along our route! HEATH: I think my biggest achievement was working with T.B. patients at one charity mission, where we were actively joining in with a charity's dedication to save people's lives.

What was the strangest thing you did on your journey wearing a tuxedo?! DOUG: Laughing Therapy in India had to be up there with one of the funniest moments. We found a man in Rishikesh who led us, along with a few other backpackers, into a hilarious session of deep belly laughing exercises! This was meant to calm you and relieve you of external stresses. We certainly had fun so I guess it worked! HEATH: Horseback riding over the mountains in Kyrgyzstan. We added a Kyrgyz robe to our tuxedos, and with robes flowing in the wind, we precariously picked our way through a mountain pass, where when you looked down you realized that one slip and you'd be falling into oblivion.

Do you have any plans for another tuxedo journey? HEATH: We intend to keep on arranging random groups of tuxedo-clad people to turn up and perform acts of charity across the globe! I am also planning another trip, but this time it will be along a superhero theme to help save the world!

"

POLAR TREK ～～～

Explorer Hannah McKeand from Berkshire, England, completed a solo, unsupported 690-mi (1,110-km) trek across Antarctica to the South Pole in less than 40 days in 2006. On skis and dragging a 220-lb (100-kg) sled, she faced temperatures lower than –40°F (–40°C) and winds of more than 70 mph (112 km/h).

GLOBE RUNNER ～～～

A man dubbed the British "Forrest Gump" ran around the world over a period of 5 years 8 months. Robert Garside from the town of Stockport in Cheshire, England, ran more than 35,000 mi (56,000 km) and crossed through 30 countries between 1997 and 2003. On the way he was jailed in China, threatened at gunpoint in Panama, and met his future wife in Venezuela.

PARTY GIRL ～～～

Evelyn Warburton of Berwick, Pennsylvania, rode to her 100th birthday party in September 2007 in a motorcycle sidecar—wearing a black leather jacket and a cool pair of sunglasses.

BLADE RUNNER ～～～

Even though his legs were amputated below the knee when he was 11 months old, South African sprinter Oscar Pistorius races against—and beats—able-bodied athletes. Pistorius can run 400 meters in 46.34 seconds—just three seconds outside Michael Johnson's world record—on carbon-fiber artificial legs that have earned him the nickname of Blade Runner.

VETERAN RUNNER ～～～

Although he never ran a full mile until he was nearly 50, George Etzweiler of State College, Pennsylvania, has been making up for lost time ever since. In June 2007, the active 87-year-old completed the Mount Washington Road Race in New Hampshire—a 7.6-mi (12.2-km) course featuring an uphill climb with a daunting 11.5 percent incline.

VETERAN JUMPER ～～～

In August 2007, an 83-year-old New York skydiver made his 100th jump from an airplane. A veteran of World War II, Leo Dean took up skydiving after he was widowed in 1998. He's now aiming for 200 jumps.

PADDLE POWER ～～～

Margo Pellegrino of Medford Lakes, New Jersey, paddled her kayak some 2,000 mi (3,220 km) along the east coast of the U.S.A. in 2007 from Miami, Florida, to Camden, Maine, covering an average of 40 mi (65 km) a day.

ECHO SKILL ～～～

Daniel Kish of Long Beach, California, is completely blind but can ride a bike using echolocation, just like a bat or a dolphin, to "see" objects with sound.

VERSATILE COOK ～～～

Krishnaveni Mudliar, a housewife from Bhopal, India, can cook nearly 65,000 different recipes. She can prepare recipes from every state in India as well as Italian, Chinese, and Burmese dishes.

AUTOGRAPH FRENZY ～～～

To promote his latest album "West Side," Singaporean pop singer J.J. Lin signed his autograph on 3,052 copies of the album's CD in 2½ hours in Tianjin, China, in July 2007.

KAYAK CROSSING

Two Australian adventurers completed a historic crossing of the Tasman Sea by kayak—less than one year after another Australian, Andrew McAuley, died while attempting the same feat. James Castrission and Justin Jones, both from Sydney, finished the arduous 2,050-mi (3,300-km) journey—known locally as "crossing the ditch"—from Forster, New South Wales, to Ngamotu Beach on New Zealand's North Island in 62 days. They arrived in early January 2008—20 days later than anticipated after strong winds and stormy seas left them floundering in circles halfway through the trip and nearly forced them to turn back. They also had to fend off the unwelcome attention of sharks.

Their voyage had taken four years' intense preparation, including sleep deprivation and isolation training. Afterward, Castrission acknowledged the value of having a companion to lean on. "Some nights when we were out there," he said, "we had each other to hold through the difficult moments."

Although the kayak was designed to combat 40-ft (12-m) waves, crossing the Tasman Sea proved a daunting prospect and sometimes Jones and Castrission had to paddle in shifts for 18 hours a day.

SUMMIT TALKS

A British climber made a cell-phone call from the top of Mount Everest in 2007. Rod Baber was able to make two calls from the 29,029-ft (8,848-m) mountain after China set up a new mobile base station. Even making a short call at such an altitude was hazardous for Baber, as talking into the handset meant removing his oxygen mask.

TWO-DAY MATCH

Brian Jahrsdoerfer and Michel Lavoie played fellow Americans Peter Okpokpo and Warner Tse in a doubles tennis match that lasted 48 hours 15 minutes at Westside Tennis Club, Houston, Texas, in April 2006.

SUPER COACH

Robert Hughes of Fort Worth, Texas, retired in 2005 with 1,333 wins to his name—more than any other high-school basketball coach in U.S history.

WINNING STREAK

The boys' football team at De La Salle High School, Concord, California, had a 12-season, 151-game winning streak from 1992 to 2004.

PUSH-UPS

Roy Berger of Ottawa, Ontario, Canada, completed more than 1,000 fist push-ups in just under 17 minutes in May 2007. He did not even break a sweat until he hit 400.

SNOWMOBILE JUMP

Ross Mercer of Whitehorse, Yukon, Canada, jumped his snowmobile 263½ ft (80.3 m) high at Steamboat Springs, Colorado, in March 2007.

CABLE CAR

In 2007, Liu Suozhu of Korla City, China, drove his pickup truck for 15 minutes along 200 yd (180 m) of parallel steel cables that were stretched more than 60 ft (18 m) in the air between two hills.

HIGH RIDERS

In April 2007, two Chilean men drove a car to an altitude of 21,942 ft (6,688 m). After two failed attempts to reach extreme altitudes, driver Gonzalo Bravo and his spotter Eduardo Canales piloted their modified 1986 Suzuki Samurai to the highest slopes of the Ojos del Salado volcano in Chile's Atacama Desert.

DANCING FOOL

The U.K.'s official state jester, as named by the national charity English Heritage, Peterkin the Fool—alias Peet Cooper—danced a jig for 28 days on a 100-mi (160-km) journey from Bristol to Northampton, England, in July 2006. He was commemorating the 100-mi jig-journey made in 1599 by Will Kemp, a Shakespearean court jester.

SENIOR HERDSMAN

Li Xicai still works as a herdsman in the mountainous Kuangshi village of China, at the age of 107. He has been herding animals all his life and still herds bulls in the mountains every day.

FLOAT ON

Keeping his hands behind his head and his toes above the surface at all times, Andrzej Szopinski-Wisla of Poland floated on water for more than two hours in 2006.

CLUB JUGGLER

Iryna Bilenka of the Ukraine can juggle three clubs for nearly two minutes—while wearing a blindfold!

When conditions were favorable, the intrepid adventurers were able to paddle at speeds of up to 6 mph (10 km/h).

Justin keeping the website account of their epic journey up to date in the kayak's sleeping quarters.

Renaissance man

Decorator Robert Burns has spent more than three years transforming the interior of his modest 1960s house in Brighton, England, into a Renaissance masterpiece. Using art books bought at rummage sales as his inspiration, he has faithfully reproduced the work of 15th-century Italian artists—mostly with emulsion paint from his local hardware store.

Robert has never been to Italy in his life, nor ever attended art school, but the books have enabled the 60-year-old father-of-four to re-create the beauty of Botticelli on his bedroom walls. A nativity scene with a

The façade of Robert's house conceals the treasures within.

trompe l'oeil (trick of the eye) gold frame dominates the dining room, while cameos of the Virgin Mary and other religious scenes are dotted throughout the house.

The hallway and lounge ceiling are adorned in a mass of fluffy clouds and blue sky, while the landing is decorated in an authentic marble effect.

Whereas Michelangelo, Leonardo da Vinci, and their contemporaries used a mixture of pigments and hundreds of egg yolks, Burns has to rely largely on household paint left over from his decorating jobs.

He adds to the Renaissance feel of the house whenever he is bored or between jobs, because it stops him going crazy waiting for the phone to ring.

He has always loved the Renaissance period and says it makes a refreshing change from his regular work. "Decorating can be a bit bland—one of my recent jobs was painting the inside of a factory with 53 liters of magnolia paint."

Ripley's ask

How did you discover your talent for painting? I didn't know I could paint. I just went out and bought some brushes and paints and started painting the walls of our house. I had never painted anything before.

Have you had any formal training? My last art lesson was while I was in primary school.

Why in the Renaissance style? I started buying Renaissance art books at car boot sales and fell in love with Renaissance art and interiors. I have never seen any of these pictures or frescoes as they are in Italy.

Did you originally plan to do only one painting? My first painting in the house was on the upstairs landing. I painted a series of Lunettes over the door frames and it developed from there—I just kept adding to it.

What is your favorite piece of art and what room is it in? I am pleased with my effort in the dining room— 'The Madonna of the Chair' by Raphael and below that 'Virgin and Child' by Antoniazzo Romano.

What reactions have you had to your work? Most people are taken aback as it's not the interior you're expecting when going into a small house; but the reaction has always been favorable.

Robert applying the finishing touches to a Renaissance masterpiece in his home.

When the ovoid is closed, you would never guess that part of this building turns itself inside out.

Inside Out

An art installation in Liverpool, England, allows visitors to see a section of a building turning itself inside out. Called "Turning the Place Over" and designed by Richard Wilson, it consists of an ovoid 26 ft (8 m) in diameter, which has been cut from the façade of a derelict building in the city center and placed on a pivot. Dramatically, the ovoid rotates three-dimensionally like a huge opening and closing window.

The unusual installation seen part way through its rotation.

WEALTHY TIMES

Businesses on Times Square in New York City generate about $55 billion a year in revenue—enough to make the city block the world's 76th largest economy.

PAINTED MOUNTAIN

In 2007, forestry officials in Yunnan, China, hired seven workers to spray-paint parts of Laoshou Mountain green. The barren patch of land had been left an eyesore by years of quarrying, but instead of planting trees, the county government decided to paint the mountainside.

NAME GAME

Citizens in Wisconsin couldn't agree on a name for their small town, so they decided to pull six letters out of a hat and name it whatever those letters spelled. Thus the town of Ixonia was born!

GOOD VIBRATIONS

The Brentwood Baptist Deaf Church in Brentwood, Tennessee, uses speakers under the floor to allow its congregants to "hear" the music through the vibrations that transmit through their feet into their bodies.

MECHANICAL MAN

In Calgary, Alberta, Canada, there is a 27-ft (8.2-m) mechanical man called Spike, made from locomotive and freight car parts. His body is a boiler, his head and ears are gears, his arms and hands are couplers, and he holds a crankshaft in his right hand.

BIG CHEESE

A concrete cheese—6 ft (1.8 m) high and 28 ft (8.5 m) in circumference—sits at Perth, Ontario, Canada, to commemorate the mammoth cheese produced in the town for the 1893 Chicago World's Fair. The real cheese weighed 22,000 lb (9,780 kg) and was made using one day's milk from 10,000 cows. It created such a stir that, in 1943, it was decided to build an exact concrete replica.

PLANE COMFORT

The Woodlyn Park Motel at Waitamo, New Zealand, offers accommodation in an old freight airplane that supplied U.S. troops in Vietnam, a railway carriage, or a range of hobbit houses! The Bristol Freighter plane has been converted into two rooms, and guests are able to sleep in a bed directly under the cockpit.

EXTRA BOUNCE

Pedestrians across the U.S.A. are feeling an extra spring in their step thanks to rubber sidewalks. Rubber panels have been tested in a number of cities—including Santa Monica, California, and Seattle, Washington—to determine whether or not they are a viable alternative to concrete.

BIG FOOT

The Golden Driller statue, dedicated to the oil industry in Tulsa, Oklahoma, stands 76 ft (23 m) tall and has size 393 DD shoes!

MONSTER GRASSHOPPER

The town of Wilkie, Saskatchewan, Canada, is home to an unusual monument—a wooden grasshopper measuring 18 x 6 ft (5.5 x 1.8 m) and weighing 4,000 lb (1,815 kg).

WINE BARRELS

A number of old wine-making barrels have been converted into bedrooms at a hotel in Stavoren, the Netherlands. The 3,830-gal (14,500-l) wooden barrels are large enough to accommodate two single beds, a small living room with TV, and a bathroom with shower and toilet.

REVOLVING HOTEL

Located in Mahallesi, Turkey, is the world's only revolving hotel, giving guests in 24 bedrooms a 360-degree view. Powered by six electric motors in the basement, full rotation of the 2,750-ton building takes between two and 22 hours.

WEIGHTY PROBLEM

The Vatican Library in Rome, Italy, closed for the first time in its 530-year history in 2007 while workers repaired the damage caused by the weight of nearly two million manuscripts.

DANCING HOUSE

Designed by Czech architect Vlado Miluni and Canadian Frank Gehry, the Dancing House in Prague is so-called because it is shaped like Fred Astaire and Ginger Rogers dancing together. The building, which was completed in 1996, acquires its unusual curves from 99 concrete panels, each a different shape and size.

SHOE HOUSE

A house near Branddraai, South Africa, is built in the shape of a giant lace-up shoe. Designed by artist Ron van Zyl in 1990, the shoe house has its entrance in the two-story heel and accommodation in the toe.

ROBOT BANK

Asked to come up with a futuristic design for the Bank of Asia building in Bangkok, Thailand, architect Sumet Jumsai took inspiration from his son's toy robot. The 20-story building is shaped like a giant robot and even has two 20-ft (6-m) lidded "eyes" that serve as windows on the top floor. The eyeballs are made of glass and the lids are metal louvers.

CUBAN PARK

The Jose Marti Park in Ybor City, Florida, is actually owned by Cuba. Named after the Cuban writer and independence leader, the park was purchased by Cuba in 1957.

LUXURY LIFEBOAT

A lifeboat moored in Harlingen, the Netherlands, has been converted into a luxury hotel. The Lilla Marras carried out 105 sea rescues between 1955 and 1979, saving 45 lives, and because it is still seaworthy, guests can pay to be taken out to sea.

VIOLIN HALL

The Chowdiah Memorial Hall in Bangalore, India, was built in 1980 in the shape of a giant violin to honor the master violinist Tirumakudalu Chowdiah.

MOLE MAN

Bruce Tracy, a construction worker, builds secret underground living quarters for himself and other homeless people in Fresno, California.

LEANING STEEPLE

A 15th-century church steeple in Suurhusen, Germany, stands 84 ft (26 m) high and leans at an angle of five degrees—a degree more than Italy's famous Leaning Tower of Pisa.

MIGHTY MUSKIE

The National Freshwater Fishing Hall of Fame Museum in Hayward, Wisconsin, is housed in a building the shape of a huge muskie fish. The monumental muskie is 143 ft (44 m) long and 41 ft (12 m) high.

PORCELAIN PALACE

A newly opened house in Tianjin, China, has more than 400 million pieces of porcelain inlaid everywhere in the architecture. Businessman Zhang Lianzhi spent $65 million decorating the China House with items he has collected over the past two decades, including 16,000 items of ancient chinaware made up of bowls, dishes, figurines, and vases.

GARDEN HIGHWAY
A Polish woman returned from holiday in 2007 to discover that the local council had built a road and a traffic island in her back garden. Alicia Ziemowit complained to Lodz Council, but was told that a change in the law meant officials could use private land for road-building without consent and without paying compensation.

VANISHING LAKE
In May 2007, a 5-acre (2-ha), 100-ft-deep (30-m) lake in Magallanes, Chile, disappeared in less than two weeks.

ELEPHANT ROCK
Located in the Valley of Fire in the Nevada Desert is a huge rock that is called Elephant Rock because it is shaped like an elephant. It was formed around 150 million years ago.

SUNNY OUTLOOK
An Italian Alpine village that never saw any sun in the winter months fixed the problem by installing a giant mirror. Lying at the bottom of a steep valley and surrounded by mountains, Viganella receives no direct sunlight between November and February, but in December 2006 the mirror—a sheet of steel measuring 26 x 16 ft (8 x 5 m)—was erected on a nearby peak to reflect sunlight onto the village square below.

PIGGY BANK
The Canadian town of Coleman, Alberta, boasts the biggest piggy bank in the world. The giant cash-collector has been converted from Ten Ton Toots, an old locomotive that used to pull cars in the town's coal mines.

CAVE DWELLERS
Centuries-old caves in Andalucia, Spain, have been connected to electricity and water supplies and fitted with modern furnishings in order to provide comfortable homes for people today.

BIG STAMP
An aluminum postage stamp measuring 8 x 6 ft (2.4 x 1.8 m) stands in Humboldt, Saskatchewan, Canada. It was built in 1999 in honor of former Canadian Prime Minister John G. Diefenbaker who, as a lawyer, defended many court cases in the town.

TREE BAR
A pub in South Africa is located in the hollow interior of a 6,000-year-old baobab tree. Inside, the tree is so spacious that the bar can hold 50 people and, because the 72-ft-tall (22-m) tree is still growing, so is the pub.

BEAR CODE
Smokey the Bear, the U.S. mascot for forest-fire prevention, has his own postal zip code for fan mail.

PRISON RODEO
The Louisiana State Penitentiary in Angola, which is home to 5,000 inmates, has thousands of acres of farm land, more than 1,500 cattle, a four-year theological seminary, its own radio station, a news magazine, and an annual rodeo.

KETCHUP CAPITAL
Already home to a 170-ft (52-m) ketchup bottle (in the form of a disguised water tower), Collinsville, Illinois, temporarily acquired a sister attraction in July 2007—a ketchup packet 8 x 4 ft (2.4 x 1.2 m), capable of holding around 127 gal (480 l) of ketchup.

SHRINKING SEA
The Aral Sea, located between Kazakhstan and Uzbekistan, has shrunk by 75 per cent during the last four decades as water is diverted for industry and agriculture.

LUXURY WASHROOM
A new public washroom in Chongqing, China, has more than 1,000 toilets, and covers an area of 3,350 sq yd (2,800 sq m). The four-story washroom has an Egyptian façade, gentle piped-in music, and even television. Some of the urinals are molded in unusual shapes—including a crocodile's open mouth!

CAVE VILLAGE
The village of Zhongdong in Guizhou, China, is located within a massive natural cave the size of an aircraft hangar.

NAKED LUNCH
In 2007, a restaurant in Greenville, Maine, offered a free prime rib sandwich to anyone willing to plunge naked into Moosehead Lake. The Black Frog Restaurant called its sandwich the Skinny Dip.

SLEEP CONCIERGE
The Benjamin Hotel in Manhattan is so concerned about its customers enjoying a good night's rest that it has its own sleep concierge. The hotel guarantees that guests will sleep as well as they do at home, or they get a free night's stay.

TREE HOMES

Canadian designer Tom Chudleigh has created a range of eco-friendly homes that can be suspended from trees or rock faces. Free Spirit Spheres are made from wood and coated in fiberglass to make them waterproof. Accessible only by rope bridge, the 11-ft-wide (3.6-m) houses can sleep four people and are fitted with a kitchen that is complete with microwave, refrigerator, and sink.

Among Jason's pencil designs is a sparkling golden arrow on the ceiling.

The stairs lead up from a Victorian parlor, so Jason copied the design of an original Victorian wallpaper pattern in the stairwell—in pencils, of course.

Pencil-Vania

Jason also created a face made of pencils—a futuristic portrait of Jaina aged 88.

A garden scene of flowers and peeping sprites is another of the mosaic's special features.

Inside a San Francisco house, artist Jason Mecier has created a wonderful, colorful mosaic from thousands of pencils. He calls it Pencil-Vania.

When Jason's friend Jaina Davis bought the 100-year-old property on Potrero Hill, San Francisco, in 1997, she invited her artist friends to design the interior. Jason conceived the idea of connecting the styles of the different rooms by a pencil mosaic winding up the staircase, and was commissioned to create just that. As a result, doors, banisters, and walls have all been decorated with brightly colored pencils that have been glued to the surfaces, inserted in specially drilled holes, or suspended from the ceiling.

Jason's amazing mosaic includes a pencil flower garden, pencil Victorian-style wallpaper, and a futuristic pencil portrait of Jaina, aged 88.

Work in progress on one of the stairwell walls.

Ripley's ask

"

How would you describe Pencil-Vania? Pencil-Vania—the "Forest of Pencils"—is a mixed media art installation in the three-story stairwell of the private home of Jaina Davis in San Francisco, California. The installation, which I designed and fitted myself, covers the walls, banisters, ceilings, molding, trim, shelves, and three doors from the first floor, up two landings, and all the way to the top of the third floor. That's 980 square feet plus 20 feet of handrails.

How many pencils are there? According to our calculations, there are 92,626.

How long did it take to create? Five years, from 1997 to 2002.

How much did it cost? $50,000.

Where did all the pencils come from? The bulk of the pencils were purchased from two local reuse centers. Others were ordered from office- and school-supply catalogs, and because the house is located between two schools, Jaina would pick up abandoned pencils on her daily excursions. She also held a garage sale that accepted no money in exchange for goods—only pencils. Sometimes boxes of pencils were even left anonymously on the doorstep.

Is there anything other than pencils in the installation? There are erasers, pencil sharpeners, a renegade pen or two, and a few assorted office supplies—staplers, rulers, compasses, scissors. There's also a huge rubber-band ball on the banister.

What inspired this unusual idea? I visited Grandma Prisbrey's Bottle Village in California as a child and learned folk arts and crafts from my own grandmother. Jaina had always loved unusual homes and dreamed that one day she would live in one of her very own.

What's it like for Jaina living within walls of pencils? She says it smells like the first day of school every day!

"

Pencil-Vania includes shelves made from pencils, many of which are home to a variety of office supplies.

REMOTE HOTEL

Birdsville Hotel and Pub, located in Australia's Simpson Desert, is 900 mi (1,450 km) from the nearest town or city, but still serves 45,000 customers a year.

MOUNTAIN TOILETS

Two toilets have been built near the snow-covered summit of France's Mont Blanc. At 13,976 ft (4,260 m), they are the highest washrooms in Europe.

PIPE HOME

A man in China has built a home using two cement pipes—and it has become a city attraction. Xin Yucai, 50, of Shenyang City, bought two cement pipes from a construction company and turned them into a real house with windows, a door, and even a chimney. He turned down the offer of living in his daughter's apartment because he loves his new home so much.

PRISON GUESTS

A hotel in Liepaja, Latvia, offers guests the opportunity to experience life in a former Soviet prison. The old Karosta jail has been converted into a hotel, but visitors must still sleep on a barren bunk in a damp cell, scrub out the toilets, and are ordered around by the "prison" staff.

QUIET TOWN

The town of Colma, California, has fewer than 2,000 residents—but more than 1.5 million bodies in its cemeteries. Perhaps unsurprisingly, the town's motto is: "It's great to be alive in Colma!"

PRIVATE PUB

In response to a 2007 ban on smoking in public places, including bars and pubs, Kerry Morgan of Briton Ferry, Wales, built a private 90-seat pub in his home.

PINK CITY

Officials in Aurangabad in Bihar, India, painted many of the buildings in their city bright pink—thinking that it would help lower the crime rate.

MEAN MOSQUITO

In Upsala, Ontario, Canada, stands a steel and fiberglass monument of a giant mosquito carrying a man and a knife and fork! The hungry mosquito, which is 16 ft (5 m) long and has a wingspan of 15 ft (4.5 m), is holding the 6-ft (1.8-m) man with its legs.

HOUSE GIFT

Hollywood photographer Jasin Boland came up with the perfect Valentine's present for fiancée Maria Moral Pena—a gift-wrapped $1-million house. He arranged for the house—in Gloucestershire, England—to be covered in 5,000 sq ft (465 sq m) of white fabric, sprinkled with red hearts, and finished with a giant pink bow.

FLOATING SHOP

Dave's Bait House offers food, drinks, and fishing bait—all from Dave Steiner's 33-ft (10-ft) boat, which he anchors some 6 mi (9.5 km) from shore in the Gulf of Mexico.

CROOKED HOUSE

A crazily shaped building in Sopot, Poland, was inspired by fairytale illustrations and has roof tiles resembling the scales of a dragon. Built in 2003, the 4,780-sq-yd (4,000-sq-m) Centrum Rezydent was created by architect Szotynscy Zaleski, who based his theme on the children's book drawings of Polish illustrator Jan Marcin Szancer. At the heart of the crooked house is a bar named... Wonky Pub.

TOILET HOME

In 2007, architect Sim Jae-duck lifted the lid on his toilet house. Built from steel, white concrete, and glass, the 4,520-sq-ft (420-sq-m) home near Seoul, South Korea, is shaped like a toilet and even has a symbolic opening in the roof. Sim, who was actually born in a restroom, designed the $1.6-million house as part of his campaign for cleaner toilets worldwide. Naturally, it has four luxury washrooms.

PINK PALACE

No two columns, doors, or even door handles are alike in the 13,155-sq-yd (11,000-sq-m) Green Citadel in Magdeburg, Germany. The last project of Austrian artist Friedensreich Hundertwasser, who died in 2000, the pink building resembles a child's drawing and, like any Hundertwasser house, there are no straight lines. The $33.8-million development—containing 55 apartments, a hotel, shops, and office space—has roofs covered in grass and the buildings are topped with gold balls.

GLASS HOUSE

The Glass House in Boswell, British Columbia, Canada, was built from half a million empty embalming-fluid bottles. It was begun in 1952 by retired undertaker David H. Brown, who traveled western Canada collecting the bottles from friends in the funeral profession and ended up with about 250 tons of them.

SECRET APARTMENT

Eight artists built and furnished a secret apartment inside a Providence, Rhode Island, shopping mall—and stayed there for four years. They used breeze blocks to build the apartment in a disused space next to a car park and overcame the absence of plumbing by sneaking out to use mall toilets.

SMALL HOUSE

Artist Jay Shafer of Sebastopol, California, lives in a house that is 96 sq ft (9 sq m)— smaller than many bathrooms. He built the tiny wooden house himself and wheeled it into a position overlooking an apple orchard. The advantages of a compact residence— little housework, for one—have led to him building small houses for other people, too.

Ripley's Believe It or Not!

Enter the Vault

HIGH FRONT DOOR

In the 1940s, Watertown, Massachusetts, was the location of this unusual front door, which had a front step 18 ft (5.5 m) above the sidewalk.

MOVING NEXT DOOR

A tornado in Lorain, Ohio, in 1928, lifted off the top story of this house and carefully set it down beside it.

TALL STORY ▶

This log cabin built in Urania, Louisiana, in the 1930s, was an astonishing 50 ft (15 m) high.

NO PARKING!

These unconventional road signs appeared either side of a downtown street in Randolph, Vermont, in the 1980s.

REDWOOD RESIDENCE

This home in Palm Springs, California, was built in the 1950s in the shape of the famous giant redwood tree General Sherman, which stands in Sequoia National Park in California.

MINI HOSPITAL

Built in the 1930s, this veterinary hospital in New York City was once billed as the smallest in the world—it measured just 3 x 15 ft (1 x 4.5 m). Its owner, Dr. J. Lebish, had his office upstairs.

LUCKY BREAK

A tornado carried away the end of this house in Elgin, Illinois, in 1934, but left every dish in the pantry intact!

TINY CHURCH

Built in the 1930s, the Little Cathedral of Festina, in the town of Festina, Iowa, is a tiny church that seats a mere eight worshipers.

NAME THAT TOWN

In 1930, Robert Ripley visited the Welsh town that until recently had the longest town name in the world. Seen here standing at the town's railway station, Ripley was visiting Llanfairpwllgwyngyllgogerychwyrndrobwllllantysiliogogogoch, whose name translates as "The church of St. Mary in the hollow of white hazel trees near the rapid whirlpool by St. Tysilio's of the red cave."

FLOATING HOUSE

In 1940, R.G. Letourneau of Peoria, Illinois, built a house that he then towed to its destination, across the Illinois River. The watertight steel house, complete with furnace, plumbing, and furniture, did not sit on a barge, but floated happily to its new home.

BEER MOUNTAIN

When property manager Ryan Froerer went to check out one of his rented apartments in Ogden, Utah, he found around 70,000 empty beer cans piled high all the way up to the ceiling, completely obscuring the furniture. The cans, which equate to 24 beers a day during the tenant's eight-year stay, were later recycled for $800.

STRESS BUSTERS
Customers at the Rising Sun Anger Release Bar in Nanjing, China, are invited to relieve stress by smashing glasses and beating up staff, who wear protective padding.

MAGIC MENU
At the Ninja Japanese restaurant in New York City, waiters perform magic tricks while serving customers their sushi.

WEIGH-IN
The town of High Wycombe in Buckinghamshire, England, is the only place in the world that weighs its mayor publicly. Mayors are weighed at the beginning and end of their year in office to see whether or not they have gained any weight at the taxpayers' expense.

HORSESHOE TOWER
The Scarrington Horseshoe Tower in Nottinghamshire, England, is 17 ft (5 m) high and 6 ft (1.8 m) in diameter—and is made up of more than 50,000 metal horseshoes.

FINDERS KEEPERS
Diamonds State Park in Arkansas has a diamond mine where visitors can search for—and keep—any gems they find.

COOL BAR
A new bar in Dubai is the coolest place to hang out—because everything is made of ice. The bar, tables, and chairs at Chillout are made of ice, as are the cups, glasses, and plates. There is also an ice sculpture that depicts Dubai's skyline, and an ice chandelier. A cover charge provides customers with a hooded coat, woolen gloves, and insulated shoes to keep out frostbite.

DOLLHOUSE MEMORIAL
The grave of Nadine Earles (1929–33) in Lanett, Alabama, is covered by a brick dollhouse with a life-sized doll, a tea set, and toys inside.

DEEP MINE
Two of the world's tallest buildings could be stacked on top of each other in the pit of the Kennecott Copper Mine in Utah and still not reach the surface!

TAAL TALE
In the Philippines there is an island in a lake on an island in a lake on an island! The first island is in Crater Lake on Volcano Island in Lake Taal on Luzon Island.

DOLLAR BAR

A bar in the Florida Keys is dripping in money. Every wall and ceiling of the No Name Pub is plastered with dollar bills donated by customers who, for the past 20 years, have been writing their names and messages on bills and stapling them to the wall. It is estimated that the bar is now covered in an estimated $100,000 worth of cash.

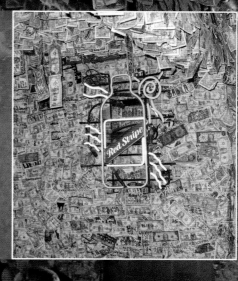

DRAINPIPE HOTEL

The Dasparkhotel near Linz, Austria, consists of three big concrete drainpipes, each of which has a double bed squashed into it. Blankets, storage space, and an electrical socket are also provided. Guests pay what they think the accommodation is worth.

OIL FIELD

The grounds of the State Capitol in Oklahoma City, Oklahoma, doubled up as a working oil field during most of the 20th century.

SENIOR PLAYTIME

In 2007, Berlin's Preussen Park opened Germany's first playground for senior citizens. The playground, which is fitted with eight steel flexibility machines, is designed to encourage elderly people to keep fit, as well as to socialize.

PLASTIC HOUSE

Tomislav Radovanovic of Kragujevac, Serbia, has spent five years building a house made out of 13,500 plastic bottles. Only the foundation of the 72-sq-yd (60-sq-m) house is concrete—even the kitchen furniture and windows are made of plastic bottles.

SALMON CARE

The Chester Creek River in Westchester, Alaska, has had its gradient reduced to make it easier for the tired salmon that have to jump upstream every year to reach their breeding grounds.

COLOR CHANGE

The water in a lake in Manitoba, Canada, has the amazing ability to change color. Little Limestone Lake, which lies some 280 mi (450 km) north of Winnipeg, is a marl lake, which means that it changes color as water temperatures rise and the mineral calcite that is dissolved in the water begins to settle. So in warm, summer weather the water can go from clear to an opaque turquoise and then to a milky blue-white.

CROC DETERRENT

Crocodiles bred in captivity in eastern India have been released into the wild in order to protect endangered animals from poachers. Creatures living in wildlife sanctuaries in Orissa and West Bengal have been threatened by poachers, but the introduction of dozens more crocodiles to the sanctuaries has successfully served as a formidable deterrent.

GRUNGE PLUNGE

Mexico City's subterranean sewers are so full that a team of men must dive into bacteria-filled waters daily to prevent them from becoming clogged.

TOURISTS' REVENGE

The Scottish town of Dunoon has a unique line of souvenirs—it sells millions of dead midges every year. The irritating little insects, which bite hundreds of tourists each year, are collected and sold at £5 ($10) for a jar of 10,000.

DEATHLY PAST

San Saba High School's Rogan Field in Texas is nicknamed "The graveyard" because it was built over a cemetery—with the bodies left in place.

SOLE STUDENT

In 2007, a school in China had just one teacher and one student. The school in Dasu, Longjing, used to have more than 400 students, but many families migrated from the mountain village, leaving Li Yongchun, who has taught in that same school for more than 25 years, to teach ever-decreasing numbers.

THE BOY BEHIND THE MASK

Little Joshua Taylor's family never know what he is going to look like from one minute to the next— because he has a collection of more than 400 masks.

Six-year-old Joshua from West Jefferson, North Carolina, has been fascinated by masks since he was 18 months old, when he watched the movie *The Haunted Mask* at every available opportunity. He started wearing a werewolf mask wherever he went before progressing to making his own masks... from food.

He would bite out eyes, nose, and mouth from bologna (sliced sausage) and even designed a mask from a tortilla. His mom Angie says: "He chewed out a face from the tortilla and put it in the refrigerator for days, and it had an old wooden look to it. It amazes me to watch his creativity."

Joshua has also made masks from papier mâché and for Christmas 2006 was given his first rubber-mask-making kit. Now the talented youngster is able to devise an amazing range of latex masks—from the grotesque to the humorous.

Angie Taylor says: "He is fascinated with facial features, noses, cheeks, and shapes and we have started to look at it as an art form. We plan on making him an area in the basement to be his workshop where he can build, create, and sculpt all he wants."

Young Joshua Taylor has more than 400 masks, many of which he has made himself. A variety of monsters, aliens, superheroes, and skeletons feature in his extensive collection.

ERASER FAN

Phoebe Syms from London, England, has collected nearly 4,000 erasers. Her obsession began at just two years of age, when she was attracted by the smell and feel of them. Fourteen years later, her collection is still going strong.

STAGE FAN

Andrea Schecter of Oceanside, New York, has a collection of approximately 2,300 playbills from the stage shows that she has seen, from New York to London.

LIGHTERS GALORE

Ted Ballard of Guthrie, Oklahoma, started collecting cigarette lighters when he was six years old and at the last count had a collection of more than 20,000.

TIE PINS

Since 1977, Kevin Godden of Kent, England, has been collecting tie pins—and he now has more than 1,300 of them.

UNIQUE ATTRACTION

In the basement of his home at Onset, Massachusetts, Dick Porter has more than 5,000 thermometers—the result of some 25 years of collecting. He calls it the world's largest and only thermometer museum.

GREEN LIGHT

A 14-year-old boy from Merseyside, England, has been given the green light to collect traffic signals. Simon Patterson already has six sets of lights, more than 30 beacons, and hundreds of photographs of traffic lights from around the world sent to him by friends on holiday. He has built up his collection, which also includes numerous road signs, by writing to councils or buying old sets on eBay at about $50 each.

BEER CANS

Australia's John Loveday has a collection of more than 6,000 beer cans from 78 countries—and he doesn't even drink! He has been collecting beer-related memorabilia for more than 15 years and also has 1,500 beer glasses, 900 beer bottles, plus assorted beer-themed coasters, matchboxes, key rings, bottle tops, and mirrors.

CONE ZONE

David Morgan's life is dedicated to traffic cones. Not only does he work for the world's largest producer of cones, but he has a collection of 500 of them at his home in Oxfordshire, England. He has been collecting them for more than 20 years, usually from roadworks, where he swaps a sought-after cone for a brand new one. Among his prized possessions are a Malaysian cone, found washed up on a beach in the Isles of Scilly off the southwest coast of the U.K., and a rare 1980 cone, which he picked up at an airport in Corsica while on his honeymoon.

POINT MADE

John Little never forgot being told off at school for not having a pencil sharpener, so now he has more than 1,500. John, from County Durham, England, has been collecting sharpeners for 20 years and has examples from all over the world in such diverse shapes as a kiwi, a banana, a red letter box, an apple, a wooden clog, and a shark.

CALL CENTER

The exterior of a small electronics store in Tokyo, Japan, is decorated with 6,000 used cell phones. The shop's owner, Masanao Watanabe, has been collecting them since 1994 and decided on the unusual display when he ran out of storage space inside. Now visitors come from all over the city to study the walls and see if they can find models they have owned.

PERFECT MATCH

Joe DeGennaro of New York City, has a collection of more than 100,000 matchcovers and matchboxes. He is a leading light of the Rathkamp Matchcover Society—named after its founder and avid matchbox collector Henry Rathkamp—which boasts more than 1,000 members across North America.

LIQUOR HAUL

Leonard White, a businessman from Vancouver, British Columbia, Canada, spent decades collecting more than 8,000 unopened miniature liquor bottles. Their shapes range from Elvis Presley to airplanes to animals.

SPACE DEBRIS

Jim Bernath of Burnaby, British Columbia, Canada, collects debris from old satellites and crashed comets. His collection includes old loaves of bread from the Russian space station *Mir* and pieces of satellites belonging to countries as far afield as Canada, Hungary, Italy, and Spain.

COOKIE-JAR MONSTER

Starting in 1975, Lucille Bromberek of Lemont, Illinois, collected cookie jars and eventually amassed more than 2,000.

BAG LADY

Carol Vaughan from Birmingham, England, has collected more than 8,000 carrier bags in all shapes and sizes. The 64-year-old, who hates throwing things away, also has a house full of 52 other collections, including 2,500 bars of soap, 500 tins, and 400 mugs.

HAMMER HOME

Germany's George Peters has been fascinated by hammers for 30 years and now has over 3,500 in his collection. His hammers come from all over the world and range in weight from a tiny 0.0006 oz (0.017 g) to a hefty 155 lb (70 kg).

FISHY BUSINESS

Bob Toelle of British Columbia, Canada, collects fish posters of the world. He has more than 700 fish posters displayed on his website, and his most recent additions include Pacific Northwest Spawning Salmon and Threatened Freshwater Fish of Croatia.

RARE CORKSCREWS

Nicholas Hunt of Sydney, New South Wales, Australia, has been collecting corkscrews from around the world for over a decade and now has more than 1,000. One of the oldest dates back to 1838.

TILL DEATH DO US PART

WELL-TRAVELED BRAIN

When Princeton pathologist Dr. Thomas Harvey performed the autopsy on Albert Einstein in 1955, he chose to remove the physicist's brain. He later had it cut into 240 pieces, which he kept in two jars stored inside a cider box at his various homes across America. From time to time he sent pieces to researchers.

In 1997, Harvey traveled to meet Einstein's granddaughter in California and took the brain with him in the trunk of his car. He accidentally left the brain at her house but she did not want it, so the following year she sent it back to Princeton.

WHERE THE HEART IS

Famous English poet and novelist Thomas Hardy (1840–1928) wanted to be buried in the village of Stinsford—his birthplace—in the picturesque English county of Dorset. When he died, however, his wife was offered the great honor of him being buried in "Poet's Corner" in London's great Westminster Abbey. To resolve the dilemma, his wife decided that his heart would be buried at Stinsford and his ashes interred in the Abbey.

HARMONIOUS HAIR

When Ludwig van Beethoven died in 1827, this lock of his hair was taken from his head as a keepsake of the great German composer. It became the property of the Royal Philharmonic Society in London, England, almost a hundred years later, and now belongs to the British Library.

HITLER'S HEAD

What are believed to be Adolf Hitler's skull and jaw are stored at the Federal Archives Service in Moscow, Russia. The skull piece is stored on two sheets of tissue in a floppy disk container. Ironically, Hitler had ordered a German officer to burn his remains because he didn't want to end up on display in the Soviet Union.

ARTIFICIAL LEGS

The artificial legs of British World War II fighter pilot Douglas Bader are on display at the R.A.F. Museum in Stafford, England. Bader heroically flew in the Battle of Britain despite losing both of his legs in a plane crash 11 years earlier.

HANDS APART

Body parts from 16th-century Spanish missionary St. Francis Xavier were in such demand as relics that they are now scattered all over the globe. His left hand is in Cochin, India, while his right is in Malacca, Malaysia.

MISSING ARM

British Admiral Horatio Nelson's right arm is said to be kept in the cathedral in Las Palmas, Gran Canaria. It was amputated after being shattered by grapeshot during an assault on Tenerife in 1797.

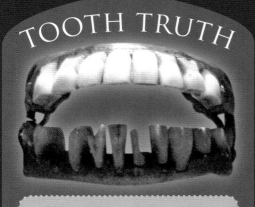

TOOTH TRUTH

Laser scans performed on George Washington's teeth at the National Museum of Dentistry in Baltimore in 2005 showed that they were not made of wood as was commonly believed. Instead, his dentures turned out to be made from gold, ivory, lead, and human and animal teeth (probably horse and donkey). The dentures had springs to help them open and were held together by bolts.

AMPUTATED LEG

Even though his right leg was nearly blown off by a cannonball during the Battle of Gettysburg, Dan Sickles calmly smoked a cigar on his way to the medical tent. After the leg was amputated, Sickles donated it to the Army Medical Museum, where he would later take friends to impress them with his bravery.

MACABRE WARNING

Oliver Cromwell died in 1658, but three years later the reinstated English monarchy under King Charles II exhumed his body and had him posthumously executed. His head was then impaled on a pike in Westminster Hall, where it remained for 20 years as a warning to others. The head now rests in a chapel in Cambridge, England.

SPINAL COLUMN

Twelve days after murdering President Abraham Lincoln, John Wilkes Booth was fatally shot in the neck. His body was later buried in an unmarked grave in Baltimore but his third, fourth, and fifth vertebrae had already been removed during the autopsy to gain access to the bullet. These parts of his spinal column are on display at the National Museum of Health and Medicine in Washington, D.C.

ELVIS'S WART

Joni Mabe, "the Elvis Babe," of Cornelia, Georgia, keeps Elvis Presley's wart in a tube of formaldehyde. She bought the wart—part of her collection of Elvis memorabilia—in 1990 from a Memphis doctor who had removed it from Elvis's right wrist when Presley joined the army in 1958.

LINCOLN RELICS

Part of President Abraham Lincoln's skull is housed at the National Museum of Health and Medicine in Washington, D.C. Also displayed are bits of his hair and the bullet that killed him.

BODY SNATCHERS

After Catherine of Siena died in 1380, pilgrims came to visit her body from all over Europe in the belief that touching it would cure their illnesses. One over-zealous worshiper removed one of Catherine's fingers and Pope Urban VI took her head.

PRESIDENTIAL TUMOR

President Grover Cleveland's tumor is kept in a jar at the Mütter Museum, Philadelphia, Pennsylvania. It was removed from the roof of his mouth in a secret operation.

FINGER OF DISCOVERY

Italian physicist Galileo (1564–1642) is credited with being the founding father of modern science. In 1737, the middle finger on his right hand was removed when his body was moved from its original grave to a mausoleum in the Santa Croce church in Florence, Italy. It eventually became the property of Florence's Institute and Museum of the History of Science in 1927, where it is now on display. The finger symbolizes how Galileo's work pointed the way toward modern science.

She's Got Sole!

Darlene Flynn has certainly taken a shine to shoes. Since starting her collection in 2000, Darlene of Romoland, California, has accumulated around 9,000 shoe-related items.

She has at least 500 different kinds of shoe memorabilia—among them shoe-shaped furniture, shoe curtains, shoe wallpaper, shoe lamps, shoe watches, shoe-themed art, shoe teapots, shoe soap, shoe purses, shoe thimbles, shoe spoons, shoe candles, shoe salt and pepper shakers, shoe-styled stationery, an electric shoe toothbrush, and a red stiletto shoe phone. Darlene's house is lined with display cases of beautiful miniature shoes. She has some 7,000 in total, including one named Ms. Vicky that is just 4 in (10 cm) wide and cost her $1,800.

Outside, a cowboy-boot birdhouse hangs from the wall and the patio is decorated with shoe-shaped flowerpots. Her collection also includes a replica of the Disney Cinderella glass slipper, Barbie shoes galore, and a shoe made from ash collected from the eruption of Mount St. Helens. She has ambitions to own a shoe-shaped car, and for her collection to appear on the *Oprah* TV show.

Darlene started her collection after visiting her cousin's house for a Halloween party. "My cousin inherited her grandmother's shoe collection and when I saw it, I knew that was something I had to do. I don't know why it had to be shoes—I just love them and the whole thing kind of got out of control."

She has about 200 pairs that she wears herself, but one of her favorite items was made by her son for Christmas 2006. He spent over 40 hours gluing together coins totalling $15.07 into the shape of a shoe. For Darlene Flynn, it was the perfect present.

"In 2006, I had a special dinner event with Raine and other shoe collectors at my home in California. Everything was shoes, shoes, shoes—we had Cinderella shoe bottle-openers, shoe silverware holders, and so on, and the big finale was the shoe dessert. It took me between six and eight months to figure something out that would be completely edible."

"These are mainly my shoe thimbles—they are all approximately an inch high."

"This curio cabinet contains some of my signed 'Just the Right Shoe' resin miniature shoe collection. 'Just the Right Shoes' were the first shoes I bought for my collection. I am ecstatic about the release of my own 'JTRS' exclusive this year—'Graffiti Gurl Black.' These shoes are so popular because of the intricate detail and creative fantasy that Raine (the artist) puts into these little treasures."

"Most of the shoes pictured here are vintage or antique shoes. I received some as gifts but mostly purchased them myself while traveling around the U.S.A. and Europe."

"My shoe pin collection is quite unique. I have a wall hanging measuring 5 x 6 ft (1.5 x 2 m) that is covered with approximately 600 shoe and boot pins. Among my favorites are the Hard Rock Cafe shoe pins, my shoe breast cancer pins, and the boot pins."

HOT WHEELS

Michael Zarnock of Deerfield, New York, has 8,128 different Hot Wheels cars—part of his collection of more than 25,000 model cars. Many of them are on display at the Children's Museum in Utica, New York, where they occupy seven glass cabinets, each 12 ft (3.6 m) in length. He says: "To this day, every birthday or holiday, everyone knows what to get me."

My Fascination with Hot Wheels!

I started collecting Hot Wheels cars when they were first released in 1968. I think the first car I bought was the Silhouette. I remembered seeing it on an episode of 'Mission Impossible' and fell in love with that car.

My mother still reminds me of the Christmas that I bought everyone in the family Hot Wheels for Christmas gifts. I knew they wouldn't want them and they would give them to me. Not a bad idea for a ten-year-old. Too bad it didn't work. I had to go out and buy everybody new gifts.

I'm also a package collector. I like the different styles of the packages from the many eras of Hot Wheels. Like I've always said, it's all about the memories for me. Hot Wheels relax me and bring me back to the easygoing childhood I once knew. I keep everything in its original package. My saying is: "Preserve the toy, preserve the boy." There isn't a day that goes by that I don't shop or look for something to add to my collection—either looking in any store that I drive by or on the Internet at the auction sites. Sadly, it's gotten to the point that there aren't too many items that I don't already have, but I always keep checking! You never know, I may get surprised and find something that I didn't know existed.

I have been obsessed with Hot Wheels cars and accessories for the past 40 years, and I look forward to continuing to collect them for the next 40 years!

MURDER MUSEUM

As well as scupltures of Charles Manson and notorious cannibals, the Serial Killer Museum in Florence, Italy, recounts the crimes of American murderers John Wayne Gacy and Ted Bundy. It also houses mock-ups of a gas chamber and an electric chair.

WALLPAPER MUSEUM

In France there is a museum devoted to wallpaper. Le Musée du Papier Peint at Rixheim has a history of wallpaper along with demonstrations of its manufacture.

MAGICAL MARBLES

As well as chronicling the history of marbles, the Marble Museum at Yreka, California, houses beautiful, hand-painted china marbles, as well as a collection of paintings about marbles.

DISCARDED OBJECTS

Artist Rebecca Wolfram of Chicago, Illinois, has set up a Museum of Objects Left on the Sidewalk—a collection of items abandoned in the street, including used fireworks, broken dolls, sweat shirts, gloves, pots and pans, and a wire coat-hanger molded into the shape of a shark.

CURIOSITY CABINET

Keswick Museum in Cumbria, England, is home to a "Cabinet of Curiosities," including a 14-ft-long (4-m), 1.5-ton xylophone made of slate, a 665-year-old cat, the Emperor Napoleon's teacup, poet Robert Southey's clogs, a spoon made from the leg bone of a sheep, and a man trap.

DRAIN TILES

Housed in the 1822 home of John Johnston, a pioneer in tile drainage technology, the Mike Weaver Drain Tile Museum at Geneva, New York, boasts a collection of more than 500 drain tiles dating from 500 BC to the modern plastic version. Marion "Mike" Weaver worked in drainage for 20 years and started his collection in 1950.

TWISTED LOGIC

In Dannebrog, Nebraska, there is a museum dedicated to liars. Nothing is as it seems at the Liar's Hall of Fame, where exhibits include a box of golf balls the size of hailstones!

SEWER MUSEUM

In Hamburg, Germany, there is a museum dedicated to objects found in the city's sewer system.

DAIRY DELIGHTS

America's Ice Cream and Dairy Museum at Medina, Ohio, has artifacts on the history of ice cream dating back to ancient Egypt. Among the most cherished exhibits is a 1905 "gaslight" soda fountain.

DRUM DREAM

Alan Buckley of Walsall, England, started collecting drum kits at the age of eight—and now he has 110 of them. The 72-year-old musician, known as "Sir Alan" after his friends bought him a "knighthood," has snares dating back to 1809 and numerous other drums from the 1920s and 1930s. His collection includes a drum from London's Windmill Theatre, famous for never closing during World War II.

TROLL COLLECTION

More than 400 trolls in different sizes and outfits are housed in a troll museum in New York City run by Jen Miller.

DEAD TICKS

The Smithsonian Institute Tick Museum in Statesboro, Georgia, has a collection of more than one million dead ticks.

SWEET SPOT

The Marzipan Museum in Keszthely, Hungary, has displays of sculpture—including dragons, shields, and miniature palaces—all made out of marzipan.

VINTAGE VODKA

In Moscow, Russia, there is a vodka museum containing 50,000 bottles of vodka, some as much as 200 years old.

NONPROFIT

The Ohio-based International Brick Collectors' Association forbids its 1,000-plus members to buy or sell bricks for money.

POPCORN MACHINES

The Wyandot Popcorn Museum at Marion, Ohio, boasts the largest collection of popcorn and peanut roasters in the world, with some items dating back to the 1890s. It has more than 50 antique popping machines, including one used by movie star Paul Newman to promote his own popcorn in Central Park, New York.

HUGE NICKEL

Among more than one million vintage pieces at the Wooden Nickel Historical Museum at San Antonio, Texas, is a wooden nickel measuring 13 ft 4 in (4 m) in diameter and weighing 2,500 lb (1,135 kg).

VOODOO EXPERIENCE

The New Orleans Historic Voodoo Museum brings together ancient and modern voodoo practices. It houses artifacts such as dolls and memorabilia relating to the 19th-century voodoo queen Marie Laveau.

ROLLER SKATING

There is a museum in Lincoln, Nebraska, that is dedicated to roller skating. The National Museum of Roller Skating has a large collection of historical roller skates and costumes.

PARASITE PARADISE

The Meguro Parasitological Museum in Tokyo, Japan, has a collection of more than 300 parasites, including a tapeworm 30 ft (9 m) long that was pulled out of a person's body.

BRAIN MUSEUM

A museum in Lima, Peru, houses almost three thousand diseased human brains. Unlike most brain collections around the world, it is open to the public. Exhibits include the brain of someone who died from the human variant of "mad cow" disease, the brains of people who died of trichinosis—the most common brain disease in Peru—which is caused by eating undercooked meat, and several human fetuses with neurological disorders.

CRYSTAL CAR

Ken and Annie Burkitt of Niagara Falls, Ontario, Canada, used more than one million genuine Austrian Swarovski lead crystals to decorate a 2004 Mini Cooper car with images of 11 of the U.S.A.'s most recognizable and enduring iconic emblems.

The mural-style design includes the Statue of Liberty, Mount Rushmore, the American flag, and the famous Hollywood sign. It took four artists six months to place each crystal individually on the "American Icon" by hand. The crystals are all the exact same size and are in 50 different shades of color to represent the 50 states of the U.S.A. Ken Burkitt said: "We wanted to create something that would pay tribute to

America in an eye-catching way. The car takes on a completely different look as the lighting changes throughout the day. The crystal design takes on a life of its own."

The sparkling car is completely functional and marked another milestone for the creative husband-and-wife team. They had previously covered a limousine in 23,000 gold coins and a double-decker London bus in 100,000 gold-plated British pennies.

THE DESIGN

Back: The White House

Roof: Bald Eagle and the U.S. flag

Left side: Hollywood Hills sign; Space Shuttle; Capitol Building and Washington Monument; New York City skyline featuring the Chrysler Building

Right side: The Alamo and Mount Rushmore

Front: The Statue of Liberty

213

PORT-A-POTTY

Inspired by the sight of a windstorm blowing portable toilets across the tarmac at a drag-car show in Texas, Paul Stender of Brownsburg, Indiana, invented his own jet-powered outhouse. Driven by a 50-year-old, 750-lb (340-kg) Boeing jet turbine, Stender's Port-o-Jet reaches speeds of 46 mph (74 km/h) and shoots out 30-ft (9-m) fireballs in its wake. While in motion, Stender sits on the toilet's original seat and looks out through a hole in the door. He tried to keep the toilet paper, but it kept getting sucked into the engine.

SPEED LIMO

An English inventor has come up with a limousine that can reach 170 mph (275 km/h), and can go from 0 to 60 mph in less than six seconds. Dan Cawley of Manchester, took a Ferrari 360 Modena, chopped it in half, and stretched it by 9½ ft (2.9 m) with a section of hand-built carbon fiber. The resulting eight-seater vehicle is 20 ft (6 m) long.

CHOCOLATE CAR

A car dealer in Qingdao City, China, coated a Volkswagen Beetle in chocolate for Valentine's Day 2007. The car was covered in plastic wrap, and then 440 lb (200 kg) of melted chocolate was spread over it.

HOG DOG

Lady Harley, a Siberian husky dog from Woodland Hills. California, has ridden more than 200,000 mi (320,000 km) on the back of owner Jeremiah Gerbracht's Harley-Davidson.

EASY TO SPOT

Artist Kelly Lyles's converted white Subaru is easy to spot—as it is covered in hundreds of them. Kelly, from Seattle, Washington, has painted the car to look like a leopard, and it has a leopard face on the hood, welded ears, and a tail. Dozens of toy leopards are glued to the bodywork, the interior upholstery is leopard skin, and Lyles herself dresses from head to toe in... leopard skin.

BOTTLE BOAT

In June 2007, Marcus Eriksen of Long Beach, California, launched a 20-ft (6-m) Viking boat made from 5,000 recycled plastic bottles at Juneau, Alaska. The bottles were held in place by fish net, and the boat's sail consisted of a collection of old shirts. The previous year, Eriksen had sailed a 14-ft-long (4.3-m) boat, the *Fluke*, made from 800 plastic bottles, on a 250-mi (400-km) Californian voyage from Santa Barbara to San Diego.

NO LICENSE

In June 2007, police in the Netherlands found that an 84-year-old man they had pulled over in a random check had been driving without a license—for 67 years.

MIRROR IMAGE

Dennis Clay of Houston, Texas, drives a Volkswagen Beetle—with an identical, upside-down Beetle on top, welded to the roof. He calls his art car creation "Mirror Image."

OXYGEN RAIL

The train service connecting Lhasa, Tibet, to China's rail system operates at such a high altitude that oxygen is provided to passengers, and those over age 60 need medical clearance before they are allowed on board.

FRUIT WAGON

Jackie Harris of Houston, Texas, transformed a 1967 Ford station wagon into the Fruitmobile—a one-of-a-kind car with plastic oranges, apples, pineapples, grapes, and other fruit attached to the bodywork.

MINI COOPER PARADE

In June 2007, no less than 273 Minis paraded at Virginia Beach, Virginia, forming a chain more than 5 mi (8 km) long. The cars came from as far away as Connecticut and Indiana.

FISH BIKE

Didi Senft from Storkow, Germany, has built a bicycle in the shape of a fish. The three-wheel monster is 10 ft (3 m) high, 30 ft (9 m) long, and made from 50,000 bicycle bells welded together. It took bicycle fanatic Didi six months to build and, fittingly, his test run in March 2007 was to a local fish restaurant. Senft, who likes to dress up as the devil when riding, also designed a bizarre bike for the 2006 soccer World Cup, which was held in Germany. That 25-ft-long (7.6-m) bicycle had wheels made from 100 soccer balls.

High & Mighty

Created by Bob Chandler, of St. Louis, Missouri, the Bigfoot 5 truck is 15 ft 6 in (4.7 m) tall, 13 ft 1 in (4 m) wide, and weighs more than 28,000 lb (12,780 kg). The huge tires 10 ft (3 m) tall, which Chandler bought from a junkyard, had previously been used by the U.S. Army on an Arctic snow train in Alaska during the 1950s.

TAXI TRIP

Not wanting to travel by air for her vacation to Greece, 89-year-old Kathleen Searles of Suffolk, England, made the 4,000-mi (6,440-km) journey by taxi instead. Although she could have flown there for $120 and the taxi fare ended up costing her $4,000 and taking three days, she insisted that it was money well spent. Taxi driver Julian Delefortrie said: "When she asked me if I'd like to drive to Europe I replied that I would love to. I never expected her to say Greece!"

PORKY TRIBUTE

Rev. Bryan Taylor of Houston, Texas, created the Jeffrey Jerome Memorial Pig car in memory of Victoria Herbert's famous pet pig, Jeffrey Jerome. The pink auto has ears, a snout, and a curly tail.

SHUTTLE SHUFFLE

It takes more than six hours for NASA to move the U.S. space shuttle 3.4 mi (5.5 km) from its hangar to the launch pad.

HIGHWAY LANDING

In July 2007, a vintage airplane made an emergency landing on a Wisconsin highway. Pilot William J. Leff from Ohio, brought the 1946 North American T-6G plane down on the northbound lanes of U.S. Highway 41 near Fond du Lac County Airport. The only damage was to the plane's right wing when it hit a number of highway signs.

MONSTER SKATEBOARD

In 2007, students at Bay College, Michigan, built a skateboard measuring 31 ft (9.4 m) long and 8 ft (2.4 m) wide, and weighing 2,400 lb (1,090 kg). It can hold 28 people.

FLYING SAUCER

A sci-fi fan who admits he knows nothing about computers has spent more than 30 years building his own flying saucer in his garage. Alfie Carrington of Clinton, Michigan, has been putting the machine together using information from aviation books, and so far the project has cost him more than $60,000.

TINY ENGINE

Iqbal Ahmed of Nagpur, India, has built a working steam engine that weighs less than 0.07 oz (2 g). It stands just 0.267 in (6.8 mm) high and is 0.639 in (16.24 mm) long and, with steam generated by ⅓ fl oz (10 ml) water, the brass-constructed engine can run for about two minutes.

ROCKET ROBERT

In 1969, Achille J. St. Onge of Worcester, Massachusetts, sent a leather-bound miniature volume of Robert Goddard's autobiography on board *Apollo 11*, the first manned space flight to the Moon. Goddard was a pioneer of rocket building and his space-flown book, with pencil markings by Buzz Aldrin, was later valued at auction as being worth between $25,000 and $35,000.

HIGH RIDE

Brad Graham of Thunder Bay, Ontario, Canada, built a two-wheeled bicycle measuring 17 ft 10 in (5.5 m) tall. He rode it for 330 yd (300 m).

GIANT RABBIT

Designer Larry Fuente of Houston, Texas, attached a huge white rabbit to a Volkswagen Beetle to create his sinister-looking art car Rex Rabbit. Fuente had previously covered a pink Cadillac with a flock of flamingos.

SPELLING ERROR

Tobi Gutt of Germany traveled 8,000 mi (12,875 km) off-course after misspelling his destination city while buying an airline ticket. Instead of Sydney, Australia, he ended up in Sidney, Montana, U.S.A.

SPEED CHASE

An 11-year-old girl was charged with drunk-driving in July 2007 after crashing while trying to escape her police pursuers at speeds of more than 100 mph (160 km/h). The girl gave police in Orange Beach, Alabama, the runaround for 8 mi (13 km) before they could catch her.

PLANE SPOTTERS

Nearly 100,000 people arrive daily at the new Suvarnabhumi Airport in Bangkok, Thailand—not to travel, but to sightsee and picnic!

SEVEN-SEATER BIKE

Eric Staller from Amsterdam, Netherlands, has invented a bicycle built for seven. The ConferenceBike, or CoBi, uses three motorcycle wheels and has seven seats in a circle. All seven riders can pedal, enabling the machine to reach speeds of up to 15 mph (24 km/h). One of the riders also takes charge of the steering wheel.

HANGING AROUND

Eelko Moorer of London, England, built a set of boots that allows him to hang upside down from safety rails in the subway. The boots have a slot in the heel that hooks over the carriage's handrail.

DOLPHIN CRAFT

New Zealander Rob Innes and Californian Dan Piazza have designed a watercraft that not only looks like a dolphin, it also behaves like a dolphin. The two-seater Seabreacher uses its 175 horsepower engine to surge through the waves, but because it is made of fiberglass, it is so light that it can fly 10 ft (3 m) in the air even at speeds of 15 mph (24 km/h). The advanced jet-ski is 15 ft (4.5 m) long and has a canopy similar to those seen on U.S. fighter jets.

Behind the exterior of John's modest home lies a replica of a 747 cockpit.

PLANE CRAZY

John Davis from Coventry, England, has spent eight years and $30,000 constructing an exact replica of a Boeing 747 cockpit in the spare bedroom of his house. The hi-tech simulator, which incorporates an autopilot system, weather radar, and engine sounds, was bought mainly over the Internet. To add to the illusion of real flight, he has erected a 6-ft (1.8-m) screen at the front of the cockpit showing panoramic views of places around the world, from the Alps to the skyline of New York. He even plays mock announcements, instructing passengers to fasten their seat belts to prepare themselves for takeoff.

John Davis studied photographs of a real Boeing 747-400 cockpit on aviation websites to make sure that the design for his home version was accurate.

CAR-TOON TRUCK

New Jersey art teacher Robert Luczun has decorated every inch of a 1928 Model AR Ford Roadster pickup truck with hundreds of comic book, comic strip, and animated cartoon characters.

Combining his twin hobbies of antique cars and comic art, he spent more than 2,800 hours over a period of 15 months airbrush-painting assorted animated icons, from 101 Dalmatians to Rat Fink and Finding Nemo to Dr. Who. The result is a rolling history of comics from 1896 to the present day.

After months of preparation, Luczun waited another three days so that he could start painting on October 18, 2004—the 108th anniversary of the first published comic, *The Yellow Kid*, whom he honored with a place on the back of the side mirror.

Each cartoon was hand-drawn twice—once on a paper layout, then again on the vehicle—and every color was masked off to prevent any spray-paint errors. He took much of the truck apart during the project. The desire to cover the entire bodywork—inside and out—forced him to paint in backbreaking positions. While drawing, he put the Where's Waldo? figure in at random and finished up with around a dozen Waldos scattered about the vehicle. Luczun's incredible cartoon truck is now a familiar sight at comic book conventions, auto shows, and art car parades.

The interior of the tailgate of Robert's car features a Ripley's Believe It or Not! cartoon (left).

The gas tank is located on the front of the windshield and has a mix of characters from Harvey, Merrie Melodies, and Warner Bros. This area was drawn and painted directly on to the truck— hanging over it!

In the interior of the car, Luczun has used a Nemo toy repainted and converted into a gearshift knob. The interior doors also feature cartoons from a wide variety of comic books.

Luczun used more than 600 research pictures of the puppies from which he chose the cutest. He has included all 101 Dalmatians from the film. At the time, the engine was out of the vehicle on roller pads, so it moved around and was easier to paint.

In Luczun's own words...

"Other airbrush artists look at me as if I'm nuts when they see the truck and what it took to get there. At least I don't have any worry about anyone trying to copy it!

My thoughts while working on each cartoon were that this was someone's favorite and this was the only one they were looking for, so it had to be perfect. One lady started hitting her husband when she saw a comic, saying: "That's the one I was talking about all these years!" Another time I had to remove the rear license plate so that a chap could get a few pictures of a cartoon—that was to be his next tattoo.

For '101 Dalmatians,' I must have collected 600 puppy pictures and I chose the cutest ones. I checked off each picture as I completed it, but just when I thought I'd finished, a piece of paper flew to the floor. It was two puppies that didn't have a check mark. So I went back and put a piece of tape on each one as I counted... 99. I put the last two in, and yes, I do have 101!

The idea to have a fun vehicle that everyone could relate to got bigger than I ever dreamed. It took on a life of its own. Some of the original cartoon artists have contributed new drawings, on 3 x 4-in plates, that I have fixed to the floor of the truck's bed. They all want to be part of what they call a comic icon.

I think the best part is the joy I get when a person says to me, 'I never thought I'd see that cartoon ever again, it was my favorite. Thanks for letting me re-live a fun part of my life!'"

ARMCHAIR RIDE

A company from DeMotte, Indiana, has designed a vehicle that enables couch potatoes to drive down the road without leaving the comfort of their armchair. Driven with a joystick and powered by either gasoline or electricity, Armchair Cruisers' range includes a Harley-Davidson chair that reaches speeds of 40 mph (64 km/h), does wheelies, and has an onboard cooler, and a two-seater sofa that can do two 360-degree turns inside an 8-sq-ft (0.74-sq-m) box. The chairs can even be customized with their own built-in stereo system.

GIRL RACER

Stephanie Beane of Grafton, Ohio, could roar around the track in a stock car at speeds of 80 mph (130 km/h)—at the age of ten. She made her stock-car debut at the Sandusky Speedway Motor-Sports Park in June 2007 and finished fifth in a field of 15, most of whom were adult men. She first got behind the wheel of a car when she was just two and started racing at four, learning to ride a go-kart before she could ride a bicycle. She was so successful—often winning trophies that were taller than she was—that she began signing autographs at age six... before she really knew how to write her name.

SUICIDE ATTACK

In August 2006, a large flock of shearwater birds bombarded a fishing boat off the coast of Alaska for unknown reasons, ramming suicidally against it for 30 minutes.

AUTHENTICITY SCAN

Zeng, an antique collector in Guangzhou, China, buys plane tickets so that he can go through the airport's X-ray scanners to verify the authenticity of artifacts that he carries with him!

VIRTUAL JOURNEY

Every Saturday in Delhi, India, around 40 passengers line up for boarding cards—for a plane that never takes off. For $4, Bahadur Chand Gupta offers people who cannot afford to fly the opportunity to experience air travel without ever leaving the ground. His Airbus 300 has only one wing, no lighting, and the toilets are out of order, but passengers happily buckle themselves in for their "virtual journey," watching safety demonstrations and listening to announcements while being waited on by flight attendants.

TOO WEAK

A 79-year-old woman from Norway was denied a driver's license renewal after losing an arm-wrestling match to her doctor.

FERRARI SALE

A red Ferrari Enzo with a top speed of 218 mph (350 km/h) was sold for more than $1 million on eBay's U.K. online auction site in 2006. Bidding started at the equivalent of $2.

TRAIN PUSH

In May 2007, a stalled commuter train in Bihar, India, was able to start again when hundreds of passengers got out and pushed!

SPOON VAN

Elmer Fleming of Columbia, South Carolina, has covered his Chevrolet pickup in kitchen utensils. He has riveted 1,480 spoons onto the bodywork.

FROZEN ORDEAL

An 11-year-old Russian stowaway survived an 800-mi (1,300-km) flight at temperatures of –58°F (–50°C) hidden in the wheel well of a Boeing 737. When Andrei Lyssov was finally discovered, many of his clothes were frozen to his body. He was then taken to hospital where doctors treated him for frostbite.

BEE ESCAPE

Some 2,000 bees escaped and buzzed off when the truck carrying their hives overturned near Billings, Montana, in September 2007. The truck was hauling 465 beehives—holding nearly 13.7 million bees—from North Dakota to California, but luckily most of the bees stayed in their hives after the accident. As the weather cooled in the evening, the escaped bees returned to their hives, too.

SITTING TALL

Michael Mooney of Asheville, North Carolina, rides tall bikes for fun. He regularly rides bikes that are 6 ft (1.8 m) and 12 ft (3.6 m) tall, but in September 2007 he decided to go all the way by riding a bike that was an amazing 44 ft (13.4 m) tall—higher than a two-story house including the roof. He demonstrated it at the Lexington Avenue Arts and Fun Festival, and managed to pedal a few yards before the machine toppled over.

VINTAGE SALE

The world's oldest working car—the steam-powered La Marquise, built in France in 1884—was sold at auction in Pebble Beach, California, in 2007 for $3.5 million. The four-seater, which is fueled by coal, wood, and paper, takes about half an hour to work up enough steam to move.

FULL SPEED AHEAD

In January 1862, John Ericsson, a Swedish engineer, completed building an ironclad ship called the U.S.S. Monitor for the U.S. Navy in just 118 days.

VIKING VESSEL

An 11th-century Viking ship has been rebuilt from the wood of 300 oak trees. The 100-ft-long (30-m) Sea Stallion is held together by 7,000 iron nails and rivets. The original vessel sank south of Copenhagen, Denmark, in 1072 and lay there for nearly 900 years until excavated.

DRIVING BACKWARD

In October 2006, a man was stopped by police near the outback town of Kalgoorlie, Australia, after driving backward down a highway for 12 mi (20 km).

CUSTOM MADE

"Flat Out" was built in just three days, but at 22 in (56 cm) high is so low that at 6 ft 4 in (1.9 m), Andy Saunders can't fit into it. Consequently, his friend Jim Chalmers gets to drive it.

Andy Saunders spent six months modeling his Picasso Citroen on the work of the Spanish artist. The headlamps and indicators were inspired by Picasso's 1937 Portrait of Dora Maar. In spite of its misplaced features, the car is still capable of reaching 65 mph (105 km/h) but can be driven only during the day, when hand signals are permissible.

Andy Saunders specializes in taking old cars and turning them into something unrecognizable. The custom-car king, from Dorset, England, is a devotee of 1950s Americana, but gains inspiration from anywhere. He works at an auto center and spends his days studying the shape of windshields, headlamps, and other parts, which he then picks up from scrapyards to use on his latest projects. His crazy creations include a car that looks like a spaceship, a Citroen 2CV redesigned in the style of a Picasso painting (left), and another vehicle that is just 22 in (56 cm) high (above).

ROLLER MAN

French designer Jean-Yves Blondeau can speed down a highway and even overtake motorbikes—just by wearing his "Buggy Rollin" suit. The plastic full-body suit has a set of rollers on most of the major joints, torso, and back, enabling him to roll along in any position at speeds of up to 60 mph (100 km/h).

MOBILE CATHEDRAL

Rebecca Caldwell of Oakland, California, has designed a car that looks like a Gothic cathedral, complete with flying buttresses, stained glass windows, and gargoyles. The framework of her "Carthedral" art car is a 1971 Cadillac hearse with a Volkswagen Beetle welded on top.

WHAT A CORKER!

Jan Elftmann of Minneapolis, Minnesota, has decorated her Mazda truck with more than 10,000 wine and champagne corks collected during her 13 years as a waitress in an Italian restaurant. To accompany the truck at art car parades, she wears a ball gown—also decorated with dozens of corks.

HEAVY METAL

A giant motorbike powered by a tank engine stands 17 ft 4 in (5.3 m) long, 7 ft 6 in (2.3 m) tall—and the engine alone weighs almost 2 tons. Dubbed the *Led Zeppelin* by its creator Tilo Nieber, the bike took a team of welders and mechanics from Zilly, Germany, almost a year to build.

CAREFUL DRIVER

A 94-year-old woman from Hereford, England, has driven over a period of 82 years more than 600,000 mi (965,600 km) without even the smallest accident. Muriel Gladwin, who taught herself to drive at age 12, has never even had a scrape—nor has she been booked for speeding.

IN THE GROOVE

Japanese engineers have created "Melody Roads" with specially cut grooves that develop pitched vibrations as a car drives over them.

GREEN MACHINE

Students at Warwick University, England, have created an eco-friendly sports car that has a body made from plants, and tires made from potatoes. Eco One uses pulped hemp injected with rapeseed oil for its bodywork, has brake pads constructed from ground cashew nuts, and runs on a fuel of fermented wheat and sugar beet. Even so, it can go from 0 to 60 mph (0 to 97 km/h) in 4 seconds and has a top speed of 150 mph (240 km/h).

BRICK TRUCK

Mark Monroe and students at Austin College, Sherman, Texas, created a station wagon that appears to be made of bricks. The Brickmobile is really a 1968 Ford Country Sedan with 839 brick-like ceramic tiles stuck to the bodywork.

MERCEDES BONZ

A Minnesota woman has spent four years covering a car in nearly 1,000 animal bones. B.J. Zander decorated her Mercedes Bonz—in reality a Volvo—with beef and chicken bones that she obtained from friends, butchers, and her dog.

WHEELCHAIR RACER

A German man was stopped by police for driving an electric wheelchair down the street at 40 mph (64 km/h)—twice the speed limit. Guenther Eichmann of Geseke had modified the wheelchair's engine so that it could go faster.

JET STOOL

If Tim Arfons fancies a quick drink, he climbs aboard his jet barstool. Powered by a gas turbine engine, the stool has reached speeds of 40 mph (64 km/h) at a raceway park in Norwalk, Ohio.

ELECTRIC TRICYCLE

To pull himself along while wearing rollerblades, Swiss figure skater Stephan Soder has designed an electric tricycle with a top speed of 12 mph (19 km/h). The Easyglider X6 has an electric-powered front wheel, a parking brake, a headlight, and three power levels. Optional extras include a music system.

PROPELLER CAR

Wanting a vehicle that he could take to both car and air shows, Dave Major of Benton, Kansas, designed the Aerocar, a cross between a little 1959 BMW 600 and an airplane. The roadworthy auto has a handmade propeller turned by an electric motor, a tail from a real airplane, and tires from a jet. Even though it never leaves the ground, it has a custom dash with a working altimeter and an airspeed indicator.

MECHANICAL SPIDER

Designers from Vancouver, British Columbia, Canada, have created a huge mechanical spider that a person can ride. Powered by a Honda engine and a system of hydraulic pumps and motors, the Mondo Spider is an eight-legged mechanical walking machine that stands 5 ft (1.5 m) high and 8 ft (2.4 m) wide with a seat at the front. The steel legs move like a spider and give it a top speed of 4 ft (1.2 m) per second, which is the equivalent of a brisk human walk.

GRASS COVERING

Ephraim Eusebio, of Minneapolis, Minnesota, drives a 1991 Toyota Previa that is covered in artificial grass salvaged from the Guthrie Theater's garbage.

LUGE RACER

Lying horizontally just a couple of inches above the asphalt, Joel King of Sussex, England, reached a speed of 112 mph (180 km/h) on a jet-powered street luge board in August 2007. He says that stopping is the hardest part. "When you've finished you turn the engine off and use your feet to brake, which at over 100 mph is quite interesting."

The Blind Adventurer

Miles Hilton-Barber during his mammoth trek across Antarctica's frozen landscape.

In April 2007, Miles Hilton-Barber piloted a tiny micro-light aircraft on a 13,360-mi (21,500-km) flight from London, England, to Sydney, Australia. The epic journey took him 55 days and involved 118 stops—but what made it truly remarkable is that Miles is blind.

The 59-year-old from Derbyshire, England, is no stranger to great adventures. Over the past decade he has circumnavigated the globe, climbed some of the world's highest mountains, trekked 150 mi (240 km) across the Sahara Desert, hauled a sled 250 mi (400 km) across Antarctica, and completed more than 40 parachute jumps.

Miles was inspired by his blind brother Geoff, who sailed solo from South Africa to Australia in 1999. "That's what made me realize the problem in my life wasn't my blindness," he says, "it was my attitude to it. The only thing holding me back was five inches—the distance between my ears."

Accompanied by sighted friend Jon Cook, Miles, who has been blind for more than 25 years, has climbed to a height of 17,500 ft (5,335 m) in the Himalayas as well as scaling Mount Kilimanjaro and Mont Blanc, the highest mountains in Africa and Europe respectively.

In 2001, Miles ran the 11-day Ultra-Marathon race across China, and the following year he completed the Siberian Ice Marathon, known as "The Coldest Marathon on Earth." Within weeks he was crossing the entire Qatar Desert nonstop in 78 hours—day and night—without sleep.

Accompanied by two disabled friends, he set off on a 93-day, 38,000-mi (61,155-km) circumnavigation of the globe in 2003, using more than 80 challenging forms of transport. These included a hot-air balloon to get him over the Nevada Desert, an elephant, and a racing car driven at 125 mph (200 km/h).

Four years later, accompanied by sighted copilot Richard Meredith-Hardy, Miles made the micro-light flight from England to Australia, flying over 21 countries and combating freezing temperatures and tropical thunderstorms along the way. Reflecting on his many adventures, he says: "The only limits in our lives are those we set for ourselves."

Miles (left) and his companion Jon Cook trek across Antarctica.

Miles (left) riding an ostrich in South Africa during his circumnavigation of the globe in 2003.

The amazing micro-light flight from London to Sydney fulfilled another ambition for Miles. "Since I was a kid I wanted to be a pilot," he says. "Then I went blind and they said I'd never fly."

Miles goes on an underwater scuba walk in the Red Sea, accompanied by his paraplegic friend Mike Mackenzie.

Climbing the icy ridges of the Cairngorms in Scotland presented a formidable challenge for Miles (right) and his sighted guide Jon Cook.

Miles abseiling down Table Mountain in Cape Town, South Africa. He was the first blind person ever to achieve this feat.

SPLASH DOWN

Darren Taylor of Denver, Colorado, can achieve a spectacular dive from a 35-ft (10.7-m) platform into a children's inflatable pool containing just 12 in (30 cm) of water. Taylor, who calls himself Professor Splash, has been diving since the age of four and has focused on shallow diving since 2000. "There really is no training for it because it's so dangerous," he says, but adds that his technique is to "skip across the water" when he makes contact with it. Don't try this at home!

He knows that with such a small target to aim at, one false move could prove fatal.

Taylor always aims to make a real splash when he lands, because the more water that splashes out of the pool, the more his fall is cushioned.

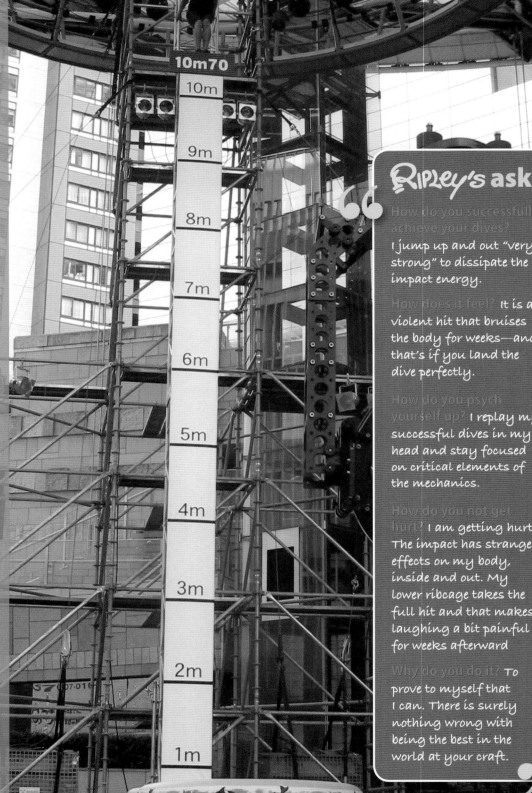

Taylor says that when he stands on the platform he makes sure he never looks down into the tiny pool below.

Ripley's ask

How do you successfully achieve your dives? I jump up and out "very strong" to dissipate the impact energy.

How does it feel? It is a violent hit that bruises the body for weeks—and that's if you land the dive perfectly.

How do you psych yourself up? I replay my successful dives in my head and stay focused on critical elements of the mechanics.

How do you not get hurt? I am getting hurt. The impact has strange effects on my body, inside and out. My lower ribcage takes the full hit and that makes laughing a bit painful for weeks afterward

Why do you do it? To prove to myself that I can. There is surely nothing wrong with being the best in the world at your craft.

MEMORY BOY

Eleven-year-old Nischal Narayanam of Hyderabad, India, can memorize and recall 225 random objects in the exact order they are presented to him.

PINT-SIZE PAPARAZZI

At age 14, Austin Visschedyk is a paparazzo. Realizing that money could be made from taking photos of famous people near his home in West Hollywood, he and his friend, 15-year-old Blaine Hewison-Jones, most nights head to favorite celebrity hangouts. The pint-size paparazzi, as they have become known, have to be home by 10.30 p.m. and then they work on their photographs before going to bed. Austin has already sold a snap of Adam Sandler exiting a gym for $500.

YOUNG BARTENDER

Chris Hardacre of Doncaster, England, is a fully qualified bartender—at 12 years old. His father David is the licensee of the Star pub and now Chris has passed all the exams necessary to serve behind the bar, with adult supervision.

BLINDFOLD DRIVER

At the age of 13, Pat Marquis of Glendale, California, was able to play table tennis and pool, drive a car, read, identify playing cards, or fence—all with his eyes completely covered by a blindfold.

FLYING CAR

In April 2007, a tornado in Indiana hurled a police cruiser 120 ft (35 m) into the air, but the driver, Detective Shayna Mireles, walked away with only bruises.

RAILWAY SLEEPER

When Alexander Fischer fell asleep on a railroad track in Berlin, Germany, he did not wake up even when a train ran over him. He escaped unhurt because his body was between the rails.

PARACHUTE PLUNGE

On his first attempt at skydiving, Benno Jacobs of Bloemfontein, South Africa, fell 3,300 ft (1,000 m) to the ground when his parachute malfunctioned. He walked away with no broken bones!

UPSIDE DOWN

In 2007, Antonio Montagno survived three days without food or water—hanging upside down—after a paragliding accident landed him in a tree near Florence, Italy.

SLEPT ON

A man in West Virginia carried on sleeping after being shot in the head. Michael Lusher of Altizer didn't realize he'd been shot until he awoke nearly four hours later and noticed blood coming from his head.

NAME DROPPER

At the age of 73, Lowell Davis of Savannah, Missouri, began to write down the names of all the persons he could remember meeting since he was three years old. At 83, in 1983, he had a 69-page binder with 3,487 names.

MIGHTY FINGER

Ji Fengshan, 56, of Harbin, China, can lift incredible weights with just one finger. Here he does pull-ups with one finger while carrying a load of bricks weighing 100 lb (45 kg) with another. Ji, who has been perfecting his finger strength for more than 40 years, has also pulled four connected taxis for a distance of 3 ft (1 m)—again with just his middle finger.

Perfect Perspective

As a child, Stephen Wiltshire was mute and did not relate to other people. Diagnosed as autistic, he had uncontrolled tantrums, lived entirely in his own world, and did not learn to speak fully until he was nine. Yet he has an incredible talent for drawing and can produce remarkably accurate and detailed pictures entirely from memory.

Just by looking once at a building, Stephen can reproduce its likeness faithfully on paper. As a 12-year-old, he drew from memory a brilliant sketch of London's St. Pancras station, which he had visited for the first time only briefly a few hours earlier. He even drew the station clock hands at 11:20, the precise time at which he had viewed them.

In 2001, after flying in a helicopter over London, he drew in three hours an aerial illustration of a 4-sq-mi (10-sq-km) area of the city, featuring 12 major landmarks and 200 other buildings, all in perfect perspective and scale. In 2005, following a short helicopter ride over Tokyo, he drew a stunningly detailed panoramic view of the city on a 33-ft-long (10-m) canvas. Since then he has drawn Rome, Hong Kong, and Frankfurt on giant canvases.

Stephen can also draw from imagination. When he was eight he was shown photographs of earthquakes in a book and promptly drew fantastic cityscapes showing the aftermath of an earthquake. His artwork is now so valued that he has his own permanent gallery in London.

The Royal Albert Hall, London

Downtown Manhattan, New York City

The Albert Memorial and Royal Albert Hall, London

UNUSUAL GENIUS

● Diagnosed with mental illness at birth, Kim Peek from Salt Lake City, Utah, reads up to eight books a day. He reads at a phenomenal rate, scanning the left page with his left eye and the right page with his right eye, and retaining around 98 per cent of the information. He can read in ten seconds a page that would take most adults three minutes.

● Tony DeBlois from Randolph, Massachusetts, was born blind but began to play the piano at the age of two. He now plays 20 musical instruments and can play more than 8,000 songs from memory.

● David Kidd can barely perform simple arithmetic, yet if he hears a random date—past, present, or future—he can immediately pinpoint on which day of the week it occurred or will occur.

● Derek Paravicini from Surrey, England, is blind and has a severe learning disability, but he can play back a piece of music after hearing it just once.

● England's Daniel Tammet can perform complex mathematical calculations at amazing speeds—he can figure out cube roots quicker than a calculator and recall pi to 22,514 decimal places. Yet because of his autism, he can't tell left from right.

● Despite being born blind with brain damage and never having had a piano lesson in his life, Leslie Lemke from Milwaukee, Wisconsin, played Tchaikovsky's Piano Concerto No. 1 after hearing it for the first time on TV.

The Chrysler Building, New York City

DRILL SWALLOWER

In Cologne, Germany, in 2007, Britain's Thomas Blackthorne had a powerful jackhammer—a drill normally used for breaking up roads—lowered 10 in (25 cm) down his gullet and turned on for five seconds—and he survived. Blackthorne said his greatest fear was that the pneumatic drill would get stuck in his throat or knock all his teeth out!

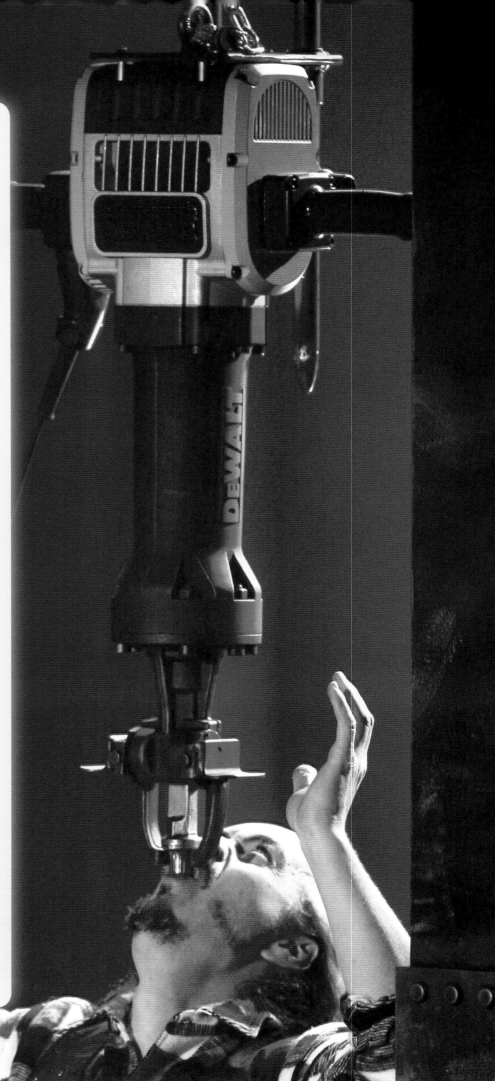

TORNADO TERROR

Caught in a tornado-like storm in New South Wales, Australia, in February 2007, German paraglider Ewa Wisnierska was sucked up in a tornado tunnel to a height of 32,600 ft (9,946 m)—higher than Mount Everest. She ascended at a rate of 65 ft (20 m) per second, causing her to lose consciousness, and in an 80-minute ordeal she survived lightning, a battering from hailstones the size of tennis balls, temperatures as low as −50°F (−45°C), and a lack of oxygen. She reagained consciousness after 45 minutes and eventually managed to come back down to earth 40 mi (64 km) away, covered in ice and gasping for air.

MATH PRODIGY

In August 2007, Hong Kong Baptist University accepted math prodigy March Tian Boedihardjo as a student—at the age of nine.

PARROT FASHION

A four-year-old autistic boy, who has severe learning difficulties and could not speak, learned his first words thanks to his pet parrot. After listening to Barney the macaw, Dylan Hargreaves of Lancashire, England, mimicked the bird's vocabulary.

CARD ACE

Ben Pridmore of Derby, England, can memorize a shuffled deck of 52 playing cards and then recall them in the correct order in less than 30 seconds.

PI PATIENCE

In 2006, Akira Haraguchi of Mobara, Japan, recited pi to 100,000 decimal places from memory. It took him more than 16 hours.

BIRD TALK

Gautam Sapkota of Nepal can talk to wild crows and make them obey simple commands. He says he can utter 13 different crow calls and get the birds to respond. A keen bird-watcher for three years, he can mimic perfectly the calls of 115 species.

BLIND MECHANIC

Despite losing his vision five years ago in an auto accident, Larry Woody has continued to work as a mechanic in Cottage Grove, Oregon. He operates by feel, and to prove that disabilities need not be a handicap, he has recently taken on a deaf assistant.

MARY POPPINS

Blown off a six-story building in Zhejiang Province, China, by a sudden gust of wind in May 2007, schoolgirl Zhang Haijing landed softly after her open umbrella slowed her fall.

LUCKY CRASH

Bryan Rocco from Vineland, New Jersey, saved his own life by crashing his car into a tree. Choking on an onion ring while driving, he blacked out and smashed into the tree. Luckily for Bryan, the impact of the car hitting the tree dislodged the food from his throat so that he could breathe again.

FELLED BEAR

In 2007, a man killed a 300-lb (135-kg) black bear that was threatening his family—by throwing a log at it. Chris Everhart felled the bear with a single blow after it raided the family's campsite in the Chattahoochee National Forest in Georgia.

HUMAN HIBERNATION

A man survived for more than three weeks in a Japanese mountain forest without food or water in the first known case of a human going into hibernation. After breaking his pelvis in a fall, Mitsutaka Uchikoshi fell asleep and when found 24 days later, his body temperature had dropped to just 71.6°F (22°C). He was also suffering from multiple organ failure and his pulse was barely detectable. Doctors believe that after he lost consciousness, his body's natural survival instincts sent him into a hibernation-like state whereby many of his organs slowed while his brain remained protected. He made a full recovery.

FLAG EXPERT

A three-year-old Indian boy can identify the names of 167 countries from their flag colors. Aazer Hussain of Bangalore learned the flags in just 11 days after his parents bought him a poster of flags of the world.

HUMAN FLAG

Canadian gymnast and acrobat Dominic Lacasse can hold himself horizontally on a bar as a "Human Flag" for 39 seconds—a feat of incredible strength.

SELF-AMPUTATION

After being pinned under a fallen tree for 11 hours, 66-year-old Al Hill of Iowa Hill, California, freed himself by using a pocket knife to amputate his own leg.

CUSHIONED FALL

A woman in Nanjing, China, survived a six-story fall in April 2007 after her landing was cushioned by a pile of human excrement. She slipped from a balcony and landed in 8 in (20 cm) of waste, which workers on the street below had just removed from the building's septic tank.

CARDBOARD CARS

Chris Gilmour makes full-sized replicas of cars, bicycles, and motor scooters out of cardboard.

Using nothing more than cardboard and glue—and with no supporting wood or metal framework—the English-born artist creates amazingly lifelike models. His "Pussy Galore" car, exhibited in New York in 2006, is an exact replica of James Bond's famous Aston Martin, right down to tire-slashers, machine guns, and rocket launchers. Although made of cardboard, it is valued at $30,000.

Gilmour uses cardboard partly because it is so easy to find—he collects discarded pieces from dumpsters near his base in Udine, Italy. Sometimes he even leaves the original printing, tape, and labels on to emphasize the fact that he is creating coveted items from what is merely waste material.

His first big piece was a cardboard cow—"to replace the cattle destroyed by B.S.E., so that the fields don't look empty"—and he has since created such diverse everyday objects as a grand piano, guitars, a coffee set, a wheelchair, and a typewriter.

He also built a series of small churches from cardboard packaging. "I needed lots of different packets," he says, "so we bought a lot of things just because of the packaging. Buying one of every item in the supermarket was fun but it did leave us with a cupboard full of food we didn't much like and couldn't tell what it was because I'd taken the wrappings off!"

Chris Gilmour's cardboard replica of a Fiat 500 car extends way beyond the simple exterior. The steering wheel, dash, and even the engine are modeled in precise detail.

Gilmour's cardboard typewriter is so realistic that visitors to his exhibitions are often tempted to press the keys.

It's hard to believe that these beautifully intricate 12-speed bicycles are made out of scrap cardboard packaging. Gilmour particularly enjoys creating objects that usually have moving parts—"you want to open the car door or turn the wheel on the bike, but of course you can't."

Gilmour says that he chose to re-create the famous 007 Aston Martin because "I wanted to take the idea of James Bond as this glamorous, invincible superhero and contrast it with an object made of total rubbish."

BMT 216A

BUMPER CRIME

A white Ford Ranger pickup truck stolen in Miami, Florida, was recovered five days later. The only things missing were 700 bumper stickers that had been covering the exterior.

FAKE BILL

Police arrested a man after he handed over a fake million-dollar bill at a Pittsburgh, Pennsylvania, supermarket and asked for change. When staff refused and confiscated the note, the man became abusive.

JESUS IMAGE

A smudge of driveway sealant said to resemble the face of Jesus was sold for more than $1,500 in an online auction. The image was found on the garage floor of the Serio family home in the town of Forest, Virginia.

DOUBLE THEFT

York Heiden of Stevens Point, Wisconsin, had his car stolen twice in one day: April 27, 2007.

LUCKY NUMBER

A woman from Devon, England, won the equivalent of $2.6 million in the lottery because she forgot the age of her son. Janet Baddick chooses numbers representing family ages, but used 26 for her son Darren, forgetting that he had turned 27 a few weeks earlier. Luckily, 26 was a winning number!

FAMILY TIES

When an off-duty jail deputy in Nevada was pulled over and charged with driving under the influence, the arresting officer was her husband. Charlotte Moore was driving her 2004 Pontiac when she was stopped by husband Mike, a deputy with the Elko County Sheriff's Department.

BOX WARS

In a craze that started in Melbourne, Australia, people fight battles wearing suits of armor made of cardboard. The rules of Box Wars—which has spread to Canada, the U.S.A., and Britain—state that only cardboard, tape, and spray paint may be used for armor and weapons. Battles last around 15 minutes each and end when no one is left wearing any cardboard.

LOVE MOTIVE

Police in Inglewood, California, arrested a man in April 2007 for stealing 26 cars that he used only to visit his girlfriend.

LUCKY MISTAKE

Derek Ladner of Cornwall, England, accidentally bought two lottery tickets with the same sequence of numbers. The numbers came up, meaning that he won a share of the jackpot—the equivalent of nearly $1 million—twice over!

LOOK, NO ARMS!

A driver in Pasco County, Florida, lost police in an 8-minute high-speed car chase in 2007 despite having no arms and only one leg. Officers said that 40-year-old Michael Wiley, who had had been sighted out in his car while legally suspended from driving, had overcome three amputations and had learned to drive with his stumps. In 1998, Wiley had also caused a highway car chase that reached speeds of 120 mph (193 km/h).

BRIDGE STOLEN

In August 2007, police in Ryazan, Russia, arrested a man for stealing an entire 16-ft-long (5-m) steel bridge.

STICKY PREDICAMENT

In March 2007, police in Magdeburg, Germany, rescued a 91-year-old man who slipped while resurfacing his roof and became glued to it by the tar.

BLIND POLICE

Many criminal investigations are solved in Belgium thanks to a blind police unit. The pioneering six-member unit specializes in transcribing and analyzing wiretap recordings and, because they have been trained to identify voices and background sounds, they often pick up evidence that sighted detectives have missed.

SILVER BEETLE

Art car enthusiast William Burge from Houston, Texas, has designed a vehicle with a gargoyle theme. Called "Phantoms," it is based on a 1968 Volkswagen Beetle and proved a scary sight at an automobile fair in Essen, Germany, in December 2007.

To celebrate the release of "The Simpsons Movie" on DVD, Donut King in Sydney, Australia, created a mighty donut that weighed nearly 4 tons—the equivalent of two rhinoceroses. Consisting of more than 90,000 individual donuts, half a ton of pink icing, and 66 lb (30 kg) of sprinklies, it measured 20 ft (6 m) in diameter and took 40 people more than nine hours to build.

MONSTER DONUT

KRYSTAL KING!

Joey Chestnut, 23, of San Jose, California, ate 103 Krystal burgers in just eight minutes at the Krystal Square Off IV World Hamburger Eating Championship at Chattanooga, Tennessee, in October 2007—that works out to 13 burgers per minute or one burger every 4.6 seconds!

△

After his incredible eating feat, Joey Chestnut said all he wanted to do was take a nap and digest his food.

Chestnut's achievement in becoming the first person to break the seemingly inconceivable 100-Krystal-burgers-in-eight-minutes barrier confirmed his position as the world's leading competitive eater.

△

FAVORITE JERSEY
David Witthoft, a young Green Bay Packers' football fan from Ridgefield, Connecticut, was so excited by his 2003 Christmas gift—a Packers' jersey with Brett Favre's No.4—that he wore it every day for four years. By the end of 2007, 11-year-old David had worn the jersey for more than 1,450 consecutive days.

SHOE SNIFFER
A man in Nagoya, Japan, was arrested in 2006 for stealing 5,000 pairs of shoes, which he took only to smell them.

FAILED CROSSING
In March 2007, a man tried to cross the fast-flowing Niagara River from Canada into the U.S.A. on an inflatable air mattress. Hearing the man's screams, guards at the Ontario Power Generation plant at Chippawa plucked him from the water as he was being swept toward Niagara Falls on a small ice floe while still clinging to the mattress.

MAIL TOWER
Artist Anne Cohen from Newcastle, England, turned a year's worth of unwanted junk mail into a garden sculpture. She put all the junk mail she received on a large metal spike outside her front door and by the end of 2007 the tower was more than 6 ft (1.8 m) tall.

BELATED GRADUATION
A Utah woman received her high school diploma in 2007—at age 94. Leah Moore Harris Fullmer missed her graduation ceremony from Provo High School in 1931 because of illness and did not pick up her diploma, but her son persuaded the school to trace her records and present it to her before her 95th birthday.

COUGHED BULLET
In October 2007, a month after he was shot in the mouth, Austin Askins of Liberty Lake, Washington, miraculously coughed up the bullet that surgeons previously had been unable to remove.

WIDE CHOICE
There were so many candidates in Bulgaria's 2007 local elections that the ballot papers were 6½ ft (2 m) long.

COMPLAINTS' CHOIR
A Finnish couple have put together a series of choirs that complain in four-part harmony about subjects ranging from bad dates to people who chew gum too loudly. Oliver Kochta-Kalleinen and Tellervo Kalleinen have started more than 20 complaints' choirs all over the world, from Melbourne, Australia, to Chicago, Illinois. In Birmingham, England, the choir sang about the country's expensive beer; in Helsinki, Finland, singers bemoaned boring dreams; and in Budapest, Hungary, choristers ranted about a neighbor practicing folk dancing in an upstairs apartment. Participants do not need to come from a musical background, but they must offer at least one complaint for possible inclusion in the performance.

CAROUSEL CONTEST

Four couples spent seven days on a rotating carousel in Xiamen, China, in an endurance contest to win a house. They had to stay on the fairground horses to eat, drink, and sleep—and were allowed to climb off only for toilet breaks. The contestants wore safety belts so that they did not fall off their horses while sleeping.

MOWER CHASE

A man accused of drunk driving tried to escape from the police on a lawn mower. The man was riding the mower near his home in Bunker Hill, West Virginia, when a sheriff's deputy pulled him over on suspicion of being drunk. The suspect attempted to speed away on the mower, but was easily outpaced by the deputy—on foot.

FOUND FRIEND

A vivid dream led a Canadian woman to a remote spot where she found a missing family friend. Jamie Lynn Cunningham of Gift Lake, Alberta, studied a sweater, a missing person's poster, and Native American Indian treaty card belonging to Michael Nahachick, who had not been seen for a month, and then dreamed Michael had fallen off a bridge at High Prairie, 25 mi (40 km) away. The next day she and fellow searchers found him, alive, at the exact spot under the bridge.

YELLOW DOOR

In 2007, Khumi Burton received a postcard sent from Poland that had been simply addressed to: Khumi, Yellow Door, Wilmslow, England.

37 SUSPECTS

When town Mayor Miguel Grima was found murdered in January 2007, police investigating the death declared all 37 residents of the village of Fago, Spain, as suspects in the case.

GOLF SPARK

In June 2007, a golfer in Reno, Nevada, struck a metal object with a golf swing and created a spark that ignited a wildfire, which destroyed 20 acres (8 ha) of land before finally dying out.

DRESS CODE

The Red Hat Society has more than 40,000 chapters in 30 countries around the world and has only two rules for its female members—they all must wear red hats and purple dresses.

BALLOON BART

Here are the Simpsons as you have never seen them before—made entirely out of balloons. They are the work of Washington State balloon artist Adam Lee, whose other creations include balloon likenesses of Jay Leno, Austin Powers, Bill Gates, Martha Stewart, and the Statue of Liberty.

237

SMASHING PUMPKINS

If you ever doubted that the pumpkin really is a squash fruit, the proof is at the Pumpkin Drop, a weird ritual that takes place each year before the Giant Pumpkin Weigh-off near Canby, Oregon. At 10 a.m. sharp, and watched by a crowd of around 4,000 admirers, a huge pumpkin (the 2007 specimen weighed 1,269 lb/575 kg) is loaded on to a crane and hoisted 100 ft (30 m) into the air above an old vehicle donated especially for the occasion. Once in position, the pumpkin is dropped from its great height onto the roof of the unoccupied van, crushing it to pieces.

POOL STOLEN
Thieves stole a 1,000-gal (4,550-l) hip-high, inflatable swimming pool from the home of Daisy Valdivia in Patterson, New Jersey—water and all!

UNEXPECTED RETURN
A man being discharged from the hospital ended up back inside after his mother hit him with her car when she went to collect him. Ron Carter was walking to meet his 84-year-old mother Lillian outside Elliot Hospital, New Hampshire, when she accidentally ran him over.

HAIRY EYE
Summitt, a dog living in Owensboro, Kentucky, has had hairs growing from the tissue of her right eye since she was a puppy.

CHICKEN RUN
Scared by a dog, a four-year-old Chinese boy let out such a loud scream that it caused a poultry stampede that killed more than 400 chickens.

ARMED SHRUBBERY
A bank in Manchester, New Hampshire, was robbed in 2007 by a man disguised as a tree. He walked in with leaves and branches duct-taped to his head and body and demanded money.

BALLOON JOURNEY
In September 2007, four-year-old Alice Maines of Manchester, England, released a balloon with a note attached—and 6,000 mi (9,660 km) and six weeks later it was recovered by 13-year-old Xie Yu Fei in Guangzhou, China.

COMPLIMENT MACHINE
Artist Tom Greaves built a machine that dispensed random compliments to passersby on 14th Street, Washington, D.C., in 2007. Placed on a street corner, the machine contained 150 pre-recorded compliments, ranging from "nice eyes" to "positive energy."

FISH ATTACK
Fisherman Josh Landin was taken to hospital in Melbourne, Florida, after a 57-lb (26-kg) king mackerel jumped into his boat, knocked him over, and bit him on the leg.

LEG HAIR
Medical student Wes Pemberton from Tyler, Texas, has a leg hair that is 5 in (13 cm) long. He spotted the stray strand growing from his left thigh in the summer of 2007 and began nurturing it by washing it daily with shampoo and conditioner.

SHOT BY DOG
A hunter in Iowa was shot in the leg by his own dog. James Harris of Tama was hunting pheasants in October 2007 when his dog stepped on his shotgun and tripped the trigger, dispatching more than 100 pellets into his master's calf.

CHEESE LOVER
Owing to a food phobia, Dave Nunley from Cambridgeshire, England, has eaten nothing but cheese for more than 25 years. He has never had a hot meal in his life—not even melted cheese—and survives by eating 238 lb (108 kg) of grated mild cheddar every year.

SLIM FIT
Artez Kenyetta Knox escaped jail in Gary, Indiana, by taking his clothes off and amazingly squeezing through the cell door's food-tray slot.

FOWL SENTENCE
Instead of giving three prisoners a 30-day jail sentence each, Municipal Judge Michael Cicconetti ordered them to stand outside the courthouse in Painesville, Ohio, wearing chicken suits.

NAME CHANGE
Scott Wiese of Forsyth, Illinois, bet that if his favorite team, the Chicago Bears, lost the Super Bowl in 2007, he would change his name to that of the opposing team's quarterback. The Bears did lose to the Indianapolis Colts and so Wiese filed to have his name legally changed to the Colts' quarterback—Peyton Manning.

GREEN SHEEP
A flock of 250 sheep in a Romanian village suddenly turned green overnight. Veterinarians discovered that the color change had been caused by a limestone solution that shepherd Cristinel Florea had given to the animals in order to cure a skin disease.

SILENT WORLD
In 2007, a boy who had taken a vow of silence when he was three years old finally spoke again for the first time in ten years. Ben Grocock of Cornwall, England, was so terrified at the prospect of a tonsil operation that he threatened never to speak again if it went ahead. True to his word, once his tonsils had been removed, he relied mainly on written notes and hand signals to communicate over the following decade.

LOTTO LUCK
The odds of winning the New York Lotto jackpot once are 22.5 million to one, but Adeline and Eugene Angelo have done it twice. In 1996, they won $2.5 million after splitting a $10 jackpot with three others, and then in 2007, with luck on their side, they picked up a $5-million prize.

HUMAN ASHTRAY
In 2007, a gravedigger in Fitchburg, Massachusetts, was charged with stealing human body parts—including a skull and a thigh bone—from a broken casket at a cemetery and taking them home to make an ashtray.

COSTLY ERROR
Instead of sending out just one winning ticket, a marketing company in Roswell, New Mexico, mistakenly dispatched 50,000 scratch-off tickets that declared the ticket holder the winner of the $1,000 grand prize. The company blamed a typographical error.

JUDGMENT DAY
Immediately after being sentenced to five years in prison for theft, David Kite of Belleville, Illinois, was married in a civil wedding ceremony—by the same judge that presided over his criminal trial.

ONE SIZE FITS ALL!

In order to make the dress, Shazneen had to transport her sewing machine up to the terrace of the building. There she had to construct a tent to protect herself from the fierce heat.

The dress was supported by thin scaffolding, which took workers more than 12 hours to erect and fit securely behind the garment.

Shazneen's dress was unveiled on a giant hanger—made of metal pipes—from the front of the Sunder Mashal building on Mumbai's Marine Drive.

Shazneen's sketch of the dress. As the building faces the sea, the weather was very windy and Shazneen had to hire three men to hold the fabric in place so that it could be stitched.

Indian designer Shazneen Chiniwala made a dress that was an incredible 70 ft (21 m) long for a fashion week in Mumbai in March 2007—that's big enough to fit more than a dozen ordinary-sized women. It took the 26-year-old two months to finish the dress, which was made of plastic and colored jute.

SLEEP WASH

Mrs. Xu, of Wuhan City, China, regularly washes the family's clothes in the middle of the night—while she is still asleep. She has been sleepwalking for more than ten years and her husband has had to put locks on the door to stop her leaving the house and washing neighbors' clothes.

ACCURATE TIPSTER

Four days before the 1959 Kentucky Derby, psychic Spencer Thornton of Nashville, Tennessee, wrote his prediction for the first three horses to finish on a piece of paper. The paper was sealed, unread, in an envelope and placed in a vault of the Third National Bank. The vault could be unlocked only by a combination of three keys, kept by two vice-presidents and its custodian—and it was not until two days after the race that the three men opened the vault and the envelope to reveal that Thornton's prediction was 100 percent correct.

COMPULSORY GOLF

Xiamen University in Fujian, China, requires all its business, law, economics, and computer students to take golf lessons.

COW CRUSHER

A couple driving through Washington State on vacation to celebrate their first wedding anniversary miraculously survived after a cow weighing 600 lb (270 kg) fell off a cliff 200 ft (60 m) high and landed on their moving minivan. Charles and Linda Everson from Westland, Michigan, escaped unhurt by the incident, but their van was badly damaged and the windshield smashed. A shocked Mr. Everson said: "It was just bam—you just saw something come down and hit the hood!"

LOST IN TRANSLATION

After having what she thought was the word "mum" tattooed on her back in Chinese letters, 19-year-old Charlene Williams was shocked to find that her tattoo actually said "Friend from hell." The mother-of-one from Dorset, England, did not realize that Chinese letters change their meaning when joined together. She has since had the tattoo covered over with a new design.

HUGE HAIRBALL

A barber for more than 50 years, Henry Coffer of Charleston, Missouri, has been collecting customers' clippings and has turned them into a huge hairball weighing over 160 lb (73 kg).

NICE PROFIT

In 2005, Ed Lee of Merrimack, New Hampshire, sold a 1913 nickel coin for $4.15 million—that's 83 million times its original value!

BURGER MISSION

Jay Barr of Cape Coral, Florida, makes an hour-long, 150-mi (240-km) flight to Kissimmee, Florida, ten times a year—just to buy hamburgers. He buys them in packs of 24 from the nearest Krystal fast-food restaurant. The Krystal company was so impressed by Mr. Barr's devotion to their burgers that it unveiled a hamburger box and drink cup with Barr's face and an airplane printed on them.

DREAM WEDDING

David Brown of London, England, sent a text message to a phone number that came to him in a dream. The woman on the other end of the text was Michelle Kitson and, intrigued, she responded. The two of them married five years later.

BIRTHDAY REMINDER

Vanda Jones of Penygroes, Wales, had the birthdays of all her five children tattooed on her arm so that she could be sure never to forget them.

ANCIENT FRUIT

In 2007, a museum in Staffordshire, England, displayed a 116-year-old orange. The blackened, dried-up fruit came from the lunchbox of coal miner Joseph Roberts, who was fatally injured in an underground explosion in 1891—sadly, before he got to eat his orange.

CANDY MAN

A snowman Pez dispenser on display at the Burlingame Museum of Pez Memorabilia in California weighs 85 lb (38.5 kg) and stands 7 ft 10 in (2.4 m) tall—that's 20 times the size of a normal Pez dispenser. It can dispense 6,480 pellets of Pez candy.

FLOATING PUB

A ship sailed 15,000 mi (24,000 km) from New Zealand to England in 2007 carrying an entire pub. When Tim Ellingham moved to London he asked friends back in New Zealand to send him his favorite Speights beer. Hearing of his predicament, the brewery decided to build a pub, fill it with beer, and ship it to the U.K. on board a cargo vessel. The pub was built in two 40-ft (12-m) containers joined together and came complete with bar, lounge, air conditioning, and plasma TV.

CHINESE VAMPIRE

Li Man-Yiu of Hong Kong was arrested in September 2007 for stealing and drinking two vials of blood from a hospital laboratory.

KIDNEY DONOR

Jamie Howard knocked on Paul Sucher's door at Twin Falls, Idaho, hoping to sell him a vacuum cleaner, but ended up giving him a kidney instead. Traveling salesman Howard learned that Sucher could not afford a new vacuum cleaner because of kidney failure three years earlier and so when he discovered that they were the same blood type, he generously offered to become Sucher's donor.

LATE ARRIVAL

A postcard sent by a Japanese soldier from Burma in 1943 finally reached its destination 64 years later. The card arrived at Shizuo Nagano's home in Japan's southwestern state of Kochi via Nagasaki, Arizona, and Hawaii.

UNWANTED GIFT

Owing to a postal mix-up, Frank and Ludivine Larmande of Cascade, Michigan, accidentally received a preserved human liver and part of a head in the mail, both intended for a lab.

THIRD EAR

Australian Stelios Arcadiou—known as Stelarc—has had an extra ear grafted onto his left arm... all in the name of art. He plans to install a microphone into the extra ear, which is made of human cartilage, and connect it to the Internet so that people everywhere can hear the sounds it picks up.

MOTORCYCLING FROG

When it comes to talented pets, Oui the frog must be unique—because she can ride a miniature motorcycle and predict winning lottery numbers! The frog's owner, Tongsai Bamnungthai of Pattaya, Thailand, says local people used to come and read Oui's stomach to determine lucky numbers, and that Oui loves to play with children's toys and to pose for photographs.

STAYING PUT

A 59-year-old prisoner in Brandenburg, Germany, has repeatedly been offered early release since 1992—but he refuses to leave the penitentiary that has become his home. The man was given life imprisonment for murder in 1972 and under German law prisoners are not obliged to leave jail before their sentences have been completed.

HALF SHARE

To protest against his pending divorce, a 43-year-old man in Sonneberg, Germany, cut his house in half with a chainsaw and then used a forklift truck to take his half away.

SPACE IMAGES

Natalie Meilinger of Chicago, Illinois, found that instead of turning on the TV for the latest news on NASA's 2007 Atlantis space shuttle, all she had to do was switch on her baby's monitor. The monitor mysteriously picked up black-and-white video images from inside the shuttle.

MEMORY LOSS

British musician Clive Wearing cannot remember anything from 1985 to the present day owing to a brain infection, but he can remember everything prior to 1985.

CRASH PREMONITION

After suffering nightmares on ten successive nights about an impending passenger-plane crash involving an American Airlines DC-10, David Booth, a 23-year-old office manager from Cincinnati, Ohio, reported his fears to the relevant authorities on May 22, 1979. Three days later, an American Airlines DC-10 crashed at Chicago's O'Hare International Airport, killing 273 people.

GHOST SHIP

In April 2007, a yacht was found off the coast of Australia with all of its emergency equipment intact and dinner on the table—but its three-member crew had disappeared without a trace.

EXPLODING TOADS

The toad population of Hamburg, Germany, was decimated in 2005 when several thousand of the creatures mysteriously exploded, sending entrails and body parts over a wide area. Witnesses said the toads swelled up to three-and-a-half times their normal size before suddenly exploding.

DEAD FISH

Millions of anchovies mysteriously washed ashore near Colunga, Spain, in September 2006, leaving the beach covered with three tons of dead fish.

DRUNK RIDER

A German man rode his horse into the foyer of a bank to sleep off his hangover. Wolfgang Heinrich of Wiesenberg had been riding his horse, Sammy, when he stopped to have a few drinks. Too drunk to ride home, he used his bank card to open up a nearby bank foyer and spent the night there with Sammy.

DARING JUGGLER

Nathan Zorchak, an American entertainer based in Brighton, England, can not only juggle scythes and bowling balls, but also three live chainsaws.

SWEET-TOOTHED BEAR

A man returned to his van in Vernon Township, New Jersey, in 2007 to find that it had been raided by a bear that had moved it 40 ft (12 m) down the street. Police believe the bear broke in to the van through the window because he could smell the Halloween candy. As he reached for the candy, the bear is thought to have dislodged the parking brake, causing the vehicle to roll down the hill.

SELF-PORTRAITS

In May 2007, U.S. artist Karl Baden exhibited contact prints of the 7,305 photographs he had taken of himself—that's one photograph a day every day since February 23, 1987. The only day he missed in that 20-year period was October 15, 1991, when he was late for a class he was teaching at Rhode Island School of Design. Baden had planned to do the picture afterward but then forgot.

GATOR WRESTLING

For $100 you can buy a day's tuition in... alligator wrestling. Colorado Gators, near Alamosa, is an alligator farm where people can learn to wrestle reptiles up to 11 ft (3.4 m) long and weighing 600 lb (270 kg). The key to success is a stealthy approach, although even experienced wrestler Jay Young gets bitten at least once a year. "These are not mild-mannered animals," he says, "and if they're breathing, they're in a bad mood."

243

CARD TOWER

Using no tape or glue, Bryan Berg built a freestanding tower of playing cards measuring 25 ft 9½ in (7.86 m) high at the 2007 Texas State Fair in Dallas. The tower, which took Berg five weeks to complete, consisted of 1,800 decks of cards and was restricted only by the height of the building in which he was working.

SLOW HAND

One of the hands on an astronomical clock in a museum at the Obizzi Palace in Vienna, Austria, requires 20,904 years to make one complete revolution.

MUMMY DEAREST

Sisters Josephine and Valmai Lamas of London, England, have kept their mother Annie in a mortician's freezer for ten years—regularly replacing her cosmetics. Instead of burying her, they have spent more than $25,000 to keep her in cold storage so that they can visit her every weekend.

HARD WORKER

Sixty-year-old Eric Weyman retired as a milkman in Herefordshire, England, in 2007 after taking just one vacation during his entire 40-year career and delivering a mammoth 10 million pints of milk.

YARD THEFT

In May 2006, a thief stole an entire front yard from a house in Adelanto, California, taking the grass, plants, and even the sprinkler system.

BULLET HALTED

Debbie Bingham of St. Petersburg, Florida, was struck by a stray bullet during a New Year's celebration—but was saved from serious injury when it lodged in her bra strap.

JAILHOUSE CROC

A saltwater crocodile that measured 7 ft 9 in (2.4 m) was captured by Australian police and kept in a cell overnight after it had threatened local fishermen. Officers in Nhulunbuy, Northern Territory, put the croc in an unused cell at the town's police station and hosed it down with water throughout the night before taking it to a farm in the morning.

COMPUTER ERROR

Denis Dixon of Dorset, England, was sent a quarterly gas bill for his two-bedroom rented apartment, which mistakenly asked for a payment of £11 million ($22 million)!

ICE COURSE

Charlie Gandy of Colorado built an 18-hole golf course on the ice of the Twin Lakes Reservoir and used microchips in the white balls so that radar could keep track of them.

NINE POSITIONS

On June 29, 2007, Brad Turney of Alexandria, Louisiana, played all nine positions for the minor league baseball team, the Alexandria Aces, during a single regulation game.

DREAM TEAM

An Australian sports fan has quit his job, sold his house in Sydney, and moved his wife and two young children to the U.S.A.—just so that he can follow the Green Bay Packers. Wayne Scullino's love affair started when he was 15 and a friend gave him a videotape of a football game between the Packers and the Minnesota Vikings.

STILL LIFE

Gisela Leibold of Munich, Germany, is blind to all movement and sees things only as a series of still frames.

COMPUTER FLOTSAM

Hundreds of computer monitors from an unknown source washed ashore in September and October 2006 on Tai Long Wan Beach in Sai Kung, Hong Kong, China.

CARD CONFUSION

Manhattan accountant Frank Van Buren ordered two replacement credit cards but received 2,000 of them instead—all with his name and account number. It took him hours to shred the surplus cards.

VALUABLE DIME

When rare-coin dealer John Feigenbaum of Virginia Beach, Virginia, flew from San José, California, to New York City in 2007, he had in his jeans pocket a 10-cent coin that was worth $1.9 million. The 1894-S dime is one of only nine known to be in existence.

MASTER LINGUIST

A ten-year-old boy from West Midlands, England, can speak 11 different languages. Arpan Sharma taught himself French, Italian, German, Spanish, Polish, Thai, Mandarin, Swahili, and the Lugandan language of Uganda. As well as English, he also learned Hindi from his parents. His teachers have described him as "extraordinary."

STAYING POWER

A couple who stopped off at a Travelodge roadside hotel in 1985 have been living in one ever since. David and Jean Davidson were so impressed by the Travelodge at Newark in Nottinghamshire, England, that they moved out of their Sheffield apartment and into the hotel. Twelve years later they finally moved—but only to a new Travelodge at nearby Grantham, where Room One has now been renamed the Davidson suite.

UNITED NATIONS

In 2006, the Lee High School soccer team in Baton Rouge, Louisiana, featured players from ten different nations: Afghanistan, China, Congo, Croatia, Honduras, Mexico, Palestine, Sudan, Togo, and the U.S.A.

TINY PARK

Mill Ends Park, an official city park in Portland, Oregon, measures only 2 ft (60 cm) across. It was built in 1948 as a leprechaun colony.

BLOCKED NOSE

Doctors in Mumbai, India, discovered what was blocking a woman's nose in 2007—a toothbrush. The 3-in (7.5-cm) brush became lodged in her nostril after breaking in two while she brushed her teeth. She could not find the upper part of the brush but started suffering bad nosebleeds and emitting a foul-smelling discharge from her nasal area. The brush was eventually removed after showing up on a CT scan.

HEAD-SPINNER

Eighteen-year-old Aichi Ono of Japan can do more than 100 spins in a minute—and he can do them standing on his head. Using his body as momentum, he demonstrated his remarkable head-spinning skills at a shopping mall in Hong Kong in December 2007.

ROADKILL TOYS

A British soft toy company has launched a range of animal characters that have all been run over. Twitch the roadkill raccoon has his tongue hanging out, one eyeball smashed in, and comes with a zipper that spills his innards and an opaque plastic body bag to keep out maggots. A label attached to his toe gives details of his grisly death. Other roadkill victims include Splodge the hedgehog and Pop the weasel.

LIZARD SMUGGLER

In 2007, a man named Jereme James, from Los Angeles, California, was accused of smuggling three rare iguana lizards into the U.S.A.—by hiding them inside his prosthetic leg. He allegedly hollowed out a secret compartment inside his false leg and used it to smuggle Banded iguanas from Fiji. According to the prosecution, James had previously admitted to selling the rare lizards for up to $10,000 each.

MULE MISSION

In 2007, Rod Maday of Boy River, Minnesota, rode his four-year-old mule, named Henry, 1,500 mi (2,415 km) to Gilette, Wyoming, in search of work. Maday, who had lost his driver's license ten years previously, rode up to 70 mi (112 km) a day and made the six-week trek in full cowboy gear.

GNOM-ADIC

The police station at Springfield, Oregon, was overrun by lawn gnomes in 2007. The 75 plastic and porcelain ornaments were recovered by officers from the front lawn of a house where they had been placed as a prank after being stolen from gardens around the town.

SHEEP ACCOMMODATION

A man in Apex, North Carolina, shared his house with 80 sheep. David Watts lived upstairs while the flock, which he considered to be pets, lived downstairs. He sometimes took selected sheep for walks on a leash around the neighborhood.

THE LAW IS AN ASS

The chief witness in a 2007 court case in Dallas, Texas, was a donkey. Buddy was led into the courtroom to help resolve a dispute between two neighbors.

KITTY COPS

Thai police chiefs have come up with a new way to discipline officers who break rules—making them wear a Hello Kitty armband. The bright pink armband has a Hello Kitty motif and two embroidered hearts and is designed to shame the wearer.

TREES MARRIED

Two trees that grew around each other in West Bengal, India, were married by villagers in 2006 in a bid to keep evil spirits at bay. More than 250 people attended the ceremony, where priests chanted hymns and decorated the conjoined trees with colorful garments.

FALLING CAT

A woman from Chongqing, China, was taken to hospital in 2007 after being knocked out by a cat falling from a high-rise apartment building. The tumbling cat hit Tang Meirong on the head as she walked along a footpath. Tang survived her ordeal but, sadly, the cat had used up its ninth life and was pronounced dead at the scene.

ALARM MIMIC

A pet parrot that loves to imitate sounds helped save a Muncie, Indiana, family from a house fire in 2007—by mimicking a smoke alarm. As flames ripped through their home, Shannon Conwell and his son slept through the real smoke alarm but were woken by Peanut the parrot's squawking imitation of it.

CROC FROCK

A woman tried to cross the border between Egypt and Gaza with three crocodiles strapped to her waist. The 20-in-long (50-cm) crocodiles had their jaws tied shut with string and were concealed under a loose robe, but the woman's "strangely fat" appearance alerted Palestinian guards at the crossing.

HEAVY HEDGEHOG

A hedgehog found in Surrey, England, weighed four times the size of a normal hedgehog. George tipped the scales at a whopping 4 lb 14 oz (2.2 kg) and was so fat that he had to be placed on a crash diet by an animal center.

Boar Island

A 250-lb (115-kg) wild boar called Babe lives a life of luxury on his own private island in the Bahamas. Babe lives on the island with its only two human inhabitants, Luke Abbott and Mona Wiethuchter, who feed him hot dogs, apples, and pasta and watch him stroll along the beach or go for a swim. For further relaxation, he enjoys a beer—but he has only one a day because with any more he can become a bit boisterous.

INDEX

ACKNOWLEDGMENTS

FRONT COVER AND TITLE PAGE Zhang Xiuke/ChinaPhotoPress/Photocome/PA Photos, Roland Berry, Alex Pang; **4** (t/l) Zhang Xiuke/ChinaPhotoPress/Photocome/PA Photos, (t/r) Gary Roberts/Rex Features, (c) Rex Features, (b/l) ChinaFotoPress/Photocome/PA Photos, (b/r) NBCUPhotoBank/Rex Features; **5** (t/l) Reuters/Sukree Sukplang, (t/r) Scott Cummins, (c) Bigfoot 4x4 Inc, (b) ChinaFotoPress/Wang Zi/Photocome/PA Photos; **8** (bgd) Alex Pang, (b) CNImaging/Photoshot, (c) Zhang Xiuke/ChinaPhotoPress/Photocome/PA Photos; **9** (sp) Zhang Xiuke/ChinaPhotoPress/Photocome/PA Photos; **10** (c) SWNS.com; **11** Reuters/Victor Kintanar; **12** SWNS.com; **13** AP/PA Photos; **14** Reuters/Lucas Jackson; **15** KNS News; **16–17** Aroon Thaewchatturat; **18** Daimler AG; **19** ChinaFotoPress/Photocome/PA Photos; **20** Peter Lawson/Rex Features; **21** (t) Steven R Kutcher, (b) AP/PA Photos; **22–23** Fredrik Fransson; **23** (b/l) NASA; **24** (l) AFP/Getty Images, (r) Yang Fan/ChinaFotoPress/Photocome/PA Photos; **25** (t) ChinaFotoPress/Zhang Yanlin/Photocome/PA Photos, (b) Bournemouth News & Pic Service/Rex Features; **26** (r) © 2007 Tony Rath Photography www.trphoto.com; **27** Javier Trueba/MSF/Science Photo Library; **28** Mike Stanford WSDOT; **29** (t) Reuters/Darrin Zammit Lupi, (b) Reuters/Finbarr O'Reilly; **30** (t) Steve Chen/AP/PA Photos, (b) Reuters/Frank Lin; **31** Reuters/Frank Lin; **32** Richard Austin/Rex Features; **33** (t) Ben Margot/AP/PA Photos, (r) Reuters/Yuriko Nakao; **34** (b/l, b/c) Cathal McNaughton/PA Archive/PA Photos, (t/r, c/r, b/r) Rick Murphy, Six Flags Discovery Kingdom; **35** (sp) Robyn Beck/AFP/Getty Images, (t/r) CNImaging/Photoshot; **36** (t) Piers Morgan/Rex Features, (c) Simon Czapp/Rex Features, (b) Chris Balcombe/Rex Features; **37** (t) S Chalker/Newspix/Rex Features, (b) ChinaFotoPress/Zhong Zhibing/Photocome/PA Photos; **38** Frogwatch (North)/Getty Images; **39** (t) Reuters/Alessandro Garofalo, (b) Colin Shepherd/Rex Features; **40** Mr.Lee/J.Perthold; **41** (t, c) Julie Peasley, (b) Mr.Lee/J.Perthold; **42** (t) Mike Stone, (b) Inaldo Perez/AP/PA Photos; **43** Camera Press/ChinaFotoPress; **44** (t, c) Newspix/Rex Features, (b) Matt Rourke/AP/PA Photos; **45** Reuters/Ho New; **46–47** Sherron Bridges; **48** (t) Douglas Fretz, (b) Jean Farley/AP/PA Photos; **49** (t) Reuters/Ali Jarekji, (b) Gary Roberts/Rex Features; **50** (t, b) www.vipfibers.com, (c) Ashne Lalin; **51** (t) Denis Poroy/AP/PA Photos, (b) Mitsuhiko Imamori/Minden/FLPA; **54** Rex Features; **55** (t) Patrick de Noirmont, (b) Barry Batchelor/PA Archive/PA Photos; **56** (b) Caters News Agency Ltd/Rex Features; **57** (t) Albanpix Ltd/Rex Features, (b) Phil Yeomans/Rex Features; **58** (t) Photocome/Photocome/PA Photos, (b) Eric Gay/AP/PA Photos: **59** Michael Steve Bean; **60** Tommy LaVergne, Rice University; **61** Wenger N.A.; **62** (t) Barcroft Media, (b) ChinaFotoPress/Photocome/PA Photos; **63** (t) Allan Bovill/Strathclyde Police/PA Wire/PA Photos, (b) Rex Features; **64** (t) Katsumi Kasahara/AP/PA Photos, (b) Reuters/Jason Lee; **65** Brandi Simons/Getty Images; **66** Choi Byung-kil/AP/PA Photos; **67** (t) John Steiner, (b) Masayuki Sumida/AP/PA Photos; **68–69** Chadwick and Spector www.chadwickandspector.com; **68** (frames) (t) Studio-54/Fotolia.com; **69** (t/l) Philip Hunton/Fotolia.com, (t/r) Aleksander Yurovskikh/Fotolia.com, (b/l) catnap/Fotolia.com, (b/r) Kirill Zdorov/Fotolia.com; **70** (t) Amia Fore, (b) AFP/Getty Images; **71** ChinaFotoPress/Wang Zi/Photocome/PA Photos; **72–73** www.anilgupta.com; **74–75** (c) Reuters/Stringer Australia; **74** (t) Newscom; **75** (t/l) Stephen Krasemann/NHPA/Photoshot, (t/r) Kelley Cox/AP/PA Photos; **76** (t) Reuters/Jason Lee, (b) AP/PA Photos; **77** Wojtek Laski/Rex Features; **78–79** (b) Manichi Rafi; **78** (t) Reuters/Kim Kyung Hoon, (c) Reuters/Marcos Brindicci; **79** (t) Joe Imel/AP/PA Photos; **82–83** (b) Peter Byrne/PA Archive/PA Photos; **82** (t) Reuters/Shaun Best; **84** Yann Arthus-Bertrand/Corbis; **85** (t) Yann Arthus-Bertrand/Corbis, (b) Rykoff Collection/Corbis; **86** (t) ChinaFotoPress/Photocome/PA Photos, (b) AP/PA Photos; **87** Don and Laura Caldwell www.AcmeBalloon.com; **88–89** Jasper Juinen/Getty Images; **90** Koichi Kamoshida/Getty Images; **91** (t) Kazuhiro Nogi/AFP/Getty Images, (b) Denis Doyle/Getty Images; **92–93** (bgd) Pete Erickson/AP/PA Photos, Kent Couch www.couchballoons.com; **94** UPPA/Photoshot; **95** (t) CNImaging/Photoshot, (b) UPPA/Photoshot; **98** (r) Dusty Bastian, (b) Brad Meyer; **99** (t) Reuters/Claro Cortes; **100–101** (t) Jin Siliu/ChinaFotoPress/Photocome/PA Photos; **101** ChinaFotoPress/Photocome/PA Photos; **102** (sp) Volker Hartmann/AFP/Getty Images, (b/l) Axel Schmidt/AFP/Getty Images, (b/r) Reinhold Kringel Münster/Germany; **103** (t) Reinhold Kringel Münster/Germany, (b) Oliver Krato/DPA/PA Photos; **104–105** Scott Ableman; **106** ChinaFotoPress/Photocome/PA Photos; **107** AFP/Getty Images; **108–109** © Veniamin's Human Slinky Author; Ioan ®Veniamin Oprea President of ®Veniamin Shows, Inc.; **110** (bgd) Courtesy of Pleasure Beach, Blackpool, (t) Martin Rickett/PA Wire/PA Photos, (b) Courtesy of Pleasure Beach, Blackpool; **111** Phil Mesibar www.mesibar.com/Paul Blair www.DizzyHips.com; **112** Babineau Photography; **113** ChinaFotoPress/Photocome/PA Photos, (b) Reuters/POOL New; **114–115** Simon de Trey-White/Barcroft Media; **116** (t) AP/PA Photos, (b) Aijaz Rahi/AP/PA Photos; **117** (t) AP/PA Photos, (b) Reuters/STR New; **118** NBCUPhotoBank/Rex Features; **119** (t) Gary Roberts/Rex Features, (b) Reuters/Ho New; **120** (t) Reuters/Stringer Shanghai, (b) Reuters/Stringer India; **121** Reuters/China Daily China Daily Information Corp – CDIC; **122** (t) Reuters/Apichart Weerawong, (b) Reuters/Stringer Shanghai; **123** Reuters/China Daily China Daily Information Corp – CDIC; **124–125** Liz Hickok; **126–127** (t) Alex Macnaughton/Rex Features; **126** (b) AFP/Getty Images; **127** (b) Reuters/Amit Dave; **128** www.brickartist.com; **129** Camille Allen www.camilleallen.com; **130–131** Althea Crome Merback; **130** (t/l) Yara Clüver; **132–133** Timothy O'Rouke/Rex Features; **134** Courtesy of Pete Goldlust/Amy Mac Williamson; **135** SWNS.com; **136** (t) Gavin Bernard/Barcroft Media, (b) Mark Beekman; **137** Gavin Bernard/Barcroft Media; **138–139** Jeff Gagliardi, The Etch A Sketch ® product name and configuration of the Etch A Sketch ® product are registered trademarks owned by The Ohio Art Company; **142–143** (b) Hu Xuebai/ChinaFotoPress/Photocome/PA Photos; **142** (t) Photocome/PA Photos; **143** (t) Caters News Agency Ltd/Rex Features; **144–145** (b) Wang Bin/ChinaFotoPress/Photocome/PA Photos; **144** (t) Barcroft Media; **145** (t) Reuters/Danilo Krstanovic; **146–147** Scott Cummins; **148** (t) Peter Macdiarmid/Getty Images, (b) ChinaFotoPress/Photocome/PA Photos; **149** Chris Jackson/Getty Images; **150–151** Tortilla Paintings © 2007 Joe Bravo; **152** (t) Reuters/Yuriko Nakao, (l) Reuters/Kiyoshi Ota, (r) Reuters/Jacob Silberberg; **153** (t) Reuters/Chip East, (b) Reuters/China Photos; **154** (t) Joe Giblin/AP/PA Photos, (b) Lindsey Parnaby/Empics Entertainment/PA Photos; **155** Srdjan Ilic/AP/PA Photos; **156** Reuters/China Photos; **157** (t/l) Daniel R. Patmore/AP/PA Photos, (t/r) Reuters/David Mercado, (b) Toru Yamanaka/AFP/Getty Images; **158** (t/l) David George Gordon, (c) ChinaFotoPress/Photocome/PA Photos, (r) Reuters/Staff Photographer; **159** (t) Tang Chhin Sothy/AFP/Getty Images, (b) Jorge Sanchez/AFP/Getty Images; **162–163** (b) Winter; **162** (t) N Connolly/Newspix/Rex Features; **163** (t) Reuters/Richard Chung; **164–165** www.carlwarner.com; **166–167** (b) Berkson Photography; **167** (t) Paul Cooper/Rex Features; **168** (t) Reuters/Chaiwat Subprasom, (b) Reuters/Sukree Sukplang; **169** (t) Reuters/Mariana Bazo, (b) AFP/Getty Images; **170** Reuters/Sergei Karpukhin; **171** (t) Ron Wurzer/Getty Images, (b) Jerome Favre/AP/PA Photos; **172–173** www.amazonswim.com; **174** Steve Colligan; **175** Antonia Bolingbroke-Kent and Jo Huxster www.tuktotheroad.com; **178–179** www.timcopejourneys.com; **180** Keith Sharples/Rex Features; **181** Gabriel Bouys/AFP/Getty Images; **182** (l, r) Juan Rivera Just Film Media, LLC, (c) Jon Ross; **183** (t) Quinn Joseph Baumberger, (b) Dr. Gregory W. Frazier www.horizonsunlimited.com/gregfrazier; **184–185** Heath and Doug, The Tuxedo Travellers; **186–187** www.crossingtheditch.com.au; **188–189** Robert Burns of Brighton; **190** Richard Wilson Turning the Place Over 2007 Courtesy Richard Wilson and Liverpool Biennial; **191** (b) Cheng Xuliang/ChinaFotoPress/Getty Images, (b/r) Reuters/Reinhard Krause; **192** Sipa Press/Rex Features; **193** Rex Features; **194–195** Richard Barnes www.jasonmecier.com; **196** Borys Czonkow/Rex Features; **197** (t) Reuters/Ho New, (b) Peter Foerster/DPA/PA Photos; **200** Ryan Froerer; **201** Victoria Simpson/Rex Features; **202–203** Angie & Jimmy Taylor; **204** (t) Phoebe Syms, (b) Ben Cawthra/Rex Features; **205** (t) Simon Jones/Rex Features, (r) Masatoshi Okauchi/Rex Features; **206** (b/l) Peter Macdiarmid/Rex Features, (b) Steve Pyke/Getty Images; **207** (l) Keith Srakocic/AP/PA Photos, (r) Institute and Museum of the History of Science, Italy; **208–209** www.darsshoeheaven.com/www.justtherightshoeheavenworldwide.com; **210** Michael Zarnock www.MikeZarnock.com; **211** (t) Daniel Graves/Rex Features, (b) Reuters/Pilar Olivares; **214–215** (dp) Bigfoot 4x4 Inc; **214** (t) Michael.J.Gallagher; **216** Dan Piazza; **217** David Burner/Rex Features; **218–219** Robert Luczun; **220** www.Armchaircruisers.com; **221** Phil Yeomans/Rex Features; **222** ChinaFotoPress/Cheng Jiang/Photocome/PA Photos; **223** (t) Tim Arfons; **223** (b) Joel King/Wrigley's Airwaves®; **224–225** Jon Cook and Miles Hilton-Barber; **226** (sp, t/l) Eric Land, (b/l) Stefan Menne; **227** Reuters/China Daily China Daily Information Corp – CDIC; **228** (c, b/l) Gary Bishop/Rex Features, (b/r) Steve Geer/iStockphoto; **229** Gary Bishop/Rex Features; **230–231** Hermann J. Knippertz/AP/PA Photos; **232–233** Courtesy Perugi artecontemporanea Italy; **234** Martin Meissner/AP/PA Photos; **235** Newspix/Rex Features; **236** The Krystal Company; **237** Adam Lee www.adamlee.net; **238–239** Your Country Escape, LLC; **241** Robert George Clegg Industries; **242** Reuters/Sukree Sukplang; **243** (t) Roger Bamber/Rex Features, (b) www.coloradogators.com; **244** Courtesy of Bryan Berg; **245** Mike Clarke/AFP/Getty Images; **246** (t) Rex Features, (b) Solent News/Rex Features; **247** Gary Roberts/Rex Features.

Key: t = top, b = bottom, c = centre, l = left, r = right, sp = single page, dp = double page, bgd = background

All other photos are from the MKP Archives and Ripley's Entertainment Inc.
Every attempt has been made to acknowledge correctly and contact copyright holders and we apologize in advance for any unintentional errors or omissions, which will be corrected in future editions.